Your Parent's
Financial Security

THE ICFP PERSONAL WEALTH BUILDING GUIDES

YOUR HOME MORTGAGE
  Michael C. Thomsett

YOUR PARENT'S FINANCIAL SECURITY
  Barbara Weltman

YOUR RETIREMENT BENEFITS
  Peter E. Gaudio and Virginia S. Nicols

Your Parent's Financial Security

Barbara Weltman

John Wiley & Sons, Inc.

New York • Chichester • Brisbane • Toronto • Singapore

In recognition of the importance of preserving what has been
written, it is a policy of John Wiley & Sons, Inc., to have
books of enduring value published in the United States
printed on acid-free paper, and we exert our best efforts
to that end.

Library of Congress Cataloging-in-Publication Data

Weltman, Barbara, 1950–
    Your parent's financial security / by Barbara Weltman.
       p.   cm. — (The ICFP personal wealth-building guides)
    Includes index.
    ISBN 0-471-54476-0 (cloth). — ISBN 0-471-54477-9 (paper)
    1. Aged—Finance, Personal. 2. Aged—Care—Finance. 3. Aged—
Housing—Finance. 4. Estate planning. I. Title. II. Series.
HG179.W466 1992
332.024'0565—dc20   91-42268

Printed in the United States of America

10 9 8 7 6 5 4 3 2 1

Printed and bound by Malloy Lithographing, Inc.

This book is dedicated with love to my mother
Ruth Obadiah Drotch

Contents

Introduction

As Americans look toward the 21st century, a new personal and financial reality is beginning to affect an ever increasing number of individuals. Retirement is no longer the last stage of life that they must plan for. After years of active retirement, more and more men and women are experiencing their retirement's final phase: old age. Until now, these extended years of life were beyond most people's plans and dreams. Developments in medicine and technology in the closing decades of the 20th century have made it possible to live many years past retirement age, to 80, 90, or even older.

There is no exact birthday that marks entry into old age. For some, it may come after 10, 20, or more years of having enjoyed an active retirement. Old age can happen gradually, without a person even noticing it, or it can occur instantaneously, in a sudden illness or an accident.

Certain ages in life have been codified. A person reaches the age of majority in most states at 18. A person can drink legally at 21. A person reaches the normal retirement age at 65. But no statute prescribes the time at which old age begins. For one person, old age may come at 70; for another, it may not come until 90! For purposes of this book, old age is defined as the time when independence gives way to requiring assistance. The ability to live on one's own diminishes. The need for help in daily life, whether in personal and/or financial matters, grows increasingly greater.

This last stage of life requires new planning initiatives. If you have an elderly parent who has not taken any initiative to plan, then you may have to plan for your parent, to ensure your parent's well-being and your own peace of mind. Millions of adult children are presently providing care for one or both of their parents. With life expectancies rising, the number of these unpaid caregivers will increase. If you are not already counted among them, you may be joining them in the future.

THE ELDER CARE CRISIS

We rarely read a newspaper, listen to the radio, or watch television without encountering a story involving problems of the elderly: instances of abuse in nursing homes, Medicare rip-offs, Alzheimer's disease's slow death, and the like. Underlying all of these stories are the themes of the skyrocketing cost and the great amount of time required for caring for the elderly, and the shortages of the money and time needed for proper care. Truly, there is an "elder care crisis."

This nationwide crisis has several contributing factors: demographic changes, soaring medical costs, and changing life-styles. No single factor is responsible; they all contribute to the problem.

Demographic Changes

Changes in demography (the science of vital statistics of populations) provide a clue to why the care of the elderly has reached crisis proportions. Americans are now living dramatically longer, because of advances in medicine. The average life expectancy of a newborn today is 27 years longer than it was for babies born at the turn of the century.

Statistically, everyone, no matter how old, has a life expectancy. The longer one lives, the greater one's life expectancy. For example, a man who is now 65 had a life expectancy at birth of 64.1 years. He has already outlived his original life expectancy. He now has a life expectancy of 80.6 years. A woman age 65 had an original life expectancy of 71.9 years. It is now 84.9 years. A man who is now 85 had a life expectancy at birth of only 54 years. Statistically, he can look forward to 5$^1/_2$ more years of life. A woman age 85 had a life expectancy at birth of 61.4 years. She can expect to live to almost 92 years! These life expectancy statistics, impressive as they are, pale against other age-related statistics.

The age 65+ group now makes up 12 percent of our population. Forty years from now, it is expected, the age 65+ group will top 21 percent of our population. By the year 2030, more than 1 out of every 5 Americans will be at least 65 years old.

The fastest growing segment of the population is the "elderly elderly"—those age 85 and over. In 1930, there were only about 300,000 people in this age group. Today, there are more than 3 million individuals age 85 and over. This represents about 1 percent of our population. By the middle of the next century, the Bureau of the Census estimates, 5 percent of Americans will be over the age of 85! This is almost 20 years beyond the current social security retirement age. Perhaps even more amazing is the fact that 35 Americans turn 100 *every day*. The Social Security Administration currently lists about 66,000 centenarians; the White House estimates that it sends out about 50 birthday cards a day to those age 100 and over. There are estimates that, by the middle of the 21st century, there will be 1.5 million Americans age 100 and over.

Just 20 years ago, only 1 in 4 Americans in their 50s had an elderly parent. A decade ago, that figure had increased to 2 in 5; today, it is even greater. People in their 50s are not the only ones with an elderly parent. Ten years ago, 20 percent of those in their 60s and 2 percent of those in their 70s had an elderly parent. By the middle of the 21st century, one-third of those between ages 60 and 74 could have an elderly parent.

Soaring Medical Costs

An important contributing factor in the elder care crisis is the runaway cost of health care. These high costs affect all individuals, regardless of age, but the elderly feel their impact more acutely because increased longevity, for many people, is accompanied by failing health.

Those age 65 and over spend from about 18 percent to as much as 33 percent of their income on out-of-pocket medical costs. As medical costs have risen 12 percent a year, income has increased only 7.1 percent.

Not all elderly people have health problems requiring extensive care. In fact, serious health problems do not typically begin before age 85. Only about 7 percent of those between the ages of 75 and 84 need nursing-home care. Others with lesser infirmities can manage very well with in-home care.

It is common knowledge that the cost of long-term care—in a nursing home or at home—is steep. The national average for a yearly nursing-home bill is about $30,000 and escalating rapidly. In some areas of the country, a bill of $60,000 or more is not uncommon. In-home custodial care can cost $25 to $75 per hour. The average cost of daily home care is now $15,000 per year but can run as high as nursing-home care.

Medicare or private insurance covers the cost of care for acute illness, such as a heart attack or cancer. It is far more likely, however, that an elderly person will face the problems of chronic illness or a disabling disease (arthritis or Alzheimer's disease, for example) rather than suffering an acute illness. Today, there are 3 million Americans with Alzheimer's disease; a half-million suffer strokes each year, and another half-million are diagnosed as having Parkinson's disease.

Medicare does not cover the costs of long-term care for these types of infirmities.

Even without serious illness or disability, many elderly will reach a point where they will have difficulty seeing to their daily needs, simply as an effect of old age. They may become incapable of shopping, cooking, and cleaning house. They may no longer be able to go to the bank, pay bills, or balance a checkbook. A trip to town to get a haircut or see a movie may become impossible. These elderly will need personal aid of some sort, to manage these activities. They must wrestle with the psychological aspects of their diminishing capability for self-care. They must also reckon with the high costs of self-care assistance. For many, this cost may be added to a high outlay for medical care.

Our country has developed into a three-class health care system. The rich can afford to pay privately for quality health care, and the poor can qualify for Medicaid. Today's high cost of health care is an onerous burden on the middle class. The elderly feel this class system most profoundly because they have the greatest health care needs. In their struggle to pay for private health care, many will use up their life's savings. Stories abound on hard-working individuals who, within a matter of months, have all their funds wiped out by payment of medical bills. Such impoverishment then entitles them to Medicaid, but they never again escape the poverty level. For couples, the well spouse, who had lived a lifetime in the middle class, often sinks into poverty so that the ill spouse can get needed health care through Medicaid. According to one study, one-half of all couples with one spouse in a nursing home had used up all their savings within 1 year. In the same 1-year period, two-thirds of single persons in nursing homes had become impoverished.

As statistics show, stories of impoverishment stemming from the high cost of today's health care are not exaggerations. To those who have lost all their assets because of illness, these horror stories are very real. Making matters worse, health care costs are projected to continue escalating at a pace that will outstrip the rate of inflation.

Many elderly meet their health care and living expenses on their own. However, increased longevity makes this task more difficult. Many have outlived the retirement period for which they had planned. Their financial resources may begin to dwindle alarmingly. Their fixed incomes have to stretch further and further, because of the erosion of their buying power. Even with a modest inflation rate of 4 percent annually, the value of the dollar drops by half in a little over 10 years. Many people who live 20 years beyond retirement age have primarily fixed incomes. At best, their dollar buys only a quarter of what they could buy with it at the time of their retirement.

The inability of the elderly to pay for their own care means that, in many cases, their children may have to step in and help. According to estimates, nearly 1 million elderly parents already receive some financial support from their adult children. This financial burden may come at a time when adult children are trying to meet their own financial goals—saving for their own retirement, living on a retirement income, paying for their own health care, or paying for their children's college education. The average American family has a median income of $27,300 and liquid assets of less than $10,000. The typical family clearly lacks the resources to shoulder the elder care burden, even when it wants to.

Changing Life-Styles

A third factor in the elder care crisis is changes in life-styles. In the past, many families remained together, with parents, children, and grandchildren living under one roof. Today, multigenerational families living in the same place are rare. Divorce has broken up many families. Job opportunities have dispersed children to all areas of the country. Parents have retired to the Sun Belt. Whatever the reason, fewer children live with, or near, an elderly parent who requires care. In the past, several on-site family members were able to share care responsibilities. Today, this may be impossible; there may be few or no relatives available to an elderly person. These life-style changes have resulted in new financial and personal burdens on everyone.

When a person has no family to call on, it is up to that person to make plans for later years. Housing options, health care decisions, and financial arrangements should be selected. There may be friends to turn to for help. Community services and other options for assistance may be available.

Couples who live apart from their children or other family members also have special planning requirements. They must plan for *two* elderly people, not one. They face twice the financial challenge. Health problems may not strike both spouses at the same time. A wife, for example, may struggle to provide home care for her husband. Still, their planning must cover more than the needs of one spouse.

Another life-style change affecting elder care is the greater presence of women in the work force. In the recent past, women who married tended to stay home. These women were full-time caregivers to their children and many continued to be available as caregivers to their parents. As more and more women work, time constraints prevent them from being available to provide that care.

For all workers, but especially working women, the challenge to provide elder care may mean difficult personal choices. They may have to quit a job, switch to part-time work, take early retirement, shoulder steep expenses, or burn their energy candle at both ends and in the middle. These unpaid caregivers typically spend 10 to 40 hours a week at this "second job." According to the Bureau of the Census, 1 of every 8 workers who cares for an elderly parent must quit his or her job, and these figures are expected to rise.

A Women's Issue?

Is the elder care crisis only a concern of women? To date, the statistics seem to show that this is generally so. About three-quarters of caregivers today are women, and they care not only for their own parents but also for their parents-in-law. Women spend an average of nearly 17 years as caregivers for their children. They may also spend about 18 years as caregivers for their parents.

This traditional view of caregiving as a "women's issue" may be changing. The number of elderly requiring care is increasing and so is the number of working women. As a result of these two developments, caregiving may well become a problem for adult children of both sexes.

The men and women caring for their parents are not the only ones affected by the elder care crisis. Employers and our nation's economy are heavily impacted by it. Almost one-quarter of workers over age 40 are providing care to elderly parents. Employers of these workers suffer absenteeism, resignations, and early retirement because of elder care responsibilities. As the work force ages, there is an increasing need to keep older workers. The elder care crisis also adversely affects the economy, especially in increased budget amounts for social security and Medicare.

A number of employers have begun to respond, in a variety of ways. Some offer direct help through counseling and referral programs. A few provide reimbursement for dependent care. Some give indirect help through liberal leave time, flexible working schedules, and job sharing.

The federal government has begun to recognize the need to protect the jobs of workers who take time off to care for parents. The Family Medical Leave Act, which provided job protection during such leave time, was passed by Congress in 1990, but then failed to become law.

It was again passed by both houses of Congress in late 1991, but final enactment is very uncertain.

Double Whammy

Many adult children who are providing elder care must carry an additional burden: caring for their own children. At present, almost 2 million women are providing care for both their parents and their children. These individuals are part of the growing "sandwich generation." They have the double responsibilities and the double financial pressures of simultaneously caring for both their parents and their children.

PLANNING FOR OLD AGE

You *can* minimize the impact of the elder care crisis on yourself and your family. No one is immune from growing old. Each of us is, or will be, directly involved in the elder care crisis and should begin planning for old age. It is never too early, or too late, to start to plan.

If your parents are young and healthy, you—and they—may view the elder care crisis as a distant concern; they may put off making any plans for old age. However, the earlier that planning begins, the more options may be available to choose from.

If your parents have already retired, you cannot afford to ignore their need to plan for their later years. If you are now caring for an elderly parent or in-law, you are well aware of the elder care crisis because it has already become a fact of your life. You may have to act, if your parent or in-law has failed to do so.

Many individuals seem never to grow old. They continue an active life, enjoy good health, and take advantage of what life has to offer. Personalities in entertainment and the arts, in sports, government, industry, and literature reappear in public over the years and seem to deny their birth certificates' dates. If your parent qualifies for this group, you are indeed fortunate. However, life is not static; things may change without warning. Statistics show that your chances of landing in the elder care crisis are very real. A slip in the shower, a missed step, a stroke, or some other unforeseen event may make a person suddenly dependent on you for personal or financial help.

Are children legally required to provide care for parents? State laws impose a parental obligation to care for children, but only half the states have a corresponding rule that children must care for their parents. In many of these states, this legal responsibility is limited to certain circumstances. No states are allowed to take the financial responsibility of a child into account in determining Medicaid eligibility. Where state law does not require a child to provide support, the child may become contractually bound to pay for a parent's care in certain circumstances.

Even where there is no overriding legal requirement to provide support for an elderly parent, most children feel a strong moral obligation to do so. This moral obligation, for many, can be as binding as a legal one.

Even if your parent is not now in need of help, it is important that you take the elder care crisis personally. Consider the options and take some action.

Avoiding a Crisis

From the increasing financial pressures of elder care, brought on by medical costs, inflation, and other expenses, a bleak picture emerges. It is self-defeating to minimize these pressures. Still, the challenges of elder care can be met without crisis. Your parent can gain a measure of protection against catastrophe, *if* you use foresight and take some simple actions before the onset of your parent's old age. Financial resources do not have to be needlessly depleted. More importantly, decisions can be made, by your parents themselves, about the quality of their future life—where to live, the type of medical treatment desired—before a crisis situation develops.

Planning for the elderly is *not* meant to be testamentary planning. It is not to ensure adult children that there will be an inheritance left over after caring for an elderly parent. Although all family members may express their needs and desires, the focus must remain on the elderly relative and ultimately that person's wishes must control.

The scope of planning for the elderly covers a wide range of psychological, sociological, and financial considerations. Very wealthy people have attorneys, accountants, financial planners, and other sophisticated advisers to assist them in planning for old age. However, most of us must rely on our own initiatives to meet the challenges of elder care.

This book helps in that endeavor by targeting for consideration certain major areas of concern to the elderly and their families. These include the role of unpaid "caregivers," medical coverage for everyday or short-term care and long-term care, medical decisions, insurance, housing options, asset management, and estate planning. The goal of each chapter is to identify a particular issue facing the elderly, present the various alternatives now available in solving this issue, and help you assess the relative merits of the alternatives for your situation.

Get Help in Planning

Elder care concerns are numerous and wide-ranging; on many issues, the law is very complex. Planning for old age is not a do-it-yourself affair. You should discuss the alternatives with other family members and seek the help of professionals. Elder care professionals include attorneys, financial planners, stock brokers, insurance agents, social workers, care managers, and religious counselors.

If you do not know where to begin finding help, you might consider seeing an attorney who is a specialist in "elder law." Attorneys practicing in this growing specialty are knowledgeable in an array of problems. They can also make referrals to other specialists, such as care managers, who deal with certain aspects of problems of the elderly. For the name of an elder law attorney in your area, contact the National Academy of Elder Law Attorneys, 655 N. Alvernon Way, Tucson, AZ 85711 (phone: 602/881-4005), or check with your state or local bar association. For the name of a care manager in your city or town, contact the National Association of Private Geriatric Care Managers, 655 N. Alvernon Way, Tucson, AZ 85711 (phone: 602/881-8008). If you are already in contact with a social worker, ask his or her advice on other professional resources.

The book's final chapter discusses recordkeeping for documents and assets. In our paper-oriented society, it is useful to know what records to keep and where and how to store them. Good recordkeeping, although tedious to organize and maintain, serves several important functions. It enables you to keep better track of your parent's property and finances *if and when* such a task becomes necessary. It gives you an overview of your parent's affairs promptly, in the event of disability or death. It serves as a handy reference when completing applications and insurance forms. Furthermore, it saves money by cutting down the amount of an attorney's time required for estate planning and probate.

The directories at the end of the book contain handy listings of various agencies, organizations, and other resources mentioned throughout the book. Help with problems such as housing, Medicare, and social security, and referrals to various professionals in the field of elder law will be available from the names on the list.

Getting Started

For many people, the most difficult thing about planning is getting started. Some individuals do not like to face their advancing age and the prospect of their own mortality. Raising certain issues with a parent is a highly delicate task for a child. It requires tact and understanding. More importantly, it requires the willingness of the child to listen to the wishes of the parent and to help with the realization of the parent's goals, even when they may be at odds with the child's own.

Some people have a notion that if they plan for old age they will succumb to it. Others have a natural reluctance to talk about death and anything associated with it. These roadblocks to planning may be understandable, but they are self-defeating and must be overcome. Invoking an overworked but helpful saying, "A journey of a thousand miles begins with one step." Take a first step now. Begin to identify the areas in which decisions must be made or actions taken.

Planning is not a one-shot deal. Even if a plan has been worked out, review it periodically. When there are births or deaths in the family, changes in health, moves to other states, changes in the tax laws, or financial windfalls, make any needed adjustments to the plan. You can and should take an active role, to help protect your parent's future personal and financial security.

A PERSPECTIVE ON ELDER CARE

The care of an aging parent or other elderly relative is a very personal endeavor for me. Growing up, I watched my mother provide care for both her mother and mother-in-law, for a great many years. I saw firsthand what it costs to provide this elder care, not only in terms of dollars but also in terms of time and emotions.

When I was a little girl, my father's mother lived with us. Long after I grew up and moved away, my grandmother, by then elderly and ill, continued to live with my mother, past the time when my mother retired to Florida. My mother cared for her until my grandmother was 88 years old and needed round-the-clock nursing care. Then the decision to place her in a nursing home had to be made, a nursing home had to be found for her, and the cost of payment had to be met. At the time when these arrangements were being made, my mother's mother was diagnosed as having terminal cancer. My mother, who lived only a short distance away from her mother, provided care and support that made it possible for her mother to live out her days in her own beloved home.

My mother's mother died in 1977; my father's mother died the following year, at the age of 90. The personal and financial cost of providing care for my grandmothers was enormous. But equally great was the knowledge that, as members of our family, they had received the quality of care that they well deserved.

Understandably, my mother's personal commitment to elder care, in terms of time and financial resources, cannot always be imitated. Adult children of an elderly parent or in-law must begin to make alternate plans for eventualities. They may have to assist an elderly parent or in-law in taking steps to protect the elderly person's independence for as long as possible. They must help an elderly parent or in-law to maximize financial resources. They must educate themselves on programs available to assist the parent or in-law in resolving problem situations.

As an elder law attorney, I have witnessed certain changes during the past few years. The number of people interested in planning for their own old age or for their elderly parents and in-laws is growing to an amazing extent. The amount of information available is also increasing. This book is intended to add to that information in a meaningful way.

I also want to dispel some misconceptions about elder care and to provide hope. Living to an advanced age does not necessarily equate with incapacity, dependence, and poverty. Planning can forestall inappropriate levels of care and the wasting of assets. There *is* help available. I especially want to give guidance to panic-stricken individuals who are suddenly beset with what appear to be overwhelming responsibilities. A myriad of resources and dedicated people can be enlisted to help with your problems. This book's goal is to provide some ways for hooking you into the elder care network.

Finally, I must emphasize that you need to continue to read about and stay current on the developments affecting elder care. Legislation is pending in Congress and in state legislatures that can have profound effects on the lives of a great many elderly individuals and their families. New ways to plan are constantly being developed. Newspapers, magazine articles, books, talk shows on television and radio, and local seminars are excellent ways to stay current. It is my profound hope, as an elder law attorney and a person with parents and an in-law, that attention focused on the elder care crisis will result in many needed changes.

I extend my sincere thanks to all the people who helped me in the preparation of this book, particularly Sidney Kess, my mentor and partner in many projects, for his support and resources, and Sherri Eisner, for her help and insight. I want to express my appreciation to my husband, Malcolm Katt, for his continuing belief in this project; to my friends, who displayed great enthusiasm on my behalf; and to my children, for tolerating my long hours at work.

1

Helping
Your Parent

Millions of today's adult children have taken a role in the care of one or both of their parents. This group of unpaid adult caregivers continues to grow impressively. At present, the great majority of children-caregivers are middle-aged. As the population grays, this ratio will change. It is estimated that, by the middle of the next century, one-third of Americans between the ages of 60 and 74 will have at least one parent still living. Many of these senior citizens will be called on to provide help for their even more elderly parent. Thus, the caregivers of the future will themselves be senior citizens.

Regardless of a child's age, it is a difficult time for an adult child when he or she realizes that the parent–child relationship has changed. Instead of providing parental care, the parent must now receive it; to a large extent, the child is already or must become the parent's parent. This realization engenders many emotions. A feeling of security that comes with knowing that Mom or Dad would always be there to provide support and assistance vanishes. It is replaced, for some children, by anger, resentment, and fear; others experience concern, sadness, loss, anxiety, and grief. Most endure a mixed bag of emotions. Whatever their response, the children's realization that they must assume a parental role for a parent can be difficult, if not traumatic.

Despite their trauma or personal feelings, children may still, of necessity, be called on to make decisions and take actions on behalf of a parent. By reading this book, you acknowledge that you have a role in your parent's future. You must begin to make that an active role, not only for your parent's benefit, but also for yours. If you fail to take an active role when your parent is still able to make plans, you may be forced to act in the future by default. If you face your role in dealing with your aging parent while your parent can actively participate, you are sparing yourself problems in the future. You are also ensuring that your parent's wishes will be best served.

In this chapter, we'll examine when a child must become involved in a parent's affairs. You'll learn how to start the planning process and how to draw up plans for your parent's benefit. We'll also examine what it means to you to become a caregiver for your parent and see what help is available to you as a caregiver. Finally, we'll explain the role of a private geriatric care manager, a professional who can work with you or for you in obtaining answers to difficult questions and providing you with needed counseling.

STARTING THE PLANNING PROCESS

A child may become involved with planning for an elderly parent in a number of scenarios. Unfortunately, the most common occurrence is a sudden illness (such as a stroke) or an accident that immediately leaves the parent dependent for personal care and even financial assistance. A child who becomes involved because of sudden illness or an accident may face a number of rushed decisions and actions, such as consenting to medical treatment, finding a nursing home, or deciding how to pay bills.

WEALTH BUILDING PROFILE *Becoming Involved in Elder Care.* Susan's mother, age 78, lived alone in New Jersey; Susan lived in New York with her teenage boys. One evening, as Susan watched TV, she received a phone call from her mother's neighbor and friend. Her mother had passed out and had been taken by ambulance to the local hospital. Susan immediately called the hospital and learned that her mother had suffered a stroke and was in intensive care. The extent of the illness was not yet known. Susan silently prayed that her mother would live. As it turned out, her prayers were answered; her mother did live, but required constant care. It was not known when and to what extent her mother would be able to take care of herself. Susan had to assume a major role in her mother's life. She had to immerse herself in the problems of elder care. She had to make arrangements for her mother's care upon discharge from the hospital, make medical decisions while her mother was unable to speak for herself, and take over the task of paying monthly bills.

Not everyone becomes involved in elder care as a result of a sudden event. Some children take on caregiving over a period of time, as they witness the gradual deterioration of a parent's faculties. Mom may not remember important things; Dad may not be able to drive his car anymore. Such children may have to begin to address the problems that accompany the aging process when each problem arises. Problems could include, for example, the wisdom of a parent's continuing to live alone or the need to get help for some of a parent's daily tasks, such as cooking or cleaning.

Wise children who have healthy and active parents anticipate the time when a parent will have a diminished capacity for self-care. These children have the luxury of time. Their parents can make plans for themselves, and decisions can be made without a crisis atmosphere.

Although a parent, regardless of age, has a right to control his or her own life, it is also true that a child can at some point become inextricably involved with the parent's affairs. This can happen by default (as when a parent suffers a debilitating condition) or by the parent's choice (as when a parent seeks out or readily accepts a child's help). It is not productive to belabor the fact that your tasks may not be pleasant when you become involved. It is far more constructive to learn what needs to be done and how best to do it.

A Three-Step Approach

Some parents make their own plans for their old age. They may move to a special community that can see to their medical care. They consult with an attorney for various documents to protect their interests. In general, they keep things under control. However, not all parents take such action.

If your parent has not taken action and has not yet faced a crisis, then you have the opportunity to initiate the planning process. *Starting* the planning process is more a matter of dealing with emotions—yours and your parents'—than of solving particular problems.

Step 1. Facing the Need to Plan

Your first step in the planning process is facing the need to take action. You must acknowledge your parent's increasing dependence and the fact that this state of affairs will not get any better as time goes on. Although it may be easy to come to this realization on an intellectual level, it may be difficult for you to do so emotionally. A lifetime of memories bolsters the view of your dependence on your parent. You remember the person who nurtured you and helped you out during your entire life. Now, the aging process works to reverse this natural order. It is hard for any child to watch a parent lose certain functions. The first signs may be only a noticeably slowed pace in walking, fading vision, or hearing loss. As time passes, walking may be difficult without a cane or walker, or reading or hearing may become impossible.

What can you do to ensure that you do not kid yourself about the importance of taking the initiative? If possible, don't take on the entire burden yourself; involve your family in the process. Talk to your brothers and sisters, your aunts and uncles. Ideally, you will be able to bounce ideas off each other and share responsibilities. This is not always possible; you may be an only child, or your aunts and uncles may be deceased or themselves in need of elder care assistance. It seems typical of many families that one sibling, by choice or by default, assumes the role of dealing with a parent. Even if you are that sibling, it may be helpful to discuss options and plans with relatives.

You can also turn to support groups for children of aging parents. These groups can give you ideas that will help you in your new role. They can provide you with the emotional support you may require at a trying time.

Your employer may offer elder care counseling as one of its benefit programs. An increasing number of Fortune 500 companies are recognizing the toll that elder care can take on an employee and are offering various benefits related to elder care. Where counseling is offered, you should find out what help is available in your parent's area.

You can turn to private geriatric care managers. These are professionals, typically social workers, who specialize in providing a wide range of care for the elderly. Reliance on care managers may be essential, if a parent lives some distance from a child. A geriatric care manager may also be helpful for a child who works and cannot provide personal care. (The role of private geriatric care managers is discussed in detail later in this chapter.)

You might consider private counseling for yourself. The whole concept of assuming a parental role for your parent is fraught with psychological implications. With professional help, it may be easier for you to sort things out.

Step 2.   Understanding Your Parent's Perspective

The second step in starting the planning process is realizing the difficulties involved for your parent. It is probably painful for a parent to realize that he or she has reached the stage in life where dependence on others is needed just to get through daily tasks. Many parents have led fully independent lives. They are proud people who are not used to asking for or accepting help. The aging process for many individuals involves a loss of control—a scary thing for a parent to face. It is not uncommon for a parent to feel threatened when a child wants to discuss finances. The parent may feel that the child is only interested in the parent's money or is trying to take that money away from the parent. It may be difficult for a parent to see that, in most cases, love, not the lack of it, drives a child to discuss a parent's money matters.

Cultural or other barriers may prevent your parent from becoming involved with his or her own planning. Mom and Dad's generation typically did not discuss personal matters with anyone. Your parent may have no experience in talking about finances, health, or other private concerns with anyone, especially you.

Another problem that you should be sensitive to, with respect to your parent's reluctance or reticence to discuss these concerns, is the fact that these issues deal to some degree with death. For example, your parent may not want to talk about a will because this means facing the fact that he or she will die.

Your understanding and sensitivity to your parent's problems and concerns will help to pave the way for necessary planning. It may also be productive to have your parent see a private counselor and get help in facing the need to plan for old age.

Step 3.   Getting Started

If your parent does not start to plan for his or her own future, then the task is left to you. If you fail to take the initiative, then you may well be forced to make decisions under emergency situations in the future. By acting before such situations arise, the maximum number of options remains open to your parent and you.

――――――――――――→ ACTION ITEM ←――――――――――――
Initiating the planning process is something helpful a child can do. Forcing a parent to take action or to take a particular kind of action is not appropriate.

How can you broach the issue with your parent? This obviously depends on your relationship with your parent. You may be able to speak directly to your parent about one aspect of elder law planning, either in person or by telephone. You can ask whether your parent has a will, a living will, or a durable power of attorney. You might feel more comfortable writing to your parent, perhaps enclosing a clipping from your local paper about a topic involving elder care (a change in Medicare, or a new adult community being constructed), as a means of breaking the ice. Whatever the method chosen for starting the conversation, the message should be clear: it is now time to begin discussing plans for the future.

?

What is the best way of starting the planning process for an elderly parent?

There is no best way to start this usually stressful process. Get other family members, friends, or professionals involved. Above all, start the process *before* the need arises, *before* a serious illness occurs.

Who is in the "sandwich" generation?

Very likely, yourself, since you are reading this book. The sandwich generation is comprised of those who care for elderly parents and raise a family at the same time.

What is elder law?

Because of the greatly increased number of elderly, elder law is becoming a new legal specialty, just as gerontology is a new medical field. You can contact a lawyers' association, The National Academy of Elder Law Attorneys (see page 245 for address information).

What is respite care?

Because of the heavy demands on a family caregiver, some private agencies have now set up respite care programs to provide a primary caregiver with some time off.

MAKING PLANS

Your parent may have made some plans for the future. Now is the time to identify your concerns for your parent and your parent's needs for the future. Then your parent can begin to seek out answers on programs, facilities, or alternatives available for solving the problems that he or she faces.

This book is designed to alert you to the various areas of concern for your parent. It then provides solutions and directs you to resources for further inquiry. You may need to work through each and every chapter—from health care issues, to housing alternatives, to legal documents for financial and personal well-being. Alternatively, you may be primarily concerned with one area at the start; for example, housing may be the key issue you focus on at this time. Later, as circumstances change, your parent may begin to plan for money management or long-term medical care. Each area is important and has an effect on other areas of planning.

It would be most helpful if your parent could complete the personal recordkeeper in Chapter 11, to show the extent of assets and other information and to indicate the planning measures that have already been taken. The recordkeeper will also be helpful for other purposes, such as to permit professional planners to assist you in Medicaid qualification (if this becomes necessary), income planning, or estate planning.

It must be emphasized that every family is different. In some families, a parent is fiercely independent and will manage his or her own affairs and make personal decisions until totally unable to do so. In this type of family, planning is wholly within the parent's control. A child cannot make plans for a parent while the parent is still competent to act on his or her own. The child can, however, express to a parent the various concerns and options available.

————————→ **ACTION ITEM** ←————————
Perhaps the only thing a child can do when a parent is in control (besides expressing feelings and concerns to the parent) is to become self-educated about the various aspects of personal and financial management related to growing older and make plans for his or her *own* future.

In other families, a parent may readily abdicate responsibility for certain things. For example, an elderly mother who has little financial experience may gladly turn over control of financial matters. In this type of family, a child can work with a parent to see that the parent understands how things will be handled and that all necessary legal documents are secured.

BECOMING A CAREGIVER

What Is a Caregiver?

A caregiver is a person who provides help to another individual. This help can take the form of financial assistance, companionship, help with daily tasks, or merely moral support. Certain caregivers, such as doctors, nurses, and nurses' aides, are paid for their services. Children of the elderly who provide assistance are, overwhelmingly, unpaid caregivers. Throughout this chapter, reference to caregivers means unpaid caregivers, unless otherwise noted.

The ranks of such caregivers are growing dramatically. Today, a great many caregivers are in the sandwich generation, caring for elderly parents while continuing to provide care for their own children. It is estimated that nearly 2 million women are in this category of caregiver. They carry a double burden, emotionally and financially.

Being a caregiver can require difficult personal choices. Of all the women caregivers, half are still working outside the home. For those who are working, becoming full-time or part-time caregivers may involve career decisions—leaving a job, turning down a promotion, switching to part-time work. Life-style and the standard of living can be affected.

A great loss of personal freedom usually occurs. Depending on a parent's condition, a child may become a "babysitter" tied to the house. Simple personal freedoms, like going out to the movies or accomplishing daily errands, may no longer be easily done.

Employers that are sensitive to the issues of caregivers provide counseling and flexible leave time. At present, only about 3 percent of U.S. companies have specific policies on helping employees who care for elderly parents; only 15 percent have flexible working hours that make caregiving a little easier. It is expected that, as the population ages, employers will improve their elder care policies.

Congress recently considered legislation requiring employers to grant leave time when employees must care for children or parents. At the time this book was prepared, enactment was uncertain.

When an Emergency Strikes

Do you dread the thought of receiving a phone call in the middle of the night telling you that your parent has suffered a medical emergency? In that one instant, like it or not, you become a caregiver. If plans have been made, then you are in the enviable position of being able to take advantage of that advance thought and work. You should gather up necessary documents that have been drawn, such as living wills, health care proxies, powers of attorney, and the like. (These documents are explained in detail in later chapters.)

If plans have not been put in place, you may be called on to make a wide range of decisions. What do you do? First, you stay calm and seek the help of professionals. As explained earlier, it may be beneficial to consult an elder law attorney, a lawyer who specializes in issues relating to the elderly. (You can obtain a referral from The National Academy of Elder Law Attorneys, 655 North Alvernon Way, Tucson, AZ 85711; phone: 606/881-4005.) Alternatively, you might consult a private geriatric care manager. This type of professional assistance is discussed later in this chapter.

Special Problems of Long-Distance Assistance

What do you do if your parent is in one part of the country and you live in another? Jim, an executive in Atlanta, called his mother in Detroit. On the phone, she sounded disoriented. She didn't seem to know him or remember a conversation from the previous week. Jim became alarmed. Was everything okay? After he hung up, he called his aunt (his mother's sister), who lived close to his mother. He explained his concerns and his aunt went over to check on his mother. It turned out that she was all right. But what if she hadn't been? How would you help your parent in case of emergency, when you are not personally able to provide care?

→ **ACTION ITEM** ←

See that someone has access to your parent's house in case of emergency. Your parent may be reluctant to give a house key to a stranger. If relationships of trust are established with neighbors, this reluctance may disappear.

You need to set up a network of contacts to act as your surrogates in providing care for your parent. Arrange with other relatives, who live near your parent, to stay in contact. Learn the names and phone numbers of your parent's neighbors. Speak to them about the situation.

Despite your best efforts to involve relatives and neighbors, you may be forced to rely on paid caregivers. There may be no relatives or neighbors on whom your parent and you can rely. It is helpful to know in advance how to tap into the caregiver system. In the directory at the end of this book, you will find a number of listings for help.

Your employer may be able to help with caregiving responsibilities. A few major corporations—for example, IBM, Colgate-Palmolive, Prudential—have consultants on hand to direct an employee to help in a parent's town, even if it is different from that of the employee.

HELP FOR CAREGIVERS

Adult Day Care

If your parent needs full-time supervision and care but you work and cannot provide the needed parental care throughout the day, you may be able to ensure proper care of your parent through an adult day-care center. As the name implies, an adult day-care center functions much like a child-care facility, except that the persons receiving care are elderly.

Adult day-care facilities vary greatly in quality and in the types of programs offered. Some facilities provide transportation. Some have special programs for certain medical problems. For example, there may be an adult day-care program near you that caters to people with Alzheimer's disease.

For further details on adult day-care, see Chapter 5.

Respite Care

Caregivers who provide full-time care for a parent are always "on duty." This 24-hour-a-day job can be emotionally and physically grueling. Caregivers need time off.

Members of large families can take turns providing coverage for a parent. One sibling may be the primary caregiver (furnishing a home and the bulk of supervision for a parent), and other siblings can take on some responsibility at certain times.

When family members or neighbors are not available for assistance in caregiving chores, outside help may be necessary. There are agencies that provide respite care for a parent, to allow the caregiver some time off. Allowances vary from a regular time off each week for a few hours, or one day each week, to a full week for a vacation or other personal reasons. Time off is essential for a caregiver. Emotional and physical "burnout" is a chief problem of caregivers, and only time away from caregiving responsibilities can alleviate it.

Congress had originally provided Medicare funds for respite care in 1988, but this coverage was repealed in 1989. Given the shape of the federal budget and the further inroads in Medicare, it is highly unlikely that respite care will be covered in the near future.

Tax Relief

You may be providing personal and financial assistance to your parent. Federal income tax law provides several tax benefits to a child who is financially supporting a parent. These include the opportunity to claim a dependency exemption, qualify as a head of household, and deduct medical expenses paid for your parent (see Chapter 2 for further details).

You may also be entitled to a tax credit. If your parent lives with you and is physically or mentally incapable of self-care, which requires you to hire assistance in order for you to work outside the home, you may be able to claim a dependent care credit. The credit percentage is scaled according to your income. The maximum tax credit that can be claimed by high-income individuals is $480.

Support Groups for Caregivers

The strains of providing care, whether they involve time, emotions, or money, can be enormous. The myriad problems and great variety of solutions can be overwhelming.

→ ACTION ITEM ←

Joining a support group can provide caregivers a double benefit. Not only will they receive support for the problems that result from being a caregiver, but the group can serve as an excellent source of information.

There are a number of groups that can help you. Check your local clearinghouse of self-help groups to see which groups are designed for caregivers. For resource information, contact Children of Aging Parents (CAPS), 2761 Trenton Road, Levittown, PA 19056; phone: 215/945-6900. Membership dues to this nonprofit organization entitles you to a newsletter, networking (if available in your area), and information on caregiver support groups throughout the country.

PROFESSIONAL CAREGIVERS

With the aging population and the increasing complexity of health care, there has been a growing need for professionals who know "the system," can counsel the elderly and their families, and can see that care is received. These specialists are private geriatric care managers.

When an individual advertises that he or she is a geriatric care manager, what does this title mean? Such a professional has an advanced degree in some field of human services—usually social work, psychology, or gerontology—or an equivalent qualification, such as a nursing degree. A geriatric care manager gets paid to provide a wide range of services: assessment, counseling, crisis intervention, care management, entitlements, psychotherapy, information, and referrals.

→ **ACTION ITEM** ←

Geriatric care managers see that a parent receives the necessary care. They also can provide the counseling often needed by children of the elderly, who face a great deal of stress from the decisions they are forced to make.

Some or all of these terms may seem alien to you. They are best understood by example. A parent has Alzheimer's disease. A child thinks the parent should be in a nursing home. Is this the correct choice? If yes, which home should be used? How will the cost of care be paid? How will the child cope with the decision? The geriatric care manager can assess the parent's physical and mental condition to determine whether nursing home placement is the appropriate level of care. Adult day care may suffice for some time, and a nursing home may not yet be necessary. If nursing home care is required, the professional can advise which nursing homes in the area can provide the type of care necessary for the parent. He or she can help in getting the parent into the right home. The care manager can also help with Medicaid eligibility and can direct the family to an elder law attorney for legal issues.

Private geriatric care managers maintain normal office hours, but generally are available 24 hours a day, 7 days a week.

Costs and Referrals

Fees for private geriatric care managers vary widely across the country. In the south, for example, fees may run as low as $50 an hour; in the northeast, they run around $125 a hour. These costs may sound steep, but they may save money in the long run. For example, the assistance of a professional (such as a caregiver or an attorney) is not required to complete a Medicaid application. However, failure to supply certain information or to answer questions properly can result in denial of the application, even if the parent is theoretically eligible for coverage. Use of a care manager in the application process may avoid rejection or the need to reapply.

For referral of a geriatric care manager in your parent's area or yours, contact the National Association of Private Geriatric Care Managers, 655 North Alvernon Way, Tucson, AZ 85711; phone: 606/ 881-8008. There is no charge for referrals.

───────── POINTS TO REMEMBER ─────────

▶ Starting the planning process means dealing with emotions first— yours and your parent's.

▶ To help get the planning process going, involve others in laying the groundwork. There are several types of individuals to seek out: your immediate family members; support groups for children of aging parents; or employee assistance programs (if available).

▶ Understand your parent's perspective in beginning the planning process.

▶ Begin composing a personal recordkeeper—a written list of financial assets, medical insurance, and other important financial and personal data for your parent.

▶ Become familiar with caregiving options: yourself as the caregiver; another family member; adult day-care centers; or professional caregivers.

2

Budgeting for Short-Term Medical Care

*A*s we grow older, medical costs become our greatest or second greatest monthly expense (after housing). This is true even if a portion of our medical costs is covered by private insurance or government programs.

MEDICAL COSTS: A MAJOR BUDGET ITEM

There are two reasons for the relative size of medical expense: need and high cost. First, the elderly need more and more medical care. As time goes on, the body, like an engine, is in ever increasing need of maintenance and repair. Those who are healthy still have an increased need for routine checkups: eye care, dental care, and various diagnostics. Some elderly are not in good health. They suffer from acute illnesses (heart disease, cancer, stroke); their care is extensive and continuing. Others have chronic illnesses requiring long-term care (Alzheimer's disease, arthritis, Parkinson's disease). Whether healthy or ill, the elderly must also pay for various forms of medical insurance.

A second reason for the relative size of medical expenses is that the costs of medical care are astronomical and are continuing to soar. In recent years, medical costs have increased at three times the rate of inflation. Assuming that this trend continues, we can expect medical costs to escalate at about 12 percent to 15 percent each year.

The individual's share of medical costs is really a middle-class issue. The poor are sheltered from the medical cost burden by government benefits. (The government program for the poor—Medicaid—is discussed in Chapter 4.) The rich can well afford to cover whatever medical costs they incur. For them, medical costs are not an "issue." It is the middle class—those too rich for government largesse and too poor for medical costs not to be a hardship—who must worry about how to meet this onerous burden.

The problem is not confined to the elderly alone. It spills over to the children of the elderly, who may have to pick up the medical tab if the parent is unable to do so. It also affects employers, especially employers that pay retiree health care costs, and the economy as a whole. Still, with some foresight, a parent's out-of-pocket costs for medical care can be reduced. Adequate insurance or other programs can greatly assist in paying for medical care.

——————————————→ **ACTION ITEM** ←——————————

Keep abreast of new rules and opportunities for handling health care costs. Medicare rules are constantly changing and new Medigap policies may be introduced.

Subcommittees in each house of Congress continue to examine the problems of medical costs for the elderly. Although major changes may not occur often, miscellaneous changes that are made each year can have personal impact. It is important to continue monitoring any modification of Medicare rules and other government programs.

Figuring Actual and Projected Medical Costs

To arrange finances, take out insurance, and make other plans to cover medical costs, it is necessary to know what to plan for. Admittedly, it is hard to budget for medical costs. No one has a crystal ball to predict his or her future health status. Doctors' charges, the cost of drugs, and insurance premiums are not static. Still, it is important to begin somewhere. Fill in the Wealth Building Worksheet on page 16. Complete all spaces that apply in your parent's case, using information from bills, check stubs, and receipts for the past year. Make estimates of costs where actual amounts are not known. This will help you to know how much your parent requires each month for medical care.

──────────── **Wealth Building Worksheet** ────────────
Monthly Medical Costs

	Actual	*Projected*
Insurance premiums	$	$
Out-of-pocket* costs for doctors	$	$
Out-of-pocket* costs for therapy	$	$
Out-of-pocket* costs for prescriptions	$	$
Other charges and costs	$	$
Total	$	$

* Out-of-pocket costs are those not covered by Medicare or insurance; they include deductibles, coinsurance amounts, and noncovered items. *Note:* When the total is multiplied by 12, you can see the annual cost of health care for your parent.

For planning purposes, make two columns of costs: one for actual expenses and one for projections of possible future expenses. In making your projections, you must take into account the impact of inflation on health care expenses. In most years, these expenses have outstripped the annual rate of inflation for other items. To project what expenses might be a year from now, boost your insurance premiums by 5 percent and increase other items by 15 percent. The information that follows in this chapter will give you an idea of the average costs of various items and services that might be needed.

Monthly Insurance Premiums

An elderly parent may have to pay for as many as four or more insurance premiums each month, including Medicare Part B (plus Part A, if coverage is not automatic), a Medigap policy, and long-term care insurance.

The monthly premium for Medicare Part B for 1992 was $31.80. This amount is deducted from the monthly check for social security benefits. If an individual is not receiving benefits, the premium is paid each month directly to the Social Security Administration.

If coverage under Part A is not automatic, then the insured pays a monthly amount ($192 in 1992).

In addition, many elderly have "Medigap" policies to cover certain coinsurance payments and deductibles not picked up by Medicare. The annual costs of Medigap policies vary; according to the General

Accounting Office of the U.S. Congress, the average annual cost in 1990 was $840, or $70 a month.

A relatively new type of insurance policy is one covering the cost of long-term custodial care. The premium for this type of policy can vary greatly, depending on the type of coverage, the age at which it is bought, the insurance company underwriting the coverage, and many other factors, as discussed in Chapter 4. The average annual cost of a long-term care policy bought today is about $1,500, or $125 a month.

Monthly Medical Costs

These costs are harder to peg than insurance premiums. Medical conditions vary from month to month. The need for treatment, drugs, and other medical items is always changing. To get a handle on monthly costs, it may be helpful to generalize. Each month, even in the absence of an acute illness, an elderly person may have regular monthly costs for prescription drugs, doctor's visits, or therapy charges. Some of these expenses (doctor's visits, therapy charges) may be partially covered by Medicare; others (prescription drugs, the cost of transportation to the doctor, pharmacy, or hospital) may not be covered at all. The cost of prescription drugs can be quite high. It is not uncommon for an elderly person to be on three or more regular medications. The monthly cost of one medication for hypertension is about $25; the monthly cost of treatment for high cholesterol is about $60. Eyeglasses or special shoes can also add considerably to the monthly budget. One pair of eyeglasses can run to $450 or more. Although this may be a once-a-year purchase, the cost works out on a monthly basis to almost $38.

Tax Savings

The high cost of medical care can be lessened somewhat by tax savings. A deduction is allowed for the cost of medical care, to the extent that it exceeds 7.5 percent of adjusted gross income. No deduction can be claimed unless deductions are itemized.

What expenses qualify for the medical deduction? The law allows a deduction above the 7.5 percent floor for any cost of diagnosis, cure, mitigation, treatment, or prevention of disease or any treatment that affects a part or function of the body. This rule is quite broad and covers a lot of territory:

▶ Professional services (fees for doctors, dentists, nurses, chiropractors);

▸ Supplies and equipment (artificial teeth, eyeglasses, crutches, orthopedic shoes);

▸ Medical treatments (hydrotherapy, radium therapy, x-ray treatments, injections);

▸ Prescription drugs;

▸ Laboratory tests (blood tests, cardiograms, urine analyses);

▸ Hospital services (use of the operating room, oxygen);

▸ Medical insurance premiums (major medical, Medicare, Medigap insurance);

▸ Transportation (use of a car at the rate of 9 cents per mile, plus parking and tolls).

The extent of tax savings from claiming a medical deduction depends on a person's tax bracket. For every dollar deductible at the 31 percent bracket, the individual effectively pays 69 cents and the federal government pays 31 cents.

Good recordkeeping is the key to cashing in on deductions. It is important to keep receipts of paid doctor's bills, prescriptions, and insurance premiums. It is essential to maintain records on the number of miles driven to a doctor, hospital, or pharmacy to obtain medical care.

UNDERSTANDING MEDICARE

Medicare: What Is It? What Does It Provide? What Does It Cost?

Medicare is a federal program of limited health coverage for the elderly (and certain younger disabled individuals). Medicare is *not* a "welfare" program. It is a program to which one is entitled by virtue of having paid into the social security system or railroad retirement system or by directly paying for coverage. Medicare coverage is available without regard to an individual's income or other financial resources. As of 1991, there were approximately 34 million Medicare participants.

There are two distinct parts to Medicare: Part A covers hospital insurance and Part B is supplemental medical insurance. For those who have paid enough into social security, there is no additional cost for obtaining Part A coverage; their only charges under

Part A are coinsurance amounts and deductibles. Part B is a voluntary program and participation depends on the continued payment of monthly premiums.

A number of arms of the federal government are involved in the Medicare program. The Social Security Administration (SSA) and the Health Care Financing Administration (HCFA) administer the Medicare program. Both of these administrations are within the Department of Health and Human Services (DHHS). This alphabet soup of red tape can be used to provide help. If an individual has a question or a problem concerning a Medicare issue, the local social security office is the first place to inquire. SSA's national toll-free number is 1-800/772-1213. The telephone number of the local office may be found in the telephone directory under Social Security Administration.

How to Begin Medicare Coverage

A person may be eligible for Medicare merely because of reaching the age of 65 and meeting certain other requirements, but coverage is not automatic. Your parent must apply for coverage. First, let's see whether your parent is eligible. Then let's cover the steps your parent must take to be covered by Medicare.

Part A coverage applies to an individual who is age 65 and older *and* (1) is eligible for social security benefits or for railroad retirement benefits, or (2) was a federal employee. Even those who are not otherwise entitled to social security or railroad retirement benefits may still obtain coverage under Part A by enrolling in the program and paying for it.

Medicare Part B is known as Supplemental Medical Insurance. An individual age 65 and older may also obtain physician's care and outpatient services by paying a monthly premium for coverage under Part B. For 1991, the monthly premium was $29.90 and for 1992 it's $31.80. Increased premiums can be expected each year.

An individual is entitled to Part B coverage if he or she is age 65 or over and (1) is entitled to Part A coverage or (2) is a resident of the United States and a U.S. citizen or permanent resident for the past 5 years.

There are two ways to enroll. The first is to begin collecting social security benefits. The second is to apply for and receive benefits under Medicare Part A. To begin collecting social security benefits, an application for them must be made on Form SSA-1-F6 at the local social security office.

Even if your parent does not apply for social security benefits (for example, your parent continues to work past the age of 65), enrollment in Medicare Part B is still advisable. This can be done by a written application submitted in the "initial enrollment period" or in a subsequent "general enrollment period." The application is the same Form SSA-1-F6 used to apply for social security retirement benefits.

The initial enrollment period is a 7-month period beginning on the first day of the third month before the month in which your parent turns 65. The general enrollment period is the first quarter of each year (January 1 through March 31).

To have coverage begin on the first day of the month in which a person turns 65, enrollment must be made before turning 65. If a person enrolls during the month in which he or she turns 65, coverage will not begin until the first day of the following month. If enrollment is *after* the month in which a person turns 65 (but during the initial enrollment period), then coverage begins on the first day of the second month after the month of enrollment. If enrollment is after the initial 7-month enrollment period, the enrollment is transferred to the next general enrollment period, and coverage begins on the first day of the fourth month after the general enrollment period.

WEALTH BUILDING PROFILE   ***When to Apply for Medicare.*** On May 1, 1992, your parent turns 65. Your parent may enroll during the initial enrollment period, which begins on February 1, 1992, and lasts through August 31, 1992 (7 months from the first day of the third month before the month of eligibility). If your parent fails to enroll by August 31, 1992, your parent must wait until the next general enrollment period (January 1, 1993, through March 31, 1993. Coverage would begin on July 1, 1993.).

Special enrollment rules apply to those over 65 who continue to work and enjoy medical coverage through an employer plan. When these persons leave employment because of retirement or termination, a special 7-month enrollment period applies. The 7-month period begins on the first day of the month in which the private insurance ends. If enrollment is made during that month, Medicare coverage begins at the start of the month after coverage under the private insurance ends. If enrollment is delayed to any other month in the special enrollment period, then coverage begins on the first day of the month following the month of enrollment.

Of the three classes in the United States today— the poor, the middle class, and the rich—which has to worry the most about medical expenses?

The middle class. Generally, the poor obtain coverage through Medicaid, and the rich have sufficient resources to take care of practically all their medical needs. The middle class, both the elderly and their children, need to be aware of the types of coverage available, and the costs and limitations of each.

In figuring projected medical costs, how much should be assumed for inflation of medical expenses?

Medical expenses have consistently been one of the fastest growing costs that anyone pays, and show little sign of slowing down their pace. Based on past experience, expect that insurance premiums will rise by 5 percent per year, and that other medical expenses will rise by 15 percent per year.

How does one enroll in Medicare?

For Medicare Part A, an individual enrolls by beginning to collect social security benefits (filling out Form SSA-1-F6) or by applying for Medicare coverage directly. Those who are not eligible for social security benefits can purchase Medicare and pay a monthly premium. Medicare Part B is available by making a direct application, and is often advisable even when an individual continues to work past age 65.

How does the 80/20 rule apply for Medicare Part B expenses?

Medicare specifies a "covered charge" for many common types of medical expenses, and pays 80 percent of this charge. The patient is responsible for the remaining 20 percent, after an annual deductible is paid, in addition to all fees over the covered charge.

How should Medigap policies (provided by private insurance companies) be evaluated?

First, know what coverage Medicare itself provides. Next, consider the special health needs of your parent. Then evaluate the value of the benefits, relative to the cost of the premiums. New federal rules have made it easier to comparison-shop for Medigap policies.

Benefits under Medicare Part A

This portion of Medicare is the hospitalization coverage. There are two requirements for eligibility to get benefits under Part A. First, a person must be covered under Part A, as we've already discussed. Second, the specific services must fall under Part A.

Part A relates to in-hospital coverage (including limited psychiatric hospital care), skilled nursing facility services, in-home skilled nursing care, and hospice care. Certain items are covered up to a fixed amount in any given "benefit period."

In-Hospital Coverage

Part A covers the cost of the room, medical and surgical services provided by interns and certain residents, specific diagnostic and therapeutic services, nursing and medical social services, the use of hospital facilities, and drugs, biologicals, supplies, appliances, and equipment.

Although these items are "covered," they are not necessarily covered in full. In a benefit period, during the first 60 days of hospitalization, all covered services are paid by Part A except the annual deductible. The deductible in 1992 was $652. In the past, there was only one deductible *per year*. Now, there is one deductible *per benefit period*. Technically, an individual who goes 60 days or more between periods of hospitalization can be required to pay *more than one* deductible within the *same* year. The individual has experienced more than one benefit period within the same year.

For the next 30 days of continuing hospitalization, Part A pays for all covered services *minus* a coinsurance amount paid by the patient. This coinsurance amount is one-quarter of the deductible for the benefit period. In 1992, it was $163 a day for 61 to 90 days. For a continuing hospital stay of the full 30 days beyond the first 60 days, this coinsurance amount was $4,890 in 1992.

During the next 60 days of continuing hospitalization, called lifetime reserve days, Part A pays for all covered services *minus* a co-insurance amount of one-half of the deductible. For 1992, this coinsurance amount was $326 a day. For a hospital stay of the full 60 days beyond the first 90 days, this coinsurance amount totaled $19,560 in 1992.

If the deductible and coinsurance amounts for a hospital stay of 150 days in 1992 were added up, a person is out-of-pocket $24,802. This figure is alarming. However, the average hospital stay by Medicare patients is only a week. A stay of 150 days is rare. Regardless of the length of hospitalization, out-of-pocket costs can be minimized by Medigap insurance, discussed later in this chapter.

Expenses after the 150th day of hospitalization are not covered by Medicare. The patient must pay the entire cost. Again, certain insurance policies can help to meet this cost.

Special rules apply to coverage for a stay in a psychiatric hospital. There is a 190-day *lifetime* limit on coverage. All costs after 190 days are borne by the patient.

Skilled Nursing Facility Services

The emphasis here is on *skilled* nursing facility (SNF) services. Medicare covers only skilled nursing care provided by a Medicare-certified facility. It does not cover lesser degrees of nursing care, such as intermediate or custodial care, or private-duty nursing or attendant care.

Skilled nursing care is the type of care needed to recuperate from an acute illness or accident. For example, a stroke victim may be sent from a hospital to an SNF for a limited stay. Intermediate or custodial care is the type of care given for chronic conditions, where help with daily personal chores is needed. For example, an arthritis victim needs daily care and help in all personal tasks.

It is important to distinguish the type of care provided from the place providing it. A skilled nursing facility may be called a nursing home. A person staying in that facility may not necessarily require or receive skilled nursing care.

To qualify for coverage for a stay in a skilled nursing facility, several conditions must be met:

1. There must be a prior hospitalization of at least 3 consecutive days.
2. Admission to the skilled nursing facility must occur within 30 days of discharge from the hospital.

3. The care required by the patient must be "skilled" nursing care.
4. The facility must be Medicare-certified.
5. The bed used by the patient must be a Medicare-certified bed (a facility can be certified by Medicare and yet not have all its beds designated for Medicare use).

To be considered "skilled" services, the treatment must be ordered by a physician and require the skills of technical or professional personnel (registered nurses, licensed practical nurses, physical therapists, occupational therapists, speech pathologists, and audiologists). Further, the services must be required on a daily basis and be of the type provided in an SNF, and they must follow, although not immediately, a period of hospitalization.

The full cost of an SNF for the first 20 days is covered under Part A. For the next 80 days, the full cost of SNF *minus* a coinsurance payment of one-eighth of the hospital deductible (or the actual cost, if less than the deductible) is covered. This coinsurance amount for 1991 was $78.50 a day. In 1992, it rose to $81.50 per day.

For stays in a skilled nursing facility after the 100th day, the entire cost is borne by the patient. Most patients requiring skilled nursing care do not need it for a full 100 days. It is important to keep in mind that, if the level of care that is required gets reduced to intermediate or custodial care, Medicare will stop paying for the care even though the patient is still in the same skilled nursing care facility.

In-Home Skilled Nursing Care

Part A covers the entire costs of skilled care and certain medical supplies and equipment provided in one's home. Although coverage of in-home services at first blush appears generous, this is not necessarily so. Several conditions must be met before services and items are covered. These conditions are not easy to satisfy, as the following list indicates:

▶ The elderly person must be confined to his or her home. (This would also apply to confinement to an institution that is neither a hospital nor an SNF.)

▶ The person must be under the care of a doctor.

▶ There must be a need for intermittent skilled care. Such care includes skilled nursing care, physical therapy, speech therapy, or occupational therapy. Occupational therapy is not a basis for qualifying for home health services. Once home health services are approved, then occupational therapy may be covered.

▸ The services must be provided by a Medicare-certified home health agency (HHA) on a visiting basis in the person's home.

The key to qualification for home health services is proving a need for intermittent care. Federal agencies have interpreted the term narrowly: "intermittent" has come to mean a few hours a day on a few days each week (e.g., 2 hours a day, on 3 days each week).

As already mentioned, once eligibility is met, coverage is extensive. Health care services, including part-time or intermittent nursing care, must be provided by a registered nurse or administered under his or her supervision. Physical, occupational, and speech therapy, and certain medical supplies and equipment are included. The costs of a part-time or intermittent home health aide are covered where the services are provided by a home health agency (HHA) or under an arrangement with an HHA. The medical services of interns and certain residents, under an approved teaching program of a hospital with which an HHA has an affiliation, would be included.

Not all in-home services and items are covered. Part A does not pay for intermediate or custodial care, for housekeeping or food services, or for transportation from home to obtain medical services.

Hospice Care

The terminally ill may prefer to obtain the type of care that is provided in a hospice. (Hospice care is explained in more detail in Chapter 4.) At present, only a limited number of hospices participate in the Medicare program.

Assuming that hospice care is the medical treatment of choice and that a Medicare-certified hospice is found, it is still necessary to qualify for hospice care. First, a doctor must state that the person's life expectancy is 6 months or less. Next, the terminally ill person must sign a statement agreeing to two conditions: (1) not to seek treatment of the terminal illness, and (2) not to claim Medicare reimbursement for other than hospice care.

Medicare covers 100 percent of the cost of hospice care for a limited period. A person is allowed only two 90-day periods of hospice care and one later 30-day period. Total covered hospice care is 210 days in a lifetime. Thus, if a person who elects hospice care outlives his or her life expectancy, Medicare does not have to cover additional costs. A hospice care election may be revoked during the 90-day or

30-day periods. This would allow the person to claim other Medicare benefits. However, if a later hospice care election is made, days already used are still counted.

Benefits and Services under Medicare Part B

Medicare Part A provides hospitalization coverage; Part B, called Supplemental Medical Insurance, is essentially a major medical policy. In general, it covers the cost of doctors and other services outside the hospital setting.

Deductibles

In addition to the monthly premium already discussed, certain deductibles must be paid by the elderly. First, there is an annual deductible, which was $100 in 1992. Additional deductibles are co-insurance payments that apply to each type of service or item covered under Part B. In general, Medicare pays 80 percent of covered charges and the elderly person pays 20 percent of these amounts. Covered charges are those amounts approved by Medicare for the particular procedure or item. They sometimes equal the actual charges, but, more commonly, the allowances are considerably less.

WEALTH BUILDING PROFILE   *Figuring Out-of-Pocket Costs.* Jim's doctor charges $100 for a visit. Medicare says that the visit should have cost $50. Thus, the covered charges are $50. Medicare will pay $40 (80 percent of $50); Jim must pay the doctor $60, the uncovered amount. Therefore, Jim's out-of-pocket cost is actually 60 percent of the expense, not the theoretical 20 percent he thought was his share.

There are two categories of exceptions to the 80 percent/20 percent rule:

▶ 100 percent covered by Medicare (no coinsurance): certain clinical diagnostic laboratory tests; home health services; certain used medical equipment; outpatient and ambulatory surgical services; pneumococcal vaccine; and the costs of obtaining a kidney for transplant (the medical costs of the kidney donor).

▶ 50 percent covered by Medicare (50 percent coinsurance): outpatient mental health services. The annual amount of reasonable charges (under Medicare guidelines) cannot exceed $1,375. This 50 percent ceiling does not apply to doctor visits for prescribing or monitoring prescription drugs.

The list of covered services and items under Part B is extensive:

▶ Doctors' services for diagnosis, therapy, surgery, and consultations. Office visits, hospital visits, and house calls are included. The term "doctors" means physicians licensed in medicine or osteopathy, dentists, podiatrists, optometrists, and chiropractors.

▶ Outpatient physical therapy, speech pathology services, and dialysis services.

▶ Diagnostic tests; x-ray, radium, and radioactive isotope therapy; mammography screening.

▶ Certain services and supplies (e.g., ambulance services in certain cases, braces, artificial limbs, and prosthetic devices).

▶ Medical equipment such as hospital beds, wheelchairs, suction and oxygen apparatus, and respirators. The equipment may be purchased new or used, or rented. This decision is made by Medicare.

Excluded Items

Medicare Part B does not cover certain major expenses that must be borne by the elderly:

▶ Routine checkups and the cost of immunizations, such as flu vaccines.

▶ Routine medical items such as eyeglasses and contact lenses (except where the natural lens has been surgically removed and the contact lens acts as a replacement), hearing aids, and orthopedic shoes.

▶ Custodial care (other than respite care).

▶ Routine dental or podiatric care.

▶ Personal comfort items, such as a television or telephone in a care facility.

RECOVERING EXPENSES
UNDER MEDICARE

Different recovery rules apply to expenses covered by Part A and those under Part B:

▶ *Part A expenses.* Medicare pays the hospital or other provider directly for the portion of expenses that it deems appropriate to cover. As a rule, the patient will be asked to show that he or she participates in the Medicare program. The patient will then sign a form requesting payment. The patient remains liable for the coinsurance amount.

▶ *Part B expenses.* The Department of Health and Human Services contracts with private insurance companies, called "carriers," to process claims and make payments to the elderly or to providers. The particular insurance company used to handle claims varies from state to state.

Medicare may pay either the patient or the doctor or other provider of services or items. Under a new rule that took effect on September 1, 1990, the doctor or other medical provider is *required* to submit claims for payment; individuals are no longer burdened with this paperwork. Doctors are not supposed to charge for this administrative service. However, as a practical matter, their fees for medical services are undoubtedly adjusted accordingly. Unfortunately, this new rule may not be as great a benefit to your parent as you might think. Your parent cannot see to it that claims are promptly submitted. This can mean that your parent may be forced to wait longer for reimbursement from Medicare than if he or she had submitted the claim directly. If the doctor fails to submit a claim, contact your parent's Medicare carrier.

If your parent pays the doctor and awaits reimbursement from Medicare, he or she receives the amount Medicare will cover, less the coinsurance amount (and the deductible, if not already met). Your parent pays the provider the full amount of the expense, making up the difference between the Medicare recovery and the amount of that expense.

Some doctors and other providers of items or services "accept assignment." This means that the patient assigns the right to reimbursement to the doctor and the doctor agrees to accept this amount, plus the patient's coinsurance, as payment in full for the services rendered. The patient in this case must pay no more than 20 percent of the reasonable charge (and the deductible).

WEALTH   *Figuring Costs When the Doctor Accepts Assign-*
BUILDING   *ment.* In early 1992, Susan paid $300 to see Dr.
PROFILE   Smith, a specialist, about a medical problem. Assume
                   that $300 is the reasonable charge for such a service.
Susan assigns her Medicare benefits to Dr. Smith, who accepts assignment. Assuming that Susan has not yet paid her deductible ($100
in 1992), her cost for this treatment is the deductible of $100 plus
$40 (20 percent of the $300 charge less the $100 deductible). Susan's
total cost is $140. Dr. Smith receives $160 from Medicare.

Unfortunately for the elderly, not all doctors accept assignment.
Your parent may have a long-time relationship with a particular doctor who does not accept assignment and may not want to make a
change on the basis of cost or convenience. This is a personal decision
for your parent to make. Fortunately for residents of Massachusetts
and Wisconsin, all doctors in those states are required to accept assignment as a condition of licensing.

Where possible, it is advantageous to assign benefits to the doctor
or other provider. Assignment means that the fee paid to the doctor or
other provider is limited to the one approved by Medicare. This translates into little or no out-of-pocket expense, even if the patient has no
Medigap insurance. If the patient has Medigap insurance, the deductible and coinsurance amount should be fully covered.

Fighting Medicare

What happens if Medicare denies eligibility? What if the program
fails to pay for a service or item that your parent thought was covered? Where does your parent turn for help?

The law sets out a step-by-step process that must be followed in
pressing a claim. *No step can be omitted*. Each deadline must be carefully met.

Eligibility Contests

If *eligibility* for Part A or Part B is denied, the appeals process is
similar to that used for contesting social security benefit denial. The
following steps must be taken.

1. File a request for reconsideration with the local office of
    the Social Security Administration (SSA) or the Health Care

Financing Administration (HCFA) or Railroad Retirement Board. This request must be made within 60 days after receiving a decision denying eligibility.

2. If the decision is not changed on reconsideration, then request an administrative hearing within 60 days.

3. If you receive a negative administrative ruling, file an appeal with the Appeals Council within 60 days.

4. If your parent still has not gotten satisfaction, file a suit in a U.S. District Court. Again, there is a 60-day period in which to begin the action.

Payment Contests

Different procedures apply when Medicare does not cover services or items the patient thought should be covered. For Part A services, there is no right of appeal if a hospital or other provider gives a notice of noncoverage. This means that the hospital or other provider will not seek reimbursement from Medicare; the patient is liable for the full charges. Upon admission to a hospital, a patient must receive a statement entitled "How to Request a Review of the Notice of Noncoverage." Such a request is made to the hospital, asking it to change its policy and treat a service or item as covered. If the hospital does not change its policy, a patient has no other recourse.

A hospital may treat a service or item as covered but Medicare can still deny coverage. In this case, there is a right of appeal, and these are the necessary steps:

1. Get your parent's claim reviewed. Administrative remedies must be sought before court action can begin. To seek administrative relief, the amount in question must be $100 or more. (This is called the amount in controversy.)

2. Take court action, if no relief is obtained at the administrative level. Your parent must take his or her appeal to a U.S. District Court. The amount in question must be $1,000 or more.

It is possible to bypass the first step. Once a reconsideration determination has been made or there has been a higher level of appeal, you can file a request with the SSA to skip additional administrative review and go directly to court.

When coverage for benefits under Part B is denied, there is a multilayered process of review. First, there are two stages for review by the carrier (the private insurance company that handles Medicare reimbursements for the federal government). The first stage is called the "review." A person must file a written request within 6 months of the notice of the initial determination. The request can be filed with the carrier, the local SSA office, or an HCFA office.

The second stage of review by the carrier is called the "hearing." It is available if the amount at stake is $100 or more. A 6-month period is allowed in which to file a written request for a hearing. This period runs from the date when notice is given of the review determination and may be extended at the carrier's option if a request is made.

If the amount in question is $500 or more, a second hearing may be held before an Administrative Law Judge (ALJ), after the ordinary hearing. Several claims may be grouped together to satisfy the $500 threshold. If an individual has a claim for $400, then the hearing at the second stage of review is the final one—no ALJ review is permitted.

If a favorable decision is not received and the amount in controversy is $1,000 or more, the decision is appealable to a U.S. District Court. Claims may be lumped together to reach this dollar threshold if they are for similar or related services provided to the same person.

WEALTH   *Fighting Denial of Payment by Medicare.* Edith
BUILDING   was denied payment for an $80 claim. She can have
PROFILE   her claim evaluated in the first stage of review. If she receives an unfavorable decision, that verdict is final. She does not have the required $100-or-more claim that would allow her to seek the second stage of review.

Assume that Edith has a second claim for $420. This claim can be carried through the first and second stages of review. If her claim is again denied, she may be able to seek review before an ALJ, if both claims are similar or related. This may be possible because her claims total $500. She could not go to court, because the amount at stake is not $1,000 or more.

Help in Fighting Medicare

There is no requirement that a person have legal representation when making or contesting a Medicare claim. If the claim is large enough, it may be advisable to consult an attorney, in order to learn your parent's rights and the probability of success. Check with the local bar association for a referral, if your parent does not already know an attorney. Your parent can also see a Health Advocacy Specialist. The

American Association of Retired Persons (AARP) runs a volunteer program to help with Medicare appeals. The program is called AARP/Medicare/Medicaid Assistance Program (MMAP). For more information, contact Health Advocacy Services, AARP, 1909 K Street N.W., Washington, DC 20049; phone: 202/434-2277. Another source of help in contesting Medicare claims is private companies that specialize in medical insurance recoveries. Check your local telephone directory for assistance.

MEDIGAP POLICIES

As the previous discussion has indicated, Medicare provides only a limited amount of coverage. Not all medical services or items are covered. Even when coverage is allowed, there are deductibles and coinsurance payments that are a patient's responsibility. Therefore, a parent should supplement Medicare coverage with other insurance. This additional coverage, available through insurance companies, is referred to as Medigap coverage. About 20 million elderly now have some type of Medigap insurance.

When Congress passed the Medicare Catastrophic Coverage Act of 1988, some elderly thought that the need for Medigap coverage was eliminated. They may have mistakenly dropped their coverage in 1989, with the expectation that the new law would be enough. The new law did not do away with all deductibles and coinsurance amounts. What is more, this law was repealed in 1989. For those who had dropped their coverage, insurers were required to provide a period for picking up coverage again. Notice was required to be sent to all those who dropped coverage in 1989. If your parent needs coverage for the first time or is considering a change, review the different types of policies available.

A Medigap policy is a Medicare supplemental policy that covers Medicare deductibles and coinsurance payments. It generally does not cover any amounts not otherwise covered by Medicare. For example, if a doctor charges $200 for medical services but Medicare deems those services worth only $150, a supplemental policy will not make up the $50 difference. However, some Medigap policies do pick up certain uncovered charges.

It is unfortunate that various insurance companies have used the term "Medigap" for a number of different types of individual policies or group plans that offer more than just Medicare supplements. These types of policies are often confused with true Medigap policies. In many cases, these other types of policies are unnecessary or are, at best, expensive for the benefits provided. These other types of policies include:

▶ A hospital indemnity policy, which pays a dollar amount (e.g., $50 per day) for a fixed number of days spent in a hospital. Some policies may also pay added benefits, such as surgical benefits or skilled nursing care for home confinements. Hospital indemnity policies pay benefits regardless of other insurance coverage. The cash may be used to pay medical expenses not otherwise covered by insurance, or for any other purpose. Caution is advised before taking this type of coverage. First, these policies are skillfully marketed by television and direct mail. The hype may be more than the help. Second, there usually is a period of hospitalization, such as 7 days, that is excluded from coverage. As already mentioned, the typical hospital stay for an elderly person is under 7 days. Thus, for the vast majority of individuals, this policy will never pay off. Premiums could be better spent elsewhere. Third, the amount of coverage is fixed at the outset of the policy. Therefore, it does not keep up with rising costs. On the plus side, the premiums are also fixed.

▶ A major medical or catastrophic benefits policy, which is designed to pay for the cost of a serious illness or injury. It may cover some costs not covered by Medicare, such as a portion of home care. It does not cover Medicare deductibles or coinsurance payments, and it may have a high deductible of its own. It is not a nursing home policy (discussed in Chapter 3). For those covered by Medicare Part A, this policy may be largely redundant.

▶ A policy ensuring the costs of treatment for a specific disease. This type of policy is not a Medigap policy, but is often marketed to the elderly. It provides for a fixed amount when the elderly person undergoes treatment for the specified disease. The cost of this type of insurance may be relatively high, because such coverage is a crap shoot. The insured is betting on getting a certain disease, such as cancer. The money spent on this type of policy could be better spent on Medigap or long-term care policies.

─────────────→ **ACTION ITEM** ◄─────────────

When looking for a Medigap policy, beware of insurance policies touted for the elderly. They may not provide a needed supplement to Medicare, they may only offer a limited type of benefit, and their cost may be considerable.

Shopping for Medigap Insurance

Medigap insurance is sold by insurance companies to individuals and through various groups. In 1991, over $8 billion in premiums was sold to about 20 million elderly individuals. Before buying any coverage in addition to Medicare, ask a few simple questions:

▶ How much will Medicare cover? Before the "gaps" can be closed, it is important to know what those gaps are.

▶ What special health needs does your parent need to address? Certain policies exclude some illnesses or conditions that your parent may have or can reasonably expect to have, in view of family medical history.

▶ Does the policy being considered offer the best benefits for the lowest premiums? As with most things, you get what you pay for. The lower-cost policy may not meet your parent's needs. Only one Medigap policy is necessary. It is generally a waste of money to carry more than one policy.

Federal Law on Medigap Standards

In 1990, a new federal law was enacted to make it easier to comparison shop Medigap policies. Hailed as a consumer protection measure, the new law requires that insurance companies must offer one "core" (basic) policy, plus up to nine other Medigap policies. Because all companies will use the same format, it will be possible to compare apples to apples and determine the best coverage for your parent.

The new law also requires that *all* Medigap policies have guaranteed renewability, except in the case of nonpayment of premiums. Insurance companies must pay out, in benefits to policyholders, a greater percentage of premiums earned. This mandate should mean better coverage.

The new law prevents the sale of multiple policies to an individual. In the past, it was not uncommon for the elderly to carry three, four, or as many as 20 or more Medigap policies. Now, a policy cannot be sold to an individual who already has coverage *unless* the policyholder puts in writing the intention to change policies *and* the insurance agent warrants that the new coverage improves on the old coverage.

The National Association of Insurance Commissioners (NAIC) has created standards (model regulations) for Medicare supplemental policies. Federal law requires that states adopt these standards by

July 31, 1992 (Massachusetts, Minnesota, and Wisconsin already did). As a minimum, a Medigap policy meeting these standards is required to include the following benefits:

▸ Coinsurance amounts for Part A from the 61st day to the 90th day of hospitalization ($163 in 1992);
▸ Coinsurance amounts for Part A in-patient reserve days ($326 in 1992);
▸ Eligible Part A hospitalization expenses not covered by Medicare (this may be subject to a 365-day lifetime cap);
▸ Cost of the first three pints of blood;
▸ Copayment of eligible expenses under Part B.

Additional benefits under the other nine policies under NAIC standards include:

▸ All or none of the Part A in-hospital deductible ($652 in 1992);
▸ Part B deductible ($100 in 1992);
▸ Part B excess (difference between doctor's bill and Medicare-approved charge);
▸ Part B excess (amount over 80 percent);
▸ Medically necessary emergency care in foreign countries;
▸ Bills or extended prescription drug benefit;
▸ Preventive medical care.

Before taking Medigap coverage, find out whether this additional coverage is necessary for your parent. If your parent is enrolled in a health maintenance organization (HMO) or a competitive medical plan (CMP) that has a contract with Medicare, no additional coverage is necessary. Also, individuals who qualify for Medicaid do not need supplemental insurance. In fact, federal law bars the sale of Medigap policies to those on Medicaid.

The HCFA has provided some tips for buying Medigap policies:

▸ Shop carefully before buying. Comparison shopping applies to Medigap insurance as it does to any other consumer product. The new federal law will help to simplify comparison shopping, once insurance companies adapt their products to it. Comparison shopping has already been simplified in some states. Massachusetts, Minnesota, and Wisconsin require that policy language be standardized.

▶ Don't buy more coverage than needed. It is estimated that half of all elderly have too much Medigap coverage. A single policy covering all desired items is better than several policies that may have duplicate or overlapping coverage. Senior Citizen Health Insurance Counseling (SCHIC), in Missouri, a group sponsored by state and local underwriting associations, provides free Medigap evaluations. This service can be used to prevent coverage duplication. There are also private businesses throughout the country that make insurance evaluations and recommendations. The new federal law mentioned earlier prevents an insurance agent from selling a policy if the individual already has coverage, unless that person signs a statement that he or she intends to drop the first policy. The NAIC model regulations require an agent to state that the new policy "materially improves" on the coverage provided by the first policy. Unfortunately, because the new federal law does not have retroactive effect, insurers are not required to give refunds for duplicative coverage. Individuals who already have more than one policy need not drop excess coverage. It is, however, advisable to review existing coverage to see where costs can be cut. Here are some suggestions:

▶ Consider alternatives to Medigap, such as HMOs or CMPs (discussed below).

▶ Check for preexisting-condition exclusions. Some policies may not pay for amounts spent on illnesses or conditions for which advice or treatment was received before buying the Medigap policy. Fortunately, in most states, preexisting-condition exclusions must be covered 6 months after the Medigap coverage is purchased. The fact that a policy does not require a medical examination prior to issuance is no protection against a preexisting-condition exclusion. Under the new federal law, Medicare beneficiaries have 6 months from their 65th birthdays to get Medigap coverage without having to take a medical examination.

▶ Check for waiting periods before changing policies. It may pay to have overlapping policies for a short time rather than be without protection for any length of time.

▶ Learn about the maximum benefits under the policy. They may be stated in terms of dollar amounts, number of days of care, or in relation to the amounts allowed by Medicare. Again, as policies become standardized, benefits should be easier to determine.

▶ Be sure that the policy is renewable automatically (unless there is a failure to pay premiums or misrepresentation in the application). The new federal law and model regulations of the NAIC require this automatic renewal.

▶ Look at the insurance company marketing the policy. Your parent wants to be sure that the company will be in business to pay off on claims. Check the company's rating with a rating service (e.g., A. M. Best & Company).

▶ Do not be pressured into a sale. Ask about a "free look" clause that gives your parent a 30-day refund period to cancel the policy.

To compare policies under consideration, use the following Wealth Building Worksheet.

———— Wealth Building Worksheet ————
Shopping List for Medigap

Feature	Policy A	Policy B	Policy C
Part A deductible	————	————	————
Part A coinsurance, 61 to 90 days	————	————	————
Part A coinsurance, reserve days	————	————	————
Part A expenses not covered	————	————	————
Three pints of blood	————	————	————
Part B copayments	————	————	————
Exclusion: preexisting condition	————	————	————
Other benefits:			
Dental	————	————	————
Private-duty nursing	————	————	————
Hospitalization in foreign countries	————	————	————
Prescription drugs	————	————	————
Automatic renewal	————	————	————
Insurance company rating	————	————	————
Premiums	————	————	————

Neither the federal government nor state governments sell or service Medigap policies. However, state insurance departments may approve policies for sale in their state. Such approval means only that the policies meet state law. It does not mean that the policies provide good coverage or are good values.

The federal government has established voluntary certification for insurers that meet certain minimum standards. The certification applies to Medigap policies that provide a certain level of benefits. A seal showing this certification may be used in marketing their products.

OTHER WAYS TO MEET MEDICAL COSTS

Veterans' Benefits

Individuals who served in our armed forces may not need to supplement Medicare by private insurance. They may be able to get medical treatment through the Veterans Administration (VA). However, because of cutbacks in the VA budget, admission to VA hospitals (for those who do not have service-related injuries) is largely restricted to those with financial need. Therefore, veterans should not assume that their medical needs will be met by a VA hospital.

See Chapter 4 for a discussion of veterans' benefits.

Prepayment Plans

An elderly person may be able to enroll in a prepayment plan that guarantees to provide health care. There are three types: a health maintenance organization (HMO), a preferred provider organization (PPO), and a competitive medical plan (CMP). To date, these plans have not attracted a great number of Medicare-eligible participants. It is estimated that only about 3 percent of Medicare-eligible persons opt for prepayment plans. However, despite these low numbers, such a plan may be worth considering in a particular case.

Under a prepayment plan, an enrollee is required to use the medical services provided by doctors and health care facilities participating in the plan. In case of emergency, outside services are permitted. All doctors' visits and related services are covered under the plan. By enrolling in a prepayment plan, an individual is choosing to have medical expenses covered under the plan rather than by recourse to Medicare. Medicare pays the plan a fixed amount monthly for each person enrolled in the plan. This entitles the enrollee to all the services that Medicare would cover. The plan may also offer other services not covered by Medicare. The enrollee continues to pay the Medicare Part B monthly premium (which is typically deducted from social security or railroad retirement benefits). In addition, the plan may charge a monthly fee to cover amounts not covered by Medicare (deductibles, coinsurance, and additional benefits).

To enroll in a prepayment plan, your parent must live in the area covered by the plan, according to its contract with Medicare, and your parent must have Medicare Part B. Your parent is free to "disenroll" at any time by giving written notice. Regular Medicare coverage resumes on the first day of the month after the written request is received by the plan. Thus, if your parent enrolls in a prepayment plan and then moves to an area not covered by the plan, your parent can pick up Medicare coverage again.

Whether a prepayment plan is advisable depends on the nature of the plan available in your particular locale. In some areas, the doctors and facilities affiliated with the plan may be excellent; in others, the number of doctors and the quality of facilities may not be satisfactory.

There are a number of benefits for participation in a prepayment plan. First, there is no need for additional Medigap insurance. All services covered under the plan are "prepaid." There is a charge for participating in the prepayment plan. Second, because all expenses are covered under the plan, there is no need to file for a claim. This eliminates the paperwork burden. Third, a variety of services (e.g., doctors' services, hospital care, diagnostic tests) may be obtained through one source.

There are some drawbacks to prepayment plans. Your parent can only see doctors in the plan, and the choice of doctors in the plan may be limited. As a general rule, your parent can see a specialist only if the primary care physician makes the referral. Coverage for care away from home is limited to emergency care. Thus, for example, if your parent typically spends the winter months in a warmer climate, the prepayment plan may not suit your parent's needs.

Employer Group Insurance

Some elderly people may continue to work past age 65 and may be covered under their employer's health insurance plan. Where an employer regularly employs at least 20 employees, those age 65 and over must be given the same coverage as younger employees. The employer's plan is considered the "primary payor" of benefits. Medicare is treated as a "secondary payor" of benefits. Medicare is also secondary for spouses age 65 or older (regardless of the age of the employee).

What does this mean in terms of Medicare coverage? It does not necessarily affect the overall cost to the individual. It merely determines whether claims are submitted first to the employer or first to

Medicare. As primary payor, the employer's plan is the first to meet
medical expenses. If the plan does not cover all that would be covered
under Medicare, then Medicare will pay the differential.

Lifetime Care Facilities

Some elderly opt for a special housing arrangement that includes medical care. This arrangement is called a lifetime care (or continuing
care) facility. There is an initial entry fee plus monthly charges that
cover housing, meals, other services, and medical expenses. Residence
in a lifetime care facility does not obviate the need for Medigap policies. For a complete discussion of lifetime care facilities, see Chapter 5.

CHILD'S PAYMENT OF PARENT'S MEDICAL EXPENSES

The cost of paying a parent's medical expenses may be dear. You may
have no alternative but to do so. In about half of the states, if the parent
is indigent, a child may be obligated under certain circumstances to pay
for a parent's support (including medical expenses) under a "relative
responsibility" statute.

In other states, you may choose to pay or not to pay a parent's medical expenses. If you choose *not* to pay, then your parent may be forced
to use up a life's savings on medical bills. Once assets are depleted,
your parent can qualify for Medicaid (see Chapter 4). This scenario
will result in the loss of any inheritance for you. If you pay your parent's medical expense, there are some important income tax advantages for you:

▸ You may be able to claim your parent as a dependent. This claim
  allowed a dependency exemption in 1992 of $2,300. You must
  provide more than one-half of your parent's support (or be entitled
  to the exemption under a multiple support agreement) and your
  parent must have gross income of less than $2,300. For this pur-
  pose, social security benefits, if not subject to tax, are not treated as
  gross income.

▸ You may qualify as a head of household if you are single and support your parent. This entitles you to use special tax brackets that
  are more favorable than those provided for other singles. It also
  enables you to claim a larger standard deduction than that allowed

for singles who are not heads of households. This provision is of no benefit to you if you are married. To qualify for head of household status, you must be entitled to claim an exemption for your parent and you must pay more than one-half of the cost of maintaining a household for your parent (either in your own home or in a separate household such as a nursing home).

▶ You may be able to deduct the medical expenses you pay for your parent. This will reduce your out-of-pocket costs for the expenses you cover. The types of expenses deductible and the extent of tax savings from claiming the deduction were explained earlier in this chapter, under Tax Savings (page 17). You can deduct the medical expenses you paid for your parent if (1) you provided over half of your parent's support, whether or not you are entitled to claim a dependency exemption for your parent, or (2) you are entitled to claim your parent as a dependent under a multiple-support agreement.

WEALTH   *Does Your Financial Support for Your Parent Entitle*
BUILDING   *You to Tax Breaks?* You are single and fully support
PROFILE   your parent in your home. You also pay for prescription
                    drugs and other items not covered by Medicare. Your
                    parent receives $600 a month in social security benefits
but has no other income. You can enjoy several tax benefits. You can claim your parent as your dependent. You can file as head of household, using favorable head-of-household tax rates. You can also add your parent's medical expenses to your own, if you itemize deductions.

What happens if your parent is incompetent and you are the legal guardian designated to receive your parent's social security benefits? You cannot claim a medical expense deduction for the portion of those benefits expended on your parent's medical care.

There is no gift tax for paying someone else's medical bills. An unlimited exclusion from gift tax covers direct payments of someone's medical care. No percentage limitations apply, as in the case of the income tax deduction. This gift tax exclusion for payments of medical expenses is in addition to the regular $10,000 annual gift tax exclusion. Thus, for example, it is possible to pay for a parent's medical costs, regardless of amount, as well as provide them with cash up to $10,000 without gift tax cost.

──────── POINTS TO REMEMBER ────────

▶ Medical costs are the first or second most expensive living cost for the elderly. Keep abreast of changes in Medicare and other health insurance programs for the elderly.

▶ Begin planning for medical care costs by estimating current and future medical expenses for your parent. Include the cost of insurance, out-of-pocket expenses such as medications, and an inflation factor.

▶ In making plans, don't overlook the tax deductions offered by medical costs.

▶ Medicare is complex and ever changing in how it is applied and used. Become familiar with its details. The first place to inquire about Medicare is at the local Social Security Administration office; call a national toll-free number (1-800/772-1213) to obtain information.

▶ Medicare is divided into Part A coverage (basic hospitalization coverage) and Part B (supplemental medical insurance). Most elderly qualify for Part A coverage, which is free to those who have made social security payments during their working lives. Part B applies to major medical expenses (doctors' care) and has a monthly premium. Both types of Medicare must be applied for.

▶ Part A Medicare coverage has an annual deductible (a cost that the user pays), scaled to the length of the hospital stay. Part B coverage has deductibles and covers 80 percent of "covered charges," which are limits set for the cost of various types of services.

▶ The eligibility for Medicare coverage for a medical expense, and the size of the payment Medicare makes, can be contested. Very explicit procedures have been worked out for appealing Medicare decisions, and the Medicare user must follow them.

▶ "Medigap" insurance is offered by private insurance companies to cover certain expenses that Medicare covers only partially or not at all. These policies are very popular (they have over 20 million users), but must be analyzed closely for their appropriateness and quality for the Medicare user.

▶ There are other ways to meet medical costs, such as through prepayment programs like health maintenance organizations (HMOs), preferred provider organizations (PPOs), and competitive medical plans (CMPs). Although not as common as straight Medicare coverage, these plans may make sense in some instances.

▶ Willingly or unwillingly, you may find yourself personally responsible for your parent's medical costs. Become aware of the tax advantages, responsibilities, and options for this situation.

3

Deciding on a Nursing Home

*P*erhaps the most difficult decision any person can make is to place a parent or other loved one in a nursing home. Once a parent loses the ability for self-care, and other types of care (for example, in-home care or a lifetime care facility) have been exhausted, the decision may become obvious, although not easy.

MAKING THE DECISION

The decision is a complicated one, for several reasons. First, many psychological and emotional issues are raised. The child is, in effect, acting as the parent. The child may for the first time be facing the parent's death—acknowledging the "beginning of the end" and all the things that have and have not been said.

Second, there are the difficulties in executing the decision: finding the right nursing home and having to discuss the move with the parent, if the parent still has an understanding of what is going on.

Third, there is the issue of cost. When nursing homes are used as places to recuperate from an acute illness, such as stroke, the cost may be covered under Medicare. When they are used to provide care for a parent who is no longer capable of self-care, the cost is not reimbursable from Medicare. Your parent, or you, must pay the bill through private savings or by resorting to Medicaid. Does your parent have sufficient income and/or assets or insurance to meet the monthly charges? Will your parent have to become impoverished in order to have Medicaid pick up the tab? Will you have to pay for part or all of the cost? The financial concerns regarding nursing-home care are addressed in Chapter 4.

Overview of Nursing Homes Today

It may come as no surprise that there is a nursing-home crisis in America. With the graying of the population, there is an increasing shortage of available nursing-home beds. There are only 16,000 nursing homes nationwide. More than 2.3 million elderly now live in these nursing homes; of these, 85 percent are women. Nearly one-quarter of the population over age 85 is now in nursing homes.

The cost of a nursing-home stay has now reached an average of $30,000 a year. That figure can be expected to rise. The $30,000 annual cost is only an *average* figure. In some areas, the cost is considerably higher. In more affluent communities, the average cost is now running between $60,000 and $80,000. In one newly opened home in Brooklyn, New York, the cost is $300 a day, or more than $100,000 annually!

Meeting the high cost of nursing-home care is difficult for most individuals, if not impossible. At present, almost half of all nursing-home bills are paid by individuals. Of this amount, less than 2 percent is financed by long-term care insurance. The other half of all nursing-home bills is paid from government sources, mostly Medicaid. This enormous price tag is putting a strain on the Medicare/Medicaid system. The unsatisfied demand for beds, the high costs of nursing-home care, and the strain on the government assistance programs all contribute to the "nursing-home crisis."

For those who have been searching for a facility for a parent, the realities are frightening. Spaces are limited, choices are few, and costs are high. For those who expect to have a need in the future, the very thought may provoke extreme concern. Whatever your situation, you need to learn the facts before you can act wisely.

Separating Myths from Facts

There are a number of myths surrounding nursing homes. Understanding the difference between facts and myths can make the nursing home decision somewhat easier.

Myth 1. *Nursing homes are used as places to "dump" elderly parents by children who do not want to take care of them.* This perception is largely incorrect. It is true that some parents who could do well with a lesser form of care are nonetheless placed in nursing homes. However, this is the exception, not the rule. In most cases, a nursing home is the choice of last resort. It is used because the type of care offered in the facility is the level of care required by the parent and the children have already exhausted other alternatives for care.

There is another reason why the perception that nursing homes are used to dump elderly parents is wrong. The high cost of nursing-home care prevents all but the very wealthy or the very poor from using this option. As already mentioned, the average cost of a year's stay in a nursing home is now $30,000 and can run to as much as $100,000.

Myth 2. *All elderly individuals will need nursing-home care at some time.* It is true that almost one-quarter of those 65 or older will spend *some* time during their life in a nursing home. However, the length of time may be short (usually, a month or less). Only a little more than 10 percent of the elderly spend more than 3 years in a nursing home.

The great majority of nursing-home residents are female. Thus, from a statistical perspective, the odds that an elderly father will need nursing-home care for an extended time are small while the odds that an elderly mother will need nursing-home care at some time are quite high.

Myth 3. *Nursing homes are elephant graveyards where the elderly go to die.* Statistics show that nursing homes are not places where people overwhelmingly go to die. Of the 1.2 million nursing-home residents in 1984 and 1985, only 28 percent died in the homes. About 37 percent of nursing-home residents were transferred to hospitals, but the rest went on to other housing arrangements.

Myth 4. *Nursing homes are horrible places.* More than a few instances of patient abuse have been revealed. Some nursing-home owners have been convicted of fraud and other crimes. Because of the acute shortage of space, homes that are substandard are seldom closed. However, nursing homes are not necessarily bad places. In a great number of homes, the elderly can receive good quality care.

In 1987, a nursing-home reform package was enacted by Congress. Many of the provisions of the new law, which took effect in 1990, were supposed to eliminate abuse of the elderly in nursing homes. However, a recent study by the Department of Health and Human Services

(DHHS) has found that the reforms have not ended all abuse. Six types of abuse are still found in some nursing homes:

▶ Physical abuse

▶ Misuse of restraints

▶ Verbal and emotional abuse

▶ Physical neglect

▶ Verbal and emotional neglect

▶ Personal property abuse.

Myth 5. Governments cannot meet the high cost of elder care without going broke. Many industrial countries now provide for long-term care for their elderly population without regard to need. Most of the Canadian provinces consider such care to be a right of every person, not just the poor. Britain, Denmark, Norway, and Sweden cover the cost of long-term care for their elderly. Japan also has a program of geriatric care without cost to the recipient. Taxes in those countries are significantly higher than taxes in this country.

The United States is one of the few industrial countries that furnishes elder care assistance largely on a welfare basis. Given the current fiscal problems of the federal government, however, the status quo is unlikely to change rapidly. It would be unwise to anticipate much government help in this area in the near future.

CHOOSING THE NURSING HOME

Some planning and information gathering before nursing-home placement is actually required may be advisable. Because of the shortage of space, many homes have waiting lists for entry. It is often necessary to queue up as soon as the prospect of need becomes apparent. If you understand what is involved in nursing-home placement and how to go about it, you will have prepared yourself and your parent, should such placement become necessary.

A problem encountered in deciding on nursing-home care is overplanning. A child who is concerned about a parent's future need for nursing-home care may make extensive arrangements for long-term care. The parent may not ever require that care. Instead, the parent may remain physically and mentally able to utilize lesser degrees of care or may benefit from alternative housing methods (see Chapter 5).

This problem, however, is the exception. Most families fail to make any plans until required to do so.

When Does Your Parent Require Nursing-Home Care?

Nursing-home placement generally is the choice of last resort. Experts agree that an elderly parent tends to function better in familiar surroundings, if the proper support is available. In-home care or some form of assisted living can and should be relied on until such time as a parent's ability for self-care becomes minimal and the need for professional full-time assistance becomes necessary.

To determine whether a parent's medical condition has reached a level that requires nursing-home care, it is essential to get a doctor's evaluation of your parent's medical condition. After an evaluation has been made, a patient review instrument (PRI) will be written. The PRI will tell a home about the level of care that a parent requires. Without a PRI, no placement can be made.

In some cases, the need for nursing-home placement may be absolutely clear.

WEALTH BUILDING PROFILE *Does a Parent Need to Be Placed in a Nursing Home?* Sam, age 79, suffered a stroke that left him paralyzed on his right side and unable to talk. His only child lives thousands of miles away. Sam will require extensive rehabilitative care and may never again be capable of self-care. Sam's child was advised by his father's doctor, as well as a hospital social worker, that the best course of treatment in Sam's case would be placement in a nursing home.

In other cases, the need for nursing-home placement may be a close call, after weighing various factors. Where the choice is difficult, it may be advisable for you to consult a social worker or other counselor. Some individuals seek psychological counseling at this juncture, because of the various issues (mentioned at the start of this chapter) that are raised by having to place a parent in a nursing home. You may need to sort out your own issues. You may need assurances about the decisions you make on your parent's behalf. You may also require more information before deciding on a nursing home.

Bases for Selection

Once the nursing-home decision has been made, there are a number of factors to consider in selecting the particular home. Depending on your parent's location, resources, and care requirements, choices may be many or few.

Type of Home

About three-quarters of all homes are privately owned businesses that are operated for profit. The balance are run by not-for-profit organizations like churches. According to a number of sources, a home's being for-profit or not-for-profit has no effect on the quality of care. There are both good and bad homes in each category. Unfortunately, the majority of homes are not first-rate. As a minimum requirement, be sure the home has a current, state-issued operating license. Check that the administrator of the home has a current license as well.

Level of Care Provided

Different homes provide different levels of care. Depending on your parent's particular illness or condition, it may be advisable, for example, to consider a skilled nursing facility (SNF), even if your parent needs only custodial care. If your parent's health deteriorates to a new long-term level, there will be no need for a transfer, to get the required level of nursing care.

Availability

You may be limited in your choice of nursing homes by the number of facilities in a particular location. If you want your parent to be close to your home, then your radius of inquiry is restricted. It is advisable that you find a nursing home near your own home, to allow you to make frequent visits. Your visits will be directly beneficial to your parent. He or she will more readily stay in touch with the "outside" world. There is an indirect benefit as well. Frequent visits ensure that the home continues to provide the quality of care you expect and your parent deserves.

Available space is a widespread problem. As already stressed, nursing-home space is limited. You may like one home, but its waiting list may be longer than your parent's condition can tolerate. If your parent happens to be in a hospital whose own beds are in demand, then the hospital generally will discharge your parent to the first available bed in a pool of nursing homes in the area.

Cost

All nursing homes are expensive; some are more costly than others. Unless money is no object, it is necessary to comparison shop. Ask to see a list of fees for basic and special services. The basic charges may not be all-inclusive. For example, there may be extra charges for hand feeding and incontinence care. Check whether the home accepts Medicaid patients. Not all homes do. If an individual needs Medicaid assistance to pay for nursing-home care, then only a home accepting Medicaid's allowances can be considered.

The shortage of space in nursing homes contributes to their high cost. Homes in some localities require large up-front fees in one form or another, before a parent can gain admittance. Some states—New York, for example—prohibit such fees. In other states, fees may be prohibited but routinely extracted under some guise. For instance, it may be necessary to "buy" a piece of equipment for the home, in order to secure a bed for a parent.

Living Conditions

Naturally, you want the best physical setup possible. See that the home is well-maintained and safe. A number of nursing-home fires have been reported in recent years. Once a fire breaks out, it is difficult to evacuate the building promptly, because all of the residents require assistance. If the building does not have proper fire exits, escape is delayed further. As a general rule, the newer the structure, the safer it is. Building codes have become stricter, resulting in more fire-resistant nursing homes. All bedrooms should open into corridors and should have windows. Exits should be clearly marked and accessible. Doors should unlock from the inside. Stairwells should be enclosed and fireproof. Hallways should have handrails. Bathrooms should have grab bars.

The home should accommodate wheelchairs. Hallways should be wide enough for two wheelchairs to pass each other without difficulty. Toilets should be wheelchair height.

Determine the type of room accommodations that your parent will receive. Some homes offer only large wards with little privacy. Others have individual rooms or semiprivate rooms. Medicaid recipients cannot have private rooms.

Check on the other facilities provided. Are there activity rooms for reading, crafts, card games, and socializing? Look at the dining room. Is it clean and are the meals appetizing?

You will want cheerful surroundings in general (the "feel" of the place). Are the rooms newly painted and well lit? Are there decorations, flowers, and other efforts to enliven the place? Visit the homes you are considering, to see the layout for yourself. If possible, bring your parent along for a personal tour.

Staffing

Check that there is a doctor on staff. Find out whether he or she makes regular visits and necessary referrals to specialists. Learn about the percentage of the staff that are registered nurses or licensed practical nurses. The federal government imposes minimum requirements: there must be 24-hour nursing, with a registered nurse on the premises at least 8 hours a day, every day of the week. This rule may be waived under certain circumstances. A doctor's visit to a patient is required every 30 days during the first 90 days of nursing-home care. Thereafter, visits at 60- or 90-day intervals are necessary.

The regulations also require that nurses' aides have or receive training. Such training consists of 75 hours during the first 4 months of employment. (Under a phase-in for the regulations, this 75-hour requirement is not yet fully effective.) Other regulations address requirements for routine dental examinations and care, and administration of drug therapy when prescribed by a physician. Social worker services are mandated for homes with more than 120 beds.

Find out the ratio of patients to attendants or nurses' aides. It is recommended that there should be no more than 10 patients for each aide. This ratio assures that each resident will have sufficient attention and care available.

Complete the following worksheet, to compare the nursing homes you are considering for your parent. There is no magical formula for selecting one home over another. Given the list of your parent's wants and needs and the spaces that are available, you may be forced to compromise. You may not find a home that meets all of your family's requirements. Be realistic in making your choice.

———————— Wealth Building Worksheet ————————
Checklist for Choosing a Nursing Home

Rate each nursing home on each feature, using this system:
1 = Fully meets needs;   2 = Acceptable;   3 = Substandard.

Features	*Home A*	*Home B*	*Home C*	*Notes*
Type of home	——	——	——	————————
Availability	——	——	——	————————
Cost	——	——	——	————————
Living conditions	——	——	——	————————
Staffing	——	——	——	————————
Other points	——	——	——	————————
(general "feel,"				————————
professionalism,				————————
sensitivity)				————————

Getting Help in Finding a Nursing Home

Given the shortage of nursing-home beds and the financial burdens that nursing-home placement presents, your choice in a nursing home may not be the one your parent ends up in. Several extraneous factors may dictate entry to another nursing home. Your parent may require immediate placement and the home you choose may not have a bed available. Or, because your parent is on Medicaid, he or she may not have access to the home you've selected.

To make an informed choice, it generally is advisable to enlist the help of care managers, social workers, or other professionals. Such professionals will be able to:

▶ Confirm your decision to seek nursing-home placement for your parent. The professionals can review the PRI to determine whether nursing-home care is necessary or whether a lesser degree of care may suffice.

▶ Help identify the facilities that are best suited to meet your parent's needs. Not all homes are equipped to treat all conditions. For example, certain individuals who suffer from Alzheimer's disease may become belligerent and difficult to handle. Some homes may not accept those whose mental conditions can cause trouble.

▶ Help with the nursing-home application process. The application
process can be quite lengthy. The home may require proof of the
ability to pay (including bank statements and a list of other assets).
If a parent is going to resort to Medicaid to pay for part or all of the
cost of the home, then even more extensive information must be
provided. Gathering this information is time-consuming, and not
all children have the time or background to undertake this task.

▶ Advise about Medicaid eligibility and help with the Medicaid application process. As with the nursing-home application process, a
great deal of information must be gathered and presented. If the
home does not handle the Medicaid application for your parent,
then you will have to deal with the bureaucracy yourself. This is not
an easy task. The help of experts may be required. (For more information about Medicaid, see Chapter 4.)

▶ Provide information and/or counseling for you about your parent's
condition. As discussed in Chapter 1, the fact that your parent has
reached a point of diminished capacity is not easy for you to deal
with. There are many emotions—guilt, anger, sadness, loss—that
may have to be confronted. For some adult children, the counsel of
professionals may be needed, to understand and cope with the
situation.

─────────────────→ ACTION ITEM ←─────────────────
**Because most professionals charge by the hour,
the more you know, the less costly their assistance
will be. You can, for example, do your own legwork
about the nursing homes in your area and then
turn to the professionals for the Medicaid application if necessary.**

─────────────────── **?** ───────────────────

What nursing care does Medicare cover?

Generally, Medicare covers only the nursing costs while a
patient is recovering from an operation or from an acute
illness that required hospitalization.

What is the average cost of nursing-home care?

The national average is estimated to be around $30,000 per year, but this can vary considerably, depending on the region of the country.

What license is the most important to ask for when evaluating a nursing home?

As a minimum, a current, state-issued operating license. The lack of a Medicare license, by itself, may simply mean that the nursing home doesn't accept Medicare patients.

ENSURING CARE WITHIN A NURSING HOME

In the past, the elderly confined to nursing homes were often treated as if they had no civil rights. Their wishes were disregarded. They were often subject to abuse. In response to growing concern, Congress established requirements relating to the rights of residents in skilled nursing facilities. These requirements apply to all facilities that receive funding through Medicare/Medicaid. These rights, which comprise the Patient's Bill of Rights, are:

1. Free choice. The right to choose a personal attending physician, to be fully informed in advance about care and treatment, to be fully informed in advance about any changes in care or treatment that may affect the resident's well-being, and (except with respect to a resident adjudged incompetent) to participate in planning care and treatment or changes in care and treatment.

2. Freedom from restraints. The right to be free from physical or mental abuse, corporal punishment, involuntary seclusion, and any physical or chemical restraints imposed for purposes of discipline or convenience and not required to treat the resident's medical symptoms. Restraints may only be imposed to ensure the physical safety of the resident or other residents, and only upon the written order of a physician that specifies the duration and circumstances under which the restraints are to be used (except in emergency circumstances) until such an order could reasonably be obtained.

3. Privacy. The right to privacy with regard to accommodations, medical treatment, written and telephone communications, visits, and meetings of family and of resident groups.

4. Confidentiality. The right of confidentiality of personal and clinical records.

5. Accommodation of needs. The right to reside and receive services with reasonable accommodation of individual needs and references, except where the health or safety of the individual or other residents would be endangered, and to receive notice before the room or roommate of the resident in the facility is changed.

6. Grievances. The right to voice grievances with respect to treatment or care that is (or fails to be) furnished, without discrimination or reprisal for voicing the grievances, and the right to prompt efforts by the facility to resolve grievances the resident may have, including those with respect to the behavior of other residents.

7. Participation in resident and family groups. The right of the resident to organize and participate in resident groups in the facility, and the right of the resident's family to meet in the facility with the families of other residents in the facility.

8. Participation in other activities. The right of the resident to participate in social, religious, and community activities that do not interfere with the rights of other residents in the facility.

9. Examination of survey results. The right to examine, upon reasonable request, the results of the most recent survey of the facility conducted by the Secretary of Health and Human Services (or of a State) with respect to the facility, and any plan of correction in effect with respect to the facility.

10. Other rights. Any other rights established by the Secretary of Health and Human Services.

Unfortunately, once a parent is too infirm to be his or her own spokesperson, pressing these rights largely becomes the job of those who are looking out for the parent's interests. It is your job, therefore, to see that your parent is accorded the proper treatment and respect guaranteed by the Patient's Bill of Rights.

Read the admission contract carefully. This contract may contain language that is worded to try to limit a patient's rights. It may be difficult, if not impossible, to get the home to change the language merely by request. More important, you may fear that your parent will suffer consequences if you make waves. If you have serious concerns, you can make a complaint to the appropriate state agency. Because homes must be licensed by the state, there is an agency that oversees nursing-home operations.

Frequent visits are the best way to check up on things. Should you suspect any violations, do not hesitate to inquire further. A staff that knows there is a strong advocate for a patient may think twice about violating that patient's rights. Again, complaints to a state agency may result in corrective action by the home.

→ **ACTION ITEM** ←

If serious violations are suspected (such as physical abuse), it may be advisable to seek the advice of an attorney who handles such matters.

IN-HOME CARE:
THE NURSING-HOME ALTERNATIVE

Nursing-home placement is often thought of as the choice of last resort. For many elderly individuals, proper assistance with care in their own homes can delay nursing-home placement.

**WEALTH
BUILDING
PROFILE**

Assessing the Need for In-Home Services. Rose, age 82, has lived alone in her apartment since her husband died 10 years ago. She is in general good health, but her arthritis has made it increasingly difficult for her to get around and see to her own personal needs. Her two daughters live some distance away. On their last visit, they noticed that there was virtually no food in Rose's refrigerator, that she would no longer get her clothes on by herself, and that it was very difficult for her to prepare meals. Her daughters concluded that she is at the point where she must get help or she'll be forced to go into a nursing home.

At present, there are about 6 million elderly who have lost the ability to see to their daily personal needs. When this happens, a parent requires custodial care to help with bathing, dressing, toileting, cooking, shopping, and other tasks. This care may be provided in a nursing home or in the person's own home. In-home care is recommended, for a number of reasons. A parent may prefer to stay at home; familiar surroundings are beneficial mentally and often physically. If both parents are infirm and one needs custodial care, reliance on in-home care can keep them together. Most in-home care is less costly than nursing-home care.

It is difficult to provide an "average cost" for in-home care. The extent of services varies with a person's needs. One parent may require only a few hours of help on a few days each week, for shopping or getting to doctors' appointments. Another may need round-the-clock attention for personal hygiene. It is not unusual to pay $250, $300, or more each week for daily in-home custodial care. This works out to about $1,250 a month or $15,000 a year. Put in another perspective, in-home custodial care is about half the cost of a nursing home. In-home care has other, nonmedical costs to consider. These are the expenses of maintaining the parent's residence (rent or mortgage payments, property insurance, utilities), food, and laundry service. These items are automatically included in the cost of a nursing home.

In-home care may be your choice, but paying for the care may dictate another option. Medicaid in most states does not cover the cost of in-home care, even though it would be cheaper for the program to do so. There are exceptions. In New York, for example, Medicaid pays for the cost of in-home care under a special program.

Currently, there are about 6,000 home health agencies (HHAs). These agencies undergo state examinations each year. Visits to patients are part of the checkup. The National Association for Home Care (NAHC) is essentially a trade association for home health care professionals. It provides its members with information and it lobbies in Congress on behalf of related issues. NAHC maintains a directory of Medicare-certified facilities throughout the country. It does not make direct recommendations for in-home care assistance, but can steer you to an agency in your state for this purpose. The National Association for Home Care is located at 519 C Street, N.E., Washington, DC 20002; phone: 202/547-7424.

The services provided by custodial care cover a wide range of activities: housekeeping and companion-type services; personal care services, such as bathing and toileting; more extensive care, such as medication supervision; and skilled nursing care or physical therapy.

A parent may require only a few hours of care a week or may need assistance on a 24-hour basis. When care is needed round-the-clock, a nursing home may in fact become cost-effective. The cost of custodial care varies greatly with the kinds of services provided and with various localities.

In the past, there was a great deal of concern about how homebound individuals were being treated by HHAs. In response, Congress created a Bill of Rights on in-home treatment by an HHA. It is very similar to the rights afforded to nursing-home patients, discussed earlier in this chapter. A person receiving in-home services under the auspices of an HHA is entitled to the following:

1. The right to be fully informed in advance about the care and treatment to be provided by the agency, to be fully informed in advance of any changes in the care or treatment to be provided by the agency that may affect the individual's well-being, and (except for an incompetent) to participate in planning care and treatment or changes in care or treatment;

2. The right to voice grievances with respect to treatment or care that is (or fails to be) furnished, without discrimination or reprisal for voicing grievances;

3. The right to confidentiality of clinical records;

4. The right to have one's property treated with respect;

5. The right to be fully informed orally and in writing of all items and services furnished, the coverage available under any federal program, any charges for items or services not covered and for which an individual may have to pay, and any changes in the charges for items and services;

6. The right to be fully informed in writing of the individual's rights and obligations;

7. The right to be informed of the availability of the state home health agency hot line.

Lifetime Care Facilities

One variation on the in-home alternative is the use of lifetime care or "continuing care" facilities. These residences contractually agree to provide nursing-home type care for life. This alternative generally is chosen well before nursing-home care is required. Lifetime care facilities are among the housing arrangements discussed in Chapter 5.

————————— **POINTS TO REMEMBER** —————————

▶ More than 2.3 million elderly live in nursing homes, where average annual cost per person has reached $30,000. Almost half of all nursing-home bills are paid by individuals; the federal government picks up most of the rest. Begin planning early for this eventuality.

▶ There are many guilt-ridden myths about nursing homes. They are not places to "dump" the elderly; they are not places where the elderly go to die; and they are not horrible places, in the majority of cases.

▶ The level of medical or caregiving attention your parent may need to receive—the reason for going to a nursing home—is determined by the patient review instrument (PRI). A doctor performs this evaluation.

▶ Choosing a nursing home can be a difficult emotional experience. Try to evaluate homes objectively, on the basis of type, cost, living conditions, staffing, and other details that may be important for yourself or for your parent.

▶ Costs of in-home custodial care are roughly half those of a nursing home. However, many states do not provide Medicaid coverage for in-home care.

4

Managing the Cost of Long-Term Care

*T*he fact that the cost of long-term care is high is not news to anyone. What may be a surprise is exactly how high that cost can be. We noted earlier that the average annual cost of nursing-home care is $30,000 per person, with considerably higher costs in many areas; in-home care can run at least half that amount (over and above the ordinary cost of maintaining the home). Perhaps one of the scariest and most troublesome times, when you are dealing with an elderly parent, is when you must come to grips with these costs. There are three main ways to pay for long-term care.

Self-insuring is the first way to pay for long-term care. This means accumulating enough assets to pay for long-term care out-of-pocket, without becoming poor. Self-insuring is a lifelong process. A complete discussion of all the financial planning strategies available to maximize wealth and ensure adequate assets for health care is beyond the scope of this book. Unfortunately, most elderly are caught short of having enough assets for this purpose: their adult children may be called on to supplement their income. (If you are the child of an elderly parent, you have the luxury of time to begin planning your finances so that they offer protection against your own future medical costs.)

The second way to pay for long-term care is to buy a special kind of insurance designed to cover nursing-home and in-home care. Again, this alternative requires some foresight because it is of little use once a parent is in immediate need of nursing-home care.

The third way to pay is to rely on government programs. These programs—Medicaid and veterans' benefits—are designed to help the poor.

Each method can be used alone or in combination with another method. The best method for your parent depends on a number of factors, the most important of which is his or her financial picture.

Before the three methods for paying for the cost of long-term care are explained, it should be pointed out that elderly parents who live in certain types of continuing care facilities have already taken care of the cost of long-term nursing care in an alternative fashion. They will receive the care they need, within the confines of the continuing care facilities, because this care is included in the cost of living within this type of facility. (Continuing care facilities are discussed in detail in Chapter 5.)

SELF-INSURING

The cost of nursing-home care is generally *not* covered by Medicare. Medicare covers only a limited number of days in a skilled nursing facility (SNF). An SNF provides the type of care needed after hospitalization for an acute illness, such as a stroke or a heart attack. Care is given by a skilled nurse (registered nurse or licensed practical nurse) who is available 24 hours a day. Medicare does *not* cover intermediate care or custodial care, even if it is provided in a nursing home. Intermediate care, a level of care below skilled nursing care, may entail supervision of medication or bandage changes. Custodial care is yet another level of care, below intermediate care. This is the type of care required by an elderly person who can no longer see to his or her daily needs. When nursing-home issues are discussed in this chapter, they refer to custodial care—the level of care typically provided in nursing homes. It is non-Medicare treatment, unless otherwise specified.

As indicated at the start of this chapter, the cost of a nursing home must be covered in one of several ways: out-of-pocket (the parent's pocket or your pocket, or both), long-term care insurance, or qualification for Medicaid or veterans' benefits. In some cases, a combination of payment methods is used. For example, proceeds from long-term care insurance may have to be supplemented with out-of-pocket payments. Before Medicaid will step in to pay, it may become necessary for the parent to spend his or her own funds on a nursing-home stay.

If your parent does not have adequate nursing-home insurance or cannot qualify for Medicaid, it may be necessary to demonstrate an ability to pay as a condition of admission to a nursing home.

Frequently, a nursing home may require a 2- or 3-month deposit. It may also ask to see a bank book or other proof of assets or payment ability. Under a federal law, a nursing home may *not* ask a child of a nursing-home patient to personally guarantee payment.

The prospect of paying for a nursing-home stay needn't be frightening. There are individuals who can afford to pay for care from their savings and need not turn to Medicaid; for those who can't, there are other alternatives. Before you panic or think that the cost of your parent's nursing-home care is insurmountable, take a few moments to analyze the situation.

→ **ACTION ITEM** ←

Determine whether your parent has sufficient assets to pay for long-term care. In making this determination, take into account several factors: the size and nature of the assets (e.g., income-producing, illiquid); a realistic return on investment; other sources of income (e.g., pensions, social security); and an inflation projection.

Assets may have to be rearranged to produce more income. Income-producing assets include, for example, dividend-paying stocks, bonds, mortgage-backed pass-through securities (for example, "Ginnie Maes"), annuities, Treasury obligations, certificates of deposit (CDs), and other similar instruments. A stamp collection (or similar asset) or raw land held for investment may be liquidated and the proceeds invested in stocks or bonds yielding current income. A parent may own a home that can be sold if he or she moves to a nursing home. In considering the assets and whether they may have to be sold, take into account the tax cost of the sale. At present, the top federal tax rate on net capital gains is 28 percent; people in states that levy income taxes may pay additional state tax on the capital gains. Under a special tax break that applies to the sale of a home, no tax may be due. (For further details, see Chapter 5.)

In making an estimate of a realistic rate of return, it is important to remember that this number is not fixed. As economic conditions change, so does the amount that can be earned on one's money. Only a few years ago, a 10 percent return was considered a conservative one; today, the return or yield on safe investments is considerably lower.

There are several sources of income to consider, in addition to return on investments. Pensions, annuities, and social security benefits are the most common sources. Some individuals have other sources of income, such as alimony, trust distributions, and, for a few lucky players, lottery winnings. It is important to explore all other possible sources of income. Individuals who own certain types of life insurance policies can, in some states, tap into the policies' proceeds *before* death, in order to pay for medical care. There are both pros and cons of "accelerated death benefits," as they are called. Their main advantage is a ready source of cash. However, using this source means that the funds are not going to be there at death, as originally intended. This may not be a problem, but it must be considered. The tax consequences of taking accelerated death benefits have not yet been determined. Unlike the tax-free receipt of life insurance proceeds upon the death of the insured, the receipt of accelerated death benefits may possibly be taxable.

When you make an inflation projection, to see whether income will be able to keep pace with rising nursing-home costs, it is important to use a realistic figure. Over the past several years, the inflation rate for health care costs has been approximately twice the rate for overall inflation. If inflation is running at a general rate of $4^1/_2$ percent, then, for purposes of determining income availability, it may be helpful to use a 9 percent inflation rate for health care costs. Again, this figure may not be precise but it will be helpful in making projections. It is impossible to know exactly how inflation will run in the future. Overall inflation (and health care costs) may continue to run at a rate similar to that of the past few years, or it may escalate greatly.

What happens to the projections when a parent in need of nursing-home care has a spouse who is not in need of such care? In this situation, projections become more complicated. Assets and income must stretch further. Although the ill spouse will live in the nursing home, the spouse who does not need care will continue to need a place to live outside the nursing home. This residence might be a home owned by the couple.

If annual income from assets, social security, pensions, and other sources falls below the cost of the nursing home, it becomes necessary to "dip into principal." There are charts that can be used to calculate how long principal will last if a portion is used each year. Eventually, however, the principal may be used up. The assets that were intended to be passed to one's heirs may become payments for lifetime care.

When assets are depleted, Medicaid can step in to cover nursing-home costs. Depletion of assets and resort to Medicaid is a one-way street. Once assets are used up, a parent is permanently poor. The media have popularized the notion that middle-class individuals can transfer their assets to their children and then qualify for Medicaid, avoiding the need to use their own assets for their care, and preserving their estate for their heirs. The viability of this and other Medicaid strategies is discussed later in this chapter.

The worksheet below will help you to determine the annual income available to your parent for support, whether at home or in a nursing home. Thus, if both your parents are alive and only one is ill, this is the total amount of income that can be used to pay for the parent who remains at home and the parent who goes into a nursing home.

———————— Wealth Building Worksheet ————————
Can Your Parent Afford to Pay?

Total assets $_____   × %* = $_____
Monthly income $_____   × 12 = $_____
      Total $_____

*This is the assumed rate of return. In setting this rate, make a realistic assumption based on what is currently available on low-risk investments such as Treasury bonds and CDs.

Supplementing a Parent's Payments

When your parent has some income and assets to pay a portion of care but not enough to foot the entire bill, you may have to make choices: contribute to your parent's care, allow your parent's assets to be depleted to the point where Medicaid will step in, or undertake some Medicaid asset-transfer planning. There is no way to simplify the choice. (The consequences of Medicaid are discussed later in this chapter.)

?

Can a nursing home *require* a child to support an elderly parent?

No, by federal law. It can, however, examine the parent's financial condition closely.

Can the assets of a life insurance policy be used before death?

Yes, if "accelerated death benefit" provisions can be used. Alternatively, the policy can simply be cashed out, but this may reduce the value obtained.

What is the "Medicaid strategy"?

Because Medicaid has financial tests that a person must meet before qualifying for coverage, some elderly impoverish themselves by transferring assets to their children before applying for coverage.

What is "spousal impoverishment"?

In 1989, Congress enacted certain rules for Medicare and Medicaid. In general, these rules provide some protection for one spouse when the other requires long-term care and seeks Medicaid coverage.

What is the time limit for asset transfers for Medicaid eligibility?

Generally, 30 months, although it can be less (depending on the size of the assets transferred). This, all by itself, makes it imperative to do advance planning before the need for Medicaid arises.

LONG-TERM CARE INSURANCE

A relatively new type of insurance is designed to cover long-term care. This policy, sometimes called a "nursing home policy," pays for the cost of a nursing home or in-home custodial care. Despite the newness of this type of insurance, interest in it is zooming. According to one source, 125,000 policies had been sold by 1987, but that number jumped to 1.5 million by 1990. These policies are now sold by about 120 insurance companies nationwide.

A long-term care policy serves a very real function. It pays for an expense not covered by government programs unless one is poor. Unfortunately, it is too expensive for most elderly persons. According to one study, 84 percent of those who are ages 65 to 79 cannot pay for the basic long-term care policy. In this same age group, 73 percent cannot pay for the least costly policy meeting certain minimum requirements. In an age category of 75 to 79 years, 90 percent could not afford the average coverage (and 80 percent could not afford the least costly coverage).

Despite these bleak statistics, it is worthwhile to investigate the possibility of long-term care insurance for your elderly parent— especially if your parent has sufficient assets that are worth protecting. There is no magic number that is a cutoff for protection, although some experts suggest a minimum of $50,000 in property before considering coverage. Family medical history may also be a deciding factor. If Alzheimer's disease has occurred in other family members, increasing the possibility of needing long-term nursing care in the future, then a nursing-home policy should be given serious thought.

In some locations, even the purchase of long-term care insurance may not be sufficient to pay for the cost of a nursing home. For example, if the policy pays $100 a day and the cost of the average nursing home is $60,000 a year, the policy would cover only about half the cost of the nursing home. Depending on a parent's assets, it may not be advisable to buy such insurance.

However, for wealthy individuals, long-term care insurance may well be worth the cost. For these people, the gift tax on transferring assets in order to become eligible for Medicaid may far outstrip the cost of long-term care insurance.

WEALTH BUILDING PROFILE

Paying for Long-Term Care versus Asset Transfers. Assume that a single parent, age 70, has $2 million in assets. This parent can afford to pay for long-term care, but may not want to deplete assets for this purpose. If the parent buys a top-of-the-line policy for $6,500 and lives out a life expectancy of about 15 years, the cost of coverage will have run about $100,000. This is not a large sum compared with the total assets, the amount of gift tax that would have been levied on a transfer of the assets, and the cost of nursing-home care.

The premium for a long-term care policy becomes fixed as of the date of purchase. (Only a few major carriers will issue a new policy for someone between the ages of 80 and 84; others offer initial coverage to age 79.) Like a whole life policy, this premium does not change with age. Thus, the earlier in life that the policy is bought, the lower the annual premiums. (Children with elderly parents should consider the viability of such insurance for themselves, because taking the coverage on at an early age means a lower annual cost.) A person's premiums cannot be raised on an individual basis, but they may be increased when the company increases its overall rates.

Factors in Selecting a Long-Term Care Policy

A great number of factors may vary from policy to policy, and all of these factors have an impact on cost.

Dollar Amount of Protection Purchased

Long-term care policies provide a fixed amount of benefits, such as $100 a day. This benefit may be referred to in the policy as the "indemnity" amount. When selecting the dollar amount desired, consider two things: the cost of care and your parent's other resources. For example, if a nursing home costs $150 a day, your parent's other resources may well cover $50 of that amount; therefore, coverage of $100 a day will be sufficient.

Length of Time Coverage Will Run

Some policies give lifetime coverage or run for a specified number of years (for example, 3, 4, 5, or 6 years). A recommended *minimum* is 2½ years. As discussed later, this time period will afford your parent the opportunity to make property transfers for Medicaid eligibility. Lifetime coverage is most desirable; it is also the most expensive type available. Where cost prevents lifetime coverage, it is difficult to select the best term. How can one guess how long coverage will be needed? Statistics show that the average stay in a nursing home is 30 months. This would seem to suggest that a 3-year coverage period should be ample. However, statistics are not always a good measure. Where confinement to a nursing home is the result of Alzheimer's disease, dementia, or other degenerative brain diseases, the period of need could run for many years. Such patients generally are physically strong even though they require long-term care.

Elimination Period

This is the time after care begins and before the insurance will pay off. It may be as short as 0 days, 15 days, or 20 days; or as long as 30 days, 60 days, 90 days, or even longer. The elimination period chosen affects the cost of the coverage. If a longer elimination period is chosen as a way of keeping down the cost of premiums, an individual should have sufficient assets to cover the full cost of a nursing-home stay for the elimination period chosen.

How does the elimination period work? Let's take an example. A parent enters a nursing home for care on April 1. If there is a 30-day elimination period, the policy's benefits will not begin until May 1. As already mentioned, the longer the elimination period, the less costly the annual premiums. However, the savings in premiums may be so minimal that it may be better to get the shortest elimination period possible.

Inflation Rider

Because the policy fixes the dollar benefit at the time it is purchased, the value of that benefit may be quite insignificant if it is not used until several years later. Its value goes down because inflation erodes the purchasing power of the dollar. The younger the person at the time of taking out the policy, the more important it is that the policy carry an inflation rider, to increase benefits as the rate of inflation increases. Congress is considering making the inflation rider mandatory in long-term care policies. Some insurance agents suggest that, if a person is already over 75 or so when the policy is taken out, then this feature may not be important. Premiums are increased to reflect the inclusion of an inflation rider.

Type of Care Covered

Some policies cover both in-home care and nursing-home care at both skilled and custodial-type facilities. Others cover only nursing-home care. The best policy is the one that covers the greatest options. However, if premium cost is an issue, the choice is difficult. It may be better to opt for coverage solely in a nursing home. Check the type of coverage carefully. Be sure that the policy covers treatment in all long-term care facilities. Some may limit coverage solely to skilled nursing homes. Others may require a period of treatment at a skilled nursing home before custodial care is covered. It is important that there be *no* requirement of prior skilled nursing care before qualifying for intermediate or custodial care. Check this carefully: the majority of policies require prior hospitalization, although the trend is away from this requirement.

Renewability

Some insurers may cancel or fail to renew policies because of a person's age or condition. Your parent wants to be able to renew the policy indefinitely. A termination option should be carefully investigated. The best policy is "noncancelable"; the insurance company must renew the policy for the same premium. An acceptable type of policy is "guaranteed renewable." This means that the policy is renewable at the parent's option. However, the company may choose to raise the premiums for an entire class of policyholders. Because the long-term care policies are relatively new, the data on which insurance companies base their premiums are limited. If it turns out that the number of claims is greater than anticipated, the company may well raise premiums for the entire class of policyholders. A policy that is "conditionally renewable" can terminate or end coverage for an entire class or locality. Some policies are "optionally renewable"—at the company's option. This type of renewability is unacceptable for a parent, and a policy with this clause should be avoided.

Preexisting Conditions and Other Exclusions

Some policies will not cover conditions that affect the parent at the time of purchase. Others have a waiting period, typically 6 months but sometimes up to 1 year. Even if a condition exists at the time of purchase, the policy will cover treatment after the waiting period has ended. Check for the shortest waiting period available. Be sure that the policy does not have a flat ban on certain conditions, such as Alzheimer's disease. This disease falls under the label "organically based mental conditions" that appears in some policies. Where the policy is silent on coverage for Alzheimer's disease, it may be wise to get assurances of coverage in writing.

Cost of Long-Term Care Insurance

It is difficult to generalize about the cost of long-term care insurance, for a number of reasons. First, many factors affect the premiums: the daily dollar amount, the age at which the policy is first bought, the elimination period, and whether there is an inflation rider. Second, the rate for a like amount of coverage varies from company to company and across the country as well. Third, as insurance companies gain greater experience in meeting claims, they will adjust premium costs accordingly. A person in his or her late 50s may pay only a few hundred dollars whereas that same type of coverage for someone nearing 80 may be several thousand dollars annually.

Shopping for a Long-Term Care Policy

As with the purchase of any insurance product, consumer savvy will help in buying the best coverage for the lowest cost. Use the Wealth Building Worksheet on page 70 to comparison shop long-term care policies.

It is difficult, in some cases, to get a fair comparison. One policy may have a feature that is lacking in another policy and could well justify additional cost. The bottom line is: obtain maximum coverage for a fair price. It is interesting to know that, because this type of insurance is so new, the insurance industry lacks sufficient claims data to accurately set a fair price. As time goes on and more claims are made, premiums will no doubt be adjusted—up or down—to support the risk borne by the insurance companies for long-term care.

Model Insurance Policies

Because long-term care insurance is fairly new, no standardized language is used in such policies. It is important to compare policies offered by different companies. In some states, comparison shopping has been eased somewhat. The National Association of Insurance Commissioners (NAIC) has written a model law for long-term policies, and more than a dozen states have already adopted this model.

The NAIC model includes the following features:

▶ Guaranteed renewable (cancellation is permitted in limited circumstances with permission of a state insurance commissioner);
▶ No exclusion for specific health conditions (e.g., Alzheimer's disease);
▶ No requirement of prior hospital or skilled nursing facility stay.

In 1991, Congress held hearings on long-term care policies. In the course of those hearings, many elderly individuals told of bad

---

─────────────── **Wealth Building Worksheet** ───────────────
Checklist for Choosing a Long-Term Care Policy

Factors	Policy A	Policy B	Policy C
1. The policy pays per day for:			
Nursing-home care	$	$	$
In-home care	$	$	$
2. The policy runs for:			
Number of years	___ years	___ years	___ years
Lifetime			
3. Hospitalization is required before benefits begin			
4. The elimination or deductible period is	___ days	___ days	___ days
5. The daily benefits are adjusted for inflation			
6. Covered services include:*			
Nursing-home care			
In-home care			
7. The policy can be canceled because of:			
8. The waiting period before preexisting conditions will be covered is:	__ months	__ months	__ months
9. The policy covers Alzheimer's disease			
10. Cost per year	$	$	$
11. Insurance company rating			

* In determining the type of care that a policy will cover, be sure to find out whether it will pay for any level of care ordered by a doctor and any level of care in a state-licensed nursing facility.

---

experiences with insurance agents who used high pressure, fear, and other questionable tactics to sell these policies. Congress has yet to act on any of its findings. The end result may be legislation along the lines of that enacted to standardize Medigap policies and to eliminate unfair practices with respect to their sales. Such legislation would make it easier to comparison shop.

─────────────────────→ ACTION ITEM ←─────────────────

When comparison shopping for a long-term care policy, do not be pressured into a sale. Take the time to compare not only the different products offered by one insurance agent but also other products offered by different agents.

───

Judging Insurance Companies

With ongoing changes in the financial markets and growing concerns over the soundness of certain insurance companies, consumers must question the fiscal responsibility of the company underwriting the long-term care policy. As when shopping for life insurance, it is advisable to check the rating of the insurance company with a nationally known rating service (e.g., A.M. Best & Company, Moody's, or Standard & Poor's). Although there may be no need for concern over the ability of most insurance companies to pay out on policies, consumers cannot be too overly cautious in this regard. Consider a policy offered only by an insurance company with an A or A+ rating by Best or another comparable rating service.

Buying Coverage for Your Parent

Even if your parent does not buy a long-term policy, you may be in a position to do so. One of the newest employee benefits, now offered by only a handful of employers, is long-term care insurance. In addition to some private employers, some states (Alaska, Ohio, Maryland, and South Carolina) now offer long-term insurance as an employee benefit for their workers. Coverage may be bought for employees, spouses, parents, and spouses' parents. At present, employees in most companies offering this benefit must pay the premiums. However, because rates are based on group coverage, premiums are lower than rates charged to individuals.

MEDICAID

Medicaid is a federally created, state-run program to provide assistance to poor individuals. (In California, the Medicaid program is called Medi-Cal.) A state pays out federal and state funds under Medicaid rules; these rules vary greatly from state to state. Medicaid covers a wide range of medical expenses including those not covered by Medicare, such as nursing-home or in-home custodial care, prescription drugs, eyeglasses, and dental care. The extent of services available depends on the state in which the elderly person lives. New York Medicaid, for example, provides two dozen services over the minimum required by Medicaid, including extensive home care services.

Medicaid is not limited to the elderly. However, because of the high cost of health care, a great number of elderly individuals have turned to Medicaid for help.

Who is eligible for Medicaid? In general, any person who is able to get public assistance. Those who qualify, for example, for supplemental security income (SSI), would be included. SSI provides income over and above social security benefits for those 65 and older who are in need. Some states are more generous. It may not be necessary to be poor enough for SSI, in order to qualify for Medicaid. It is critical to check the income eligibility level for Medicaid in your state. Another exception exists for those collecting social security. If a person would have been eligible for Medicaid except for the fact that social security benefits were adjusted for inflation, then that person is treated as eligible.

What is the level of need? The answer depends on two factors: marital status and the state in which your parent lives. Married individuals may have more income and more assets than single individuals. Some states provide more liberal allowances than others. More than a dozen states provide coverage for those who are considered "medically needy individuals." These are people who are not necessarily poor but do not have the ability to meet their medical expenses. All of these rules are extremely complicated. They are also subject to change very frequently.

Overview of Recent Medicaid Changes

In 1988, Congress passed the Medicare Catastrophic Coverage Act, a law that contained a number of provisions affecting Medicaid as well as Medicare. One provision was designed to prevent one spouse from becoming poor when the other spouse required long-term care and applied to Medicaid to pay for it. This package was known as the "spousal impoverishment rules." The law extended the "look-back period" (the time in which asset transfers can prevent Medicaid assistance) from 24 months to 30 months.

In 1989, Congress repealed *most* of the Medicare Catastrophic Coverage Act, not all of it. Most of the important changes that relate to Medicaid were retained. The spousal impoverishment rules were kept. In some states, this was a blessing. Without the rules, those states stripped away all assets, leaving the well spouse virtually without anything. However, in other states, keeping the spousal impoverishment rules created a burden. Some states had allowed spouses to retain all property in their name. The spousal impoverishment rules set strict limits on property retention and permissible income.

Look-Back Period

Before the 1988 Medicare Catastrophic Coverage Act, there was a 24-month asset-transfer time. Transfers in that time frame could result in Medicaid ineligibility for nursing-home coverage. The Act extended the look-back period to 30 months. (The 30-month period applies to transfers after June 30, 1988. States were permitted to apply a 24-month transfer rule before July 1, 1988.) The extended look-back period also survived the repeal process.

What does the look-back rule mean? When an application is made for Medicaid assistance to cover the cost of nursing-home care, the individual's financial dealings for the past 30 months are examined in detail. If the individual is married, the couple's finances for that period are taken into account. Where assets were transferred during those 30 months for less than full value (meaning the assets were given away rather than sold), Medicaid eligibility can be denied until the earlier of (1) 30 months, or (2) a number of months equivalent to the value of the resources transferred, divided by the average monthly cost of a nursing home in the area ("regional cost").

WEALTH BUILDING PROFILE   *Figuring the Period of Ineligibility for Medicaid.* A parent gave $20,000 to his child (his only property). One month later, the parent needed nursing-home care and sought Medicaid help. If the average monthly cost of a nursing home in the area is $4,000, the parent has to wait 5 months before becoming eligible for assistance ($20,000 transferred, divided by $4,000).

Transferring Assets

Certain transfers are permitted in the look-back period, without hurting eligibility.

First, assets may be transferred to the "community spouse" (the spouse who is well and remains in the community) without any problems. These include any transfers after October 1, 1989. (Before that date, a different rule applied to transfers between spouses.) Assets transferred between spouses cannot exceed the amount that the community spouse can retain under the resources rules spelled out below. The transfer of additional assets has to be spent down, whether owned by the institutional spouse or the community spouse, unless the community spouse refuses to contribute to the support of the institutional spouse. (The approach of "saying no" by the community spouse is discussed later in this chapter.) The community spouse may also transfer individually owned assets to anyone, without affecting the eligibility of the ill spouse. However, the community spouse may not *retransfer* assets. This means that the ill spouse can transfer assets to the community spouse, making them separate assets, but the community spouse cannot turn around and transfer those same assets to a child.

Second, a residence may be transferred to certain relatives without jeopardizing Medicaid eligibility. These relatives include a spouse; a child who is blind, disabled, or under age 21; a brother or sister who has an ownership interest in the home and who has lived there at least 1 year before the institutionalization occurs; or an adult child who has been living in the home and providing care for the parent. This care must be identified as having postponed institutional care for at least 2 years.

Third, transfers may be allowed if it is found that they were made for reasons other than Medicaid qualification. It is not clear what these reasons might be.

Resources

Only poor individuals qualify for Medicaid. The law defines what is meant by "poor" for this purpose. Different rules apply, depending on whether a parent is single (or widowed) or is legally married.

Singles

Assets of a single individual generally cannot exceed $3,050. The term "assets" generally means:

1. Property under the person's control. For example, an elderly person may not refuse to take property to which he or she is entitled. In one case, a spouse's right of election against the other spouse's will was treated as an asset of the surviving spouse.

2. Property able to be converted into cash, within reason. If someone owns illiquid assets that he or she does not want to be counted for Medicaid purposes, it may be necessary to prove that the property cannot be sold because of the nature of the asset, market conditions, or another negative factor.

3. Property that is not "exempt property." "Exempt property" includes:

▸ Personal residence (regardless of value) if there is a dependent relative living there or if there is an intention to return home on the part of the parent placed in the nursing home. This so-called "homestead exemption" applies to a one-, two-, or three-family house and the adjoining property, regardless of value. In more than a dozen states, a time limit (6, 9, or 12 months) is placed on protection of the home, once the parent enters a nursing home and if no dependent relative is living in the residence. Some states can have a lien on the residence; other states provide a right of recovery for the value of the home (which is legally different from a lien).

▸ Personal property and household furnishings up to $2,000.

▸ One wedding ring and one engagement ring (regardless of value).

▸ One car valued at no more than $4,500. No limit is placed on the car's value if it is adapted for a handicapped person's use.

▸ Life insurance with a cash surrender value up to $1,500.

▸ Burial plot (regardless of value).

▸ Burial costs up to $1,500, if segregated from other assets.

Thus, the total amount that can be retained is $3,050 *plus* exempt assets.

Once on Medicaid, the individual must turn over social security benefits and other income. A small allowance, such as $50 a month, may be retained.

A person who is not responsible for an elderly person's support (such as a child, brother or sister, or friend) may be able to provide help without jeopardizing Medicaid eligibility. In some states, gifts of money count as the person's own income. In other states, it is possible to pay for bills and provide property in kind (such as food) without any problems.

Married Persons

Even though both spouses are elderly, one may be ill while the other is quite well. The ill spouse is referred to as the "institutionalized spouse." The other spouse—the one who remains at home—is called the "community spouse."

At the time when the institutionalized spouse needs nursing-home care, the assets and income of the couple are carefully examined. A "snapshot" is taken of the couple's finances as of that date. The snapshot rule only applies to those who enter a nursing home after September 30, 1989. Anyone who entered a nursing home before that date and stays there is not subject to the snapshot rule.

Certain assets, called "exempt assets," can be kept by the community spouse. They differ slightly from the exempt assets of a single person. Included are:

▶ Personal residence (regardless of value);

▶ Personal effects, including jewelry (regardless of value);

▶ Household goods and furnishings (regardless of value);

▶ Car (regardless of value);

▶ Life insurance with a cash surrender value up to $1,500;

▶ Burial plot (regardless of value);

▶ Burial costs up to $1,500, if segregated from other assets.

As for the family residence, if the community spouse dies before the spouse in the nursing home *and* the house was in joint name, the exemption for the house ends at that time. The time limits for singles (discussed above) may then apply. The house may have to be sold and the proceeds spent down, to continue Medicaid assistance for the spouse remaining in the nursing home. If the nursing-home patient dies first, or if the community spouse owned the house in his or her name alone and dies first, Medicaid cannot make a claim to the house.

In 1992, depending on state limits, the community spouse is allowed to retain assets (over and above exempt assets) but no more than $68,700. The ceiling amount is adjusted annually for inflation.

These limits are perhaps best understood by examples. In the following cases, the unadjusted figures are used for simplicity's sake.

▶ Mr. and Mrs. P had nonexempt assets of $12,000. All of these assets can be retained by the community spouse without jeopardizing Medicaid qualification.

▶ Mr. and Mrs. Q had nonexempt assets of $200,000. Technically, the most that can be retained by the community spouse is $68,700. However, there are other ways to maximize the resources of the community spouse (discussed below). (A higher limit is allowed on a case-by-case basis if a fair hearing by Medicaid or a court so orders it.)

A community spouse may also keep a certain monthly income. This "monthly maintenance allowance" is made up of two components: enough income to raise the community spouse's income to a certain level (133 percent of the federal poverty line for a couple; 150 percent after June 30, 1992) *plus* a special shelter allowance for high housing costs. This special shelter allowance is the amount by which the mortgage, property taxes, utilities, and property insurance total more than 30 percent of the basic allowance. Altogether, the monthly maintenance allowance cannot exceed a monthly ceiling of $1,500 (adjusted for inflation). States may choose to figure the monthly maintenance allowance or to use the flat $1,500 (adjusted for inflation) limit. As in the case of asset retention, a higher limit may be ordered by a fair hearing or a court.

The Medicaid Decision

The very idea of making oneself poor, by transferring assets or by spending money on care, runs counter to the American dream of working for wealth. Yet, for many elderly individuals, the high cost of a nursing home leaves few options. Their resources may not be sufficient to meet the nursing-home bill for very long. A child may volunteer to pay the nursing-home tab. Under federal law, a nursing home may not require a child to underwrite the bill as a condition for admitting the parent to obtain quality care. However, for many children, there is a strong moral feeling about helping a parent.

Other elderly individuals may not have a child or other relative to help them, or their child may not be in a financial position to help. There may be no choice but to seek Medicaid. Of all the alternatives, Medicaid may be the best. To get Medicaid for those who are not poor requires becoming poor.

If a person has few assets or low income, there is really no decision to make. An application for Medicaid assistance is necessary in order to receive nursing-home care. However, for a person who has lived his or her life in the middle class—owning a home and other assets, receiving an income—there may be an agonizing choice to make. Does the person spend a lifetime's savings on nursing-home care or attempt to qualify for Medicaid?

When Medicaid eligibility means a spend down, there are several factors to consider before acting.

Personal Considerations

There may be natural reluctance against accepting welfare. If Medicaid offers the only means of financing long-term care, this reluctance needs to be overcome.

There may be a moral dilemma for a middle- or upper-income parent. The law was designed for the poor. Should a person of means be able to "play the game" by transferring assets solely to qualify for Medicaid? It is clear that the law provides its own limits on transferability—no more than 30 months of ineligibility—if a person chooses to transfer assets for Medicaid purposes. Thus, for many, the moral dilemma has been resolved by the rules on transfers.

Difficulty in Qualifying

The asset and income limits have already been explained. Qualifying is especially difficult when there is a community spouse to consider. It is not necessarily easy to transfer property or liquidate assets. For example, what about jointly owned assets? If a person has a bank account in joint name with a brother or sister, how is this asset viewed for Medicaid? The answer differs from state to state. In New York, for example, it is presumed that one-half belongs to the Medicaid applicant. That presumption may be altered by tracing assets to the nonapplicant. The Medicaid applicant would have to spend down his or her one-half share of the bank account.

Even if a person wants to transfer assets, it is not always apparent to whom they should be transferred. For a parent who has one child, the choice would seem easy. But what happens if that child is married to someone who wields control over money, or is in a troubled marriage and perhaps heading for divorce? The assets transferred to the child may not be very secure. A trust can be used to add protection, but not all individuals are comfortable with using trusts. If a parent has more than one child and assets are other than cash, transferring assets becomes more complicated. For example, assume that a parent with three children owns an interest in a business. It may not be easy to divide that interest equally. Even if assets of equal value are transferred to those children, the assets may have differing income tax consequences. One asset may have a potential capital gain, and another, a potential capital loss. Where cash is transferred, there is no income tax consequence at all.

Further, bureaucratic problems are entailed in making an application. Records of assets, such as bank statements, must be provided for the past 2½ years. The parent's social security card and information about social security benefits must be produced. Needless to say, it is not always easy to furnish this information, yet failure to do so may delay or prevent Medicaid help. If the social security card cannot be located and benefit information is not available, someone must file to become a representative payee for the parent. Application for this status must be made at the parent's local social security office. The bureaucratic quagmire can be simplified somewhat if the nursing home or a social worker assists in the application process.

Limitation of Choice

Medicaid operates to limit choice. Not all nursing homes throughout the country accept Medicaid patients. Homes that accept Medicaid may delay admittance if qualification is questionable or difficult. Medicaid patients are restricted to a semiprivate room. For those who want or need privacy, Medicaid may be a severe drawback.

Medicaid can have a voice in determining the level of care that a person receives. Medicaid can rule that an elderly person does not need skilled care and can be managed with custodial care. Or, it can decide that nursing-home care is no longer required. If there is substantial evidence to support Medicaid's determination, then a person is without recourse. Patients have the opportunity to contest a Medicaid determination at various administrative hearings and through the courts. But if the Medicaid decision is upheld, a person may, in rare circumstances, find he or she is out of a nursing home and without any assets to boot.

Irreversibility

Medicaid eligibility is irreversible. Once a person has spent down assets to qualify for Medicaid, he or she can never (short of the lottery or an unexpected inheritance) escape the poverty level again. Even assets that have been retained up to allowable levels are still at risk: there may be a lag between the date a person enters a nursing home and the date Medicaid begins to pay for it. The Medicaid application process is lengthy. Until it is completed and Medicaid starts to pay, a person may have to use exempt assets to pay current nursing-home bills.

There is limited relief from this problem. Under a 3-month recovery rule, a person can be reimbursed from Medicaid for nursing-home bills. This is called reimbursement of retroactive expenses. The 3-month period runs from the date when services were rendered.

Planning for Medicaid Eligibility

Someone who is poor qualifies for Medicaid; no planning is required. A person who is not poor must take two steps to qualify: plan for eligibility, and "spend down" to the Medicaid eligibility limits. This means that assets (other than exempt assets) must be used up by making transfers, by paying for care, or by otherwise dissipating funds in order to bring the person's assets within the resource limits discussed earlier.

Is it legal for an otherwise middle-class person to arrange his or her affairs so as to qualify for Medicaid? Yes, it is legal. Some would challenge the ethics of doing so, but the law does not consider this to be a problem.

Considered here are some methods used for becoming eligible for Medicaid. Some of them depend on how long prior to institutionalization planning begins.

Long-Term Planning

An elderly person may grow increasingly infirm, with the possibility of needing nursing-home care in the future. For such a person, it may be advisable to begin asset transfers in anticipation of Medicaid eligibility. This is especially recommended for a middle-class person whose assets may not be great enough to pay the cost of long-term care but are too great for immediate Medicaid eligibility. Theoretically, even millionaires can qualify for Medicaid, if they transfer sufficient assets; they can only be prevented from qualifying for a period of 30 months from the time of the transfer.

For asset transfers, gifts can be made to relatives. The transfers should be sufficient to deplete the individual's assets to the Medicaid eligibility level. This should be done at least 30 months prior to needing Medicaid.

In making transfers, consider the gift tax consequences of this action. Assets can be transferred free from gift tax up to $10,000 annually for each recipient ("donee"). For example, if an elderly mother has four children and six grandchildren, she can give away, tax-free, up to $100,000 each year ($10,000 times 10 donees). What is more, an individual has a lifetime transfer opportunity of $600,000 over and above the $10,000 annual amounts.

Although there is *gift* tax relief for the parent transferring the property, there are *income* tax consequences to consider for the donees. However, there may be a trade-off. If a gift of the property is made now, the recipient loses the "stepped-up basis" enjoyed on property transferred at death. The recipient of a gift gets not only the property but the tax potential as well. For example, an elderly parent owns a home worth $200,000 for which she paid $50,000. The house has a potential gain of $150,000. If it is given to the child, the child's basis in the house is the same as the parent's ($50,000). If the child then sells the house, the $150,000 gain is taxed to the child. If the parent holds on to the house until death, the child inherits the house with a $200,000 basis. If the child sells the house at that time for what it is worth, there is no gain to the child and no tax to pay.

Another planning tool is the so-called Medicaid trust. A person may set up a trust with the goal of protecting assets from Medicaid. At the outset, even before this trust is explained, be forewarned that the effectiveness of this type of trust is limited and even highly questionable.

In the past, a trust could have been set up to protect both income and principal from the reach of Medicaid. The trustee was given discretion to decide when and if the elderly person could get proceeds from the trust and in what amount. Because the trustee made this decision and the elderly person could not compel a different result, the trust assets as well as its income were protected from Medicaid. However, the Medicaid rules changed and the concept of a "Medicaid qualifying trust" was introduced.

A Medicaid qualifying trust is a trust set up by a Medicaid applicant *or* a spouse. If properly structured, it is hoped that it can be used to protect principal. The trust must give the trustee discretion to make distributions. This means that the trustee can use his or her judgment in making distributions to the Medicaid person. The trust cannot fix the amount of distributions. The trust must be "irrevocable." Once an irrevocable trust is set up, the person setting it up ("the grantor") cannot change his or her mind. The assets transferred to the trust cannot be recovered.

The terms of the trust must be carefully drawn. As already stated, if the trust is written properly, assets in the trust may be protected. Should the elderly person be discharged from a nursing home, he or she will not have been impoverished to the extent of assets remaining in the trust that can be used for his or her benefit. If the person dies in a nursing home, then the assets pass to heirs and Medicaid cannot recover from the trust.

However, all income from the trust that can be used for the nursing-home patient is reachable by Medicaid. Medicaid can take the most liberal interpretation of the trustee's discretion to make distributions to a nursing-home patient. Excess income goes to Medicaid and not to the individual.

In one case in New York, the whole viability of a Medicaid trust has been called into question. The law, and what planning options are available, remains unclear.

If the trust is set up within 30 months of institutionalization, there is the problem of the 30-month rule. The assets themselves are taken into account and can postpone Medicaid eligibility.

The bottom line to the use of trusts is extreme caution and limited optimism. It may be possible, with careful drafting, to gain a measure of protection. However, the full protection that could be achieved in the past through the use of a trust is no longer possible.

Another extreme planning measure has been acted on by some couples. A divorce is instituted to alleviate the community spouse's obligation of support and to protect the assets of that spouse. An undertaking such as divorce, particularly for members of the currently elder generation, should not be considered lightly, and personal choice may far outweigh financial considerations. If one spouse is already incapacitated, there may be legal impediments to getting a divorce.

Short-Term Planning

Even when a nursing home confinement is imminent (i.e., within 30 months), there are still some planning opportunities, especially for married couples.

▸ Maximize the exemption for the residence. If the couple owns a residence and it is only in the name of the institutional spouse, it is advisable to transfer title to the community spouse. You may need the services of an attorney to make this transfer; it must be done legally and recorded as required by local law. When the house belongs to the community spouse, Medicaid will have no claim on it. It may also be advisable to use excess assets to make repairs and capital improvements to the house, buy major appliances and home furnishings, or pay off the mortgage. These moves may boost the equity in the house (an exempt asset) and reduce a community spouse's income needs for housing costs. An opportunity is created for increasing the value of the house that belongs to the community spouse.

▶ Buy exempt assets. If the couple does not own a home, it may be worth considering the purchase of one. For example, $100,000 of nonexempt assets can be used to buy a condominium for the use of the community spouse. The purchase of a family car may also be explored, if the community spouse could use it. Another spend down approach is to use funds to buy necessities for the community spouse.

▶ Generate income up to allowable monthly limits. Convert nonexempt assets to income. For example, buy an annuity for the community spouse. This approach is helpful only where the annuity income is not above monthly maintenance limits.

▶ Make permissible asset transfers. Certain transfers are not taken into account for the 30-month rule. These include transfers to a spouse and transfers to a disabled child. Generally, a spouse may not retransfer assets to a child. However, a retransfer of the community spouse's assets to the child will not affect the ill spouse's eligibility, if that retransfer is made *after* the ill spouse has entered a nursing home. They also include transfer of a residence to certain individuals (spouse, disabled child, caretaker child, and sibling with an ownership interest), as discussed earlier.

▶ Wait out the ineligibility period. As explained earlier in this chapter, assets can be transferred without defeating Medicaid eligibility forever. The outer limit is only 30 months; faster qualification is permitted where the dollar value of assets transferred is less than about $150,000.

Even if a parent is entering a nursing home tomorrow, it is still possible to transfer assets and qualify before 30 months, depending on the value of property transferred and the average cost of a nursing-home stay in your parent's area. There is a "rule of halves" that has come to be used to obtain maximum transferability with the quickest Medicaid eligibility. To generalize, if your parent's nursing-home costs are about the same as the average cost of a nursing home in the area, then it is possible for a parent to transfer half of his or her assets, use the balance to pay for care during the period of ineligibility, and be able to go on Medicaid when the remaining assets are used up.

WEALTH   *Transferring Assets at the Last Minute.* Arthur,
BUILDING   who is single, has $200,000 in assets and is about to
PROFILE   enter a nursing home in an area where the average
monthly cost of a home is $5,000. He can transfer $100,000 of his assets to his child and be able to qualify for Medicaid in 20 months ($100,000 assets transferred, divided by $5,000 average monthly cost of a home in the area). By making the transfer, he has protected $100,000 and still qualified before the end of 30 months. (Remember that the parent still has $100,000, which should be enough to cover the cost of care during the period of ineligibility.)

Even more aggressive transfer strategies than the "rule of halves" have been developed. These are best discussed with an elder law attorney.

In the spend down process, do not overlook the need for a reserve for taxes. There may be gift taxes on the transfer. As described earlier, it is possible to transfer $600,000 completely free from federal gift taxes. However, there may be state gift taxes due.

There may also be income taxes on the sale of assets: there may be gains on which taxes will be owed. For example, an individual sells stock on which there is a $20,000 gain. As much as $5,600 may be due in federal income taxes. If state taxes are also due, a larger reserve is required. The transfer of a house or other property to someone other than a spouse may result in gift tax. Again, this tax liability can affect the spend down process.

There is yet another approach that married couples can use, if a community spouse feels he or she cannot live on the income and resources limits provided by law. That spouse can refuse to make extra amounts available. In that case, Medicaid can look only to the income and resources of the ill spouse. Medicaid can then sue the community spouse for support. This approach is not guaranteed to succeed in all localities. Moreover, it may require that a parent who has been married for many years adopt a legal position that is morally difficult to accept.

It is essential for the community spouse to ask the advice of an attorney before adopting this approach.

Medicaid Coverage for In-Home Care

The preceding discussion is largely applicable to Medicaid qualification when a parent enters a nursing home. New York is among the states that provide Medicaid coverage for in-home care. Different eligibility rules apply in this situation. The asset transfer rules do not apply.

VETERANS' BENEFITS

Individuals who served in our armed forces may not need to seek Medicaid. They may be able to get medical treatment through the Veterans Administration (VA). According to one estimate, there are about 7.2 million veterans over the age of 65. Of these, 1.5 million are over the age of 75!

Treatment in a VA nursing home is available to veterans age 65 or over, regardless of whether their illness or injury is related to military service. Treatment in a VA nursing home for service-connected conditions is free of charge. Treatment in a VA nursing home for non-service-connected conditions is provided free of charge only if the veteran meets an eligibility requirement. The veteran must be eligible for Medicaid, or receive a VA pension, or meet an income test. In 1992, if the veteran is single, annual income must be $18,172 or less. If the veteran has a dependent, annual income must be $21,806 or less, plus $1,213 for each additional dependent.

Veterans whose income exceeds these levels are responsible for the Medicare deductible for 90 days of coverage each year ($652 in 1992), plus $5 for each day of care. However, such cost for a 90-day period cannot exceed the in-patient Medicare deductible. Veterans' disability benefits are also reduced for a veteran living in a VA nursing home who does not have any dependents.

The Veterans Administration runs a number of homes that provide a level of care somewhat below that of a nursing home. These homes are called "domiciliaries." Use of these homes is restricted to needy veterans. There is also "community residential care"—VA-sponsored facilities to which a veteran may be referred if he or she does not need hospitalization or nursing-home care but is unable to live independently.

——————————→ ACTION ITEM ←——————————
**For assistance with veterans' benefits, contact the
local Veterans Administration office. Some cities
and towns also have veterans' benefits counselors
who can advise about programs available.**

————————— **POINTS TO REMEMBER** —————————

▶ Generally speaking, there are three ways to pay for nursing-home
care: through your parent's or your own financial assets; through
special private insurance programs; and through government programs—Medicaid or Veterans' Administration benefits. Medicare
does not provide coverage beyond the skilled nursing care needed
after hospitalization for an acute illness.

▶ Evaluate the cost and value of a long-term care insurance policy
carefully, just as you would any other type of personal insurance.
The cost of the coverage needs to be balanced against the length of
coverage, the elimination period, the daily benefits, the covered
services, and other criteria.

▶ Medicaid is a federally created, state-run program to provide assistance to the poor. The primary qualification for the elderly is financial need, but the definition of need varies from state to state.

▶ Many families prepare for Medicaid coverage by transferring assets
from the parent to a spouse, child, or grandchild, in order to meet
need-based criteria. "Look-back" evaluations going back 30 months
from the date of Medicaid application are now in force. They can
limit Medicaid eligibility based on financial dealings in the prior
30 months.

▶ The total amount of assets that an individual can retain and still
qualify for Medicaid is $3,050 plus certain exempt assets. These as-
sets can include a personal residence, some personal property, wedding and engagement rings, a car, and a few other items.

▶ For Medicaid coverage in the case of a married couple, distinctions
are made between the "institutionalized spouse" (the one needing
the nursing home or other types of care) and the "community"
spouse. Spousal "impoverishment rules" seek to protect the community spouse's financial assets.

5

Finding the Ideal Housing Alternative

Not every parent who grows old will wind up in a nursing home. Your parent may not be infirm, and may only need some special help or facilities, or a more appropriate space to match a change in financial or physical circumstances. There is a great variety of housing arrangements to consider. These arrangements are designed to maintain your parent's independence while ensuring his or her safety.

The first alternative is for your parent to remain in his or her own home or apartment. A number of private and government programs are designed to assist in making this choice possible, financially and otherwise. There are also services and devices to promote safety for an elderly person. A second alternative is downsizing. An elderly parent with a large house might consider selling in order to buy a smaller unit. A third option is an adult community. This alternative may have some health care benefits to offer, in addition to a place to live. A fourth alternative is to move in with family. Among other alternatives, your parent might consider moving in with strangers—becoming a roommate.

This chapter focuses on the benefits and disadvantages of these housing alternatives. We will examine the many housing options available. The decision on where a parent should live depends on four key factors: health, personal preference, financial resources, and available housing alternatives. For a parent who is not in need of round-the-clock nursing care or supervision, the health factor may play only a limited role; personal preference, financial resources, and housing availability will govern the choice. Each of the alternatives has advantages and disadvantages for your parent. The factors must be balanced, in order to make a decision that your parent can live with and you can be comfortable with.

A housing decision may not be a one-time thing. Your parent may be able to live independently for many years to come. However, at some point, his or her capabilities may change. Your parent may then need more assistance with personal tasks, which may make independent living less appealing. At that point, other housing alternatives will need to be reviewed.

REMAINING AT HOME

Many elderly individuals prefer to remain fully independent. They like their privacy and familiar surroundings and would choose to stay in their own homes, if possible. Their homes are furnished with cherished possessions and are situated in the neighborhood where they have lived for many years. With failing health and financial pressures, this choice may not be ideal for everyone, but it still may not be necessary to uproot an elderly parent. There are several financial considerations for opting to remain at home. A host of governmental and private programs are designed to provide in-home assistance to the elderly. To the extent that medical care is needed, it may be provided in the home. Finally, there are ways to make a home safe and better adapted for use by an elderly person.

Financial Considerations

For some elderly parents, their home has long since been fully paid for. The ancillary costs of property taxes, insurance, and utilities may be manageable. For others, however, the monthly bills for staying at home may be a considerable strain. There are a number of ways to reduce monthly costs and/or to obtain additional funds for expenses.

Long after a mortgage is paid off, property taxes continue to be levied. In some areas, such taxes may be steep. Many localities now offer property tax abatements for seniors whose incomes are below set minimums. Contact the local taxing authority to find out about your parent's eligibility for property tax abatement programs.

For those who rent rather than own their own homes, there may also be special breaks. Some cities set rent increase limits for elderly individuals with low incomes. For example, in New York City, the Rent Stabilization Board helps to fix a ceiling on the rent that can be charged to the elderly by private landlords in certain buildings. These limits are not automatically given to the elderly. Tenants must apply for them.

Local utilities may also offer some programs designed to ensure that the delivery of electricity or gas used by the elderly is not terminated because of an inability to pay or a failure to promptly pay outstanding bills. For example, the utility may offer a budgeting or level billing program, quarterly (as opposed to monthly) billing, or some other means of easing payment burdens on the elderly. Ask your parent's utility company about its programs for the elderly.

Reverse Mortgages

One reason why an elderly parent may not be able to remain at home is cost. Even with tax abatements and other cost-cutting measures, income may be too low to live on, in the present circumstances. Social security benefits, company pensions, and income from individual savings may not be sufficient to pay monthly bills.

Where the mortgage has been paid off, there is an opportunity for generating the additional cash that will enable your elderly parent to remain in an owned home. It is estimated that three-quarters of the elderly in this country own their own homes; of these, more than 80 percent have no mortgages on the homes. The homes may be impressive sources of cash for their owners. If his or her home were sold today, your parent would realize the present value of the home, referred to as "equity." This equity can be unlocked for use by the owner *without* a sale.

Traditional borrowing methods may not be useful to the elderly. Taking out a new mortgage or home equity loan would require immediate repayment of principal and interest in the form of monthly payments. This would produce a big chunk of cash up front but would not solve monthly cash-flow problems. Monthly bills would be *increased*. There is another alternative loan that can meet the needs of the elderly: the reverse mortgage.

The concept of a reverse mortgage was born in the early 1980s. The reverse mortgage allows a homeowner to borrow against the equity in the home. The bank makes a loan to the homeowner (typically up to 75 percent of the equity) and the loan is secured by the home. When it first started, the reverse mortgage was poorly designed. The loan proceeds were paid out in the form of monthly payments (a good method), they ran for a set period of time, such as 3 to 12 years (not a bad payout period), and there was no repayment of principal or interest during the payout period (a very good point). However, after the proceeds were fully paid out, the entire balance of principal and interest immediately became due (a very bad factor). To pay off the debt, a homeowner had to either obtain another loan or sell the home.

Today, there are several variations on the reverse mortgage; they vary from state to state and lender to lender. The key points to check are:

▸ How much equity can be borrowed?
▸ How are the loan proceeds paid to the homeowner?
▸ What are the payback details?

In some states, the old form of reverse mortgage, with full repayment at the end of a set number of years, is still being offered. The almost certain "forced sale" at the end of the payout period is, needless to say, a major drawback. Still, where this is the only form available, the arrangement may still be of benefit to some individuals who need the cash for the short term and anticipate additional future funds (e.g., the expectation of an insurance settlement or a lawsuit award). It may also be useful to those who are planning to sell the home and move before the end of the loan term.

Another form of reverse mortgage, available in about a half-dozen states, is called the individual reverse mortgage account (IRMA), sometimes referred to as a "tenure" mortgage. Under this alternative, monthly payments continue for the life of the owner. The IRMA can be viewed as a life annuity. The size of the monthly payments is fixed to reflect the owner's life expectancy. Thus, the payments vary with the owner's age at the time the loan is taken. Principal and interest become due at the death of the owner or a prior sale.

A couple of states offer a variation on the IRMA loan. Instead of payments continuing for life, they are made only for an agreed-on term, such as 10, 15, or 30 years. This type of IRMA is called a split-reverse mortgage. Again, repayment is required only when a sale or death occurs.

In a handful of states, there is a repayment alternative. In conjunction with a reverse mortgage, the bank is permitted to take part of the home's appreciation instead of repayment. The bank's share of the home's appreciation, which could be as much as 25 percent, is realized when the home is sold. This type of loan is referred to as a shared appreciation reverse mortgage.

Another innovation being developed in some states is a line-of-credit reverse mortgage. This arrangement allows a homeowner to draw funds from a set credit line at the time and in the amount desired. This arrangement, similar to a home equity loan, provides the flexibility of borrowing only the amount that is required.

Although reverse mortgages currently are available in only about a quarter of the states, there is reason to expect that their availability will expand. The federal government launched a pilot program in 1989 that continued until September 1991. Under the pilot program, the Federal National Mortgage Association (Fannie Mae) insured up to 2,500 reverse mortgages. The government guaranteed that the private lender would receive the entire loan balance when it comes due. This guarantee applies even if home prices decrease and sale proceeds are insufficient to meet principal and interest obligations. There was a cost for loans covered in this program: a homeowner had to pay a two-part premium—an annual charge of $1/2$ of 1 percent of the principal balance of the loan, plus 2 percent of the home's value or the maximum Federal Housing Authority (FHA) loan amount. This pilot program was extremely successful. There were many more applicants than loans available, which may encourage the government to extend the program.

Encumbering a property with a reverse equity mortgage makes transfer of the home for Medicaid eligibility purposes more difficult. A transfer of the home from a parent to child would still result in immediate acceleration of the outstanding mortgage, just as if the parent had sold the home to strangers. This aspect of planning should not be overlooked where there is a possibility of needing costly nursing-home care some time in the future.

For more details on reverse mortgages, obtain a free manual entitled *Consumer's Guide to Home Equity Conversion* from AARP, Home Equity Information Center, 1909 K Street N.W., Washington, DC 20049; phone: 202/434-2277. You might also contact Commission on Legal Problems of the Elderly, American Bar Association, 1800 M Street, N.W., Washington, DC 20036; phone: 202/331-2297.

—————————→ **ACTION ITEM** ←—————————

Contact the above agencies, your local bank, or local senior-citizen resource centers for information on reverse mortgages. Find out the advantages and disadvantages of making this financial decision, before committing to other choices for maintaining or disposing of the home.

Increasing Monthly Income by Renting a Room

Your parent may be able to stay in an owned home and enjoy additional income by renting out a portion of the home. Shared living arrangements are discussed in more detail later in this chapter.

Selling the Home to an Adult Child and Renting It Back

One of the most frequently asked questions is whether an adult child should acquire his or her parent's home by purchase or gift. There is no right or wrong answer; a great many factors must be considered.

If the home is transferred to the child, the parent may continue to live in it. When the transfer is accomplished by sale, the arrangement is called a sale and leaseback. This permits the elderly parent to cash in on the home equity built up over the years, without having to move. The arrangement is really quite simple. An adult child buys the home and then rents it back to the parent. This arrangement can be fashioned in a number of ways.

A child can buy the home from the parent, using a combination of cash plus a mortgage on the home. The parent pockets the full value of the home and can use part of it to pay the monthly rent. The balance of the proceeds can be invested to produce additional income. The balance can be available for other purposes, such as vacations or medical emergencies.

If the earnings on the proceeds are not sufficient to meet the rent, then principal must be used for this purpose. Before entering into a sale-leaseback arrangement, it should be determined how long the principal can be expected to last, if it is tapped regularly for rent and other expenses. In making this projection, take into account the monthly amount required and the rate of return that can be earned on the money. Be sure to include increases in the rent because of inflation.

Alternatively, the parent can use the money to purchase a commercial annuity. Such an annuity will provide monthly payments for life. Commercial annuities are sold by life insurance companies and brokerage firms that handle life insurance products. In buying a commercial annuity, it is advisable to check the rating of the insurance company being considered. This is especially true today, given the fact that the soundness of some carriers has been called into question. Insurance companies are rated by A. M. Best Company, the most respected independent rating organization for life insurance companies. The highest rating given by Best is A+/Excellent. Other rating companies include Moody's and Standard & Poors.

The parent may have little or no tax consequences as a result of the sale-leaseback. If the parent is 55 or over and has owned and lived in the home for 3 out of the past 5 years, then he or she qualifies to make a one-time election to exclude from gross income up to $125,000 of profit from the sale.

WEALTH BUILDING PROFILE

Selling a Home Tax-Free. A parent's home cost $50,000. Over the years, improvements totaling $25,000 were added. Therefore, the tax basis of the home is $75,000 ($50,000 cost plus $25,000 improvements). Gain (a tax word for profit) is the difference between what the home sells for and its tax basis. (There are certain tax refinements that need not be considered here.) If the home is sold for $200,000, there is no tax on the sale. Gain in this case is $125,000 (the difference between the sale proceeds of $200,000 and the basis of $75,000). The full amount of gain may be excluded under the $125,000 election.

If the selling price is greater than $200,000, gain will be treated as capital gain and taxed accordingly.

The top federal tax rate on capital gains is 28 percent. If the parent has already used the $125,000 exclusion or for some other reason does not qualify for it (for example, the parent has not owned or used the home long enough), then the economics of the sale-leaseback arrangement may not make sense.

From the child's side, there are economic and tax considerations to this arrangement. You must be able to afford the initial down payment. The balance of the purchase can be financed with a bank loan. The monthly rent from the parent will help to defray the cost of mortgage payments. However, even a fair rent may not be sufficient to meet this obligation plus other carrying costs (real estate taxes, insurance on the property, maintenance expenses).

The arrangement's tax incentives should be taken into account. Mortgage interest, property taxes, property insurance, depreciation on the house, and other related expenses are deductible. However, under the "passive loss rules," expenses in excess of rental income may not be currently deductible. Current deductibility depends on your income and your other rental activities and tax shelters. If your parent's house is your only rental or tax shelter activity, you would be able to write off expenses up to $25,000 in excess of rental income against your other income, provided your adjusted gross income does not exceed $100,000. If your adjusted gross is between $100,000 and $150,000, the $25,000 allowance is phased out accordingly.

Let's take an example of the impact of the sale of your parent's house on you. Assume that the home is sold for $150,000 and you can expect to receive a rent of about 6 percent of that value, or $9,000 annually ($750 a month). (Rents typically range between 5 percent and 9 percent of the house's value, depending on the area in which the home is located and other market conditions.) You pay $30,000 down and get a 30-year fixed-rate mortgage at 8.5 percent for the balance ($120,000). Your monthly mortgage payments are $922.70, or $11,072.40 annually. In the early years of the mortgage, the greater part of these payments is interest. Assume that property taxes, insurance, and maintenance are $5,000 annually, and that the annual depreciation on the home is $4,364 (depreciation of house, not land, of $120,000 divided by 27.5 years). Annual write-offs in excess of rental income would yield an annual federal tax savings of about $6,450 (assuming that you are in the top tax bracket and your adjusted gross income does not exceed $100,000 or you have additional passive activity income to permit the full write-offs). Even with this tax savings, you would pay out-of-pocket about $9,600 annually, but this investment may mean that you do not need to contribute directly to your parent's support. Besides, you would benefit from any appreciation in the value of the home.

→ **ACTION ITEM** ←

If you retain an accountant to calculate your annual federal and state taxes, enlist that professional's help in working out the complexities of the tax consequences of buying your parent's home.

The tax benefits to adult children were greater before the Tax Reform Act of 1986 because of higher income tax brackets and greater depreciation allowances. Still, the remaining tax incentives should not be ignored. In fact, for those in states with high income taxes, the out-of-pocket costs can be further reduced by state tax savings. As Congress continues to raise the tax brackets, a process that started in 1990 and can be expected to be repeated, the tax benefits become more important.

Public and Private Services for In-Home Care

Some elderly who can otherwise live on their own may require personal assistance. They have difficulty with such tasks as shopping, meal preparation, transportation, doctor visits, or self-care. There are a number of public and private programs that can help. How can you find out what is available in your parent's area?

First, contact your city, county, or state agency that oversees issues of the elderly, to learn what public programs are being offered. Check the blue pages of your local telephone directory for listings under such titles as Council (or Office) on Aging, Elderly, Senior Citizens, Health Department, Department of Social Services, and Department of Human Services. A complete listing of state agencies may be found in the appendix.

Available Services

State and local governments may offer a variety of free or minimal-cost in-home services. These services usually include escorted shopping, house cleaning, small repairs (e.g., light bulb changes), and transportation for doctors' appointments. For example, in 1989, New York set up an Expanded In-Home Services for the Elderly program. The state spent $14.5 million on workers who could provide various personal assistance services. These in-home services were bathing, shopping, banking, and bill paying.

Localities have also begun to devise programs to benefit the elderly who need in-home assistance. Some localities have enlisted the help of neighborhood nonprofit organizations such as churches, schools, and social clubs. Programs such as Meals-on-Wheels bring hot meals to those who are homebound. Other programs provide companionship through visits or phone calls by volunteers.

Public programs may not be available or may not meet all of your parent's needs. An even greater number of private organizations, both nonprofit and for-profit, offer a full range of services. In some states, public gas and electric companies must offer quarterly billing to the elderly, to simplify their check-writing responsibilities.

To learn what organizations may be of help to your family, check telephone listings under Family Services Agencies, Geriatric Counselors/Care Managers, Geriatric Physicians and Nurses, Churches, Community Civil and Service Groups, Associations (such as the Arthritis Foundation), and Caregiver Support Groups. If you fail to contact a helpful source, you might seek a local referral from the National Council on the Aging, Inc., 600 Maryland Avenue, S.W., Washington, DC 20024; phone: 202/479-1200.

Day Care

Is your parent not able to be left alone for extended periods of time, yet not in need of 24-hour nursing care? Does he or she need some care during the hours when relatives are at work? Or, does your parent simply want to socialize with other contemporaries? Increasingly, the elderly and their families are turning to adult day-care centers for these types of assistance. Presently, there are about 2,200 adult day-care centers nationwide and the number is growing rapidly each year. Some of these centers are private (both nonprofit or for-profit), some are employer-sponsored, and some are VA facilities.

Day-care centers generally provide some meals (breakfast and lunch). They also offer a wide range of recreational activities. Varying from center to center, social activities offered may include exercise classes, arts and crafts, and local outings. The center may also offer a number of support services: counseling, occupational therapy, physical therapy, speech therapy, health screening, medical and social evaluations, and personal care. The centers may or may not provide transportation from and to home.

→ **ACTION ITEM** ←

Make an appointment to tour local adult day-care facilities in your community, if you live in the vicinity of your parent. Talk with friends who may have themselves arranged such a placement for their parents. Become familiar with the strengths and weaknesses of the facilities in your parent's area.

The great majority of states (but not all) have certain *minimum* standards to which these centers must adhere. You should personally check out the center that you are considering for your parent, to make your own assessment. The ratio of staff to clients should be as low as possible. The center should be able to handle the specific needs of your parent. For example, a parent with Alzheimer's disease should use only a day-care center that is staffed for that ailment. Some day-care programs specialize in persons with a particular ailment (e.g., Alzheimer's disease) and can offer more than just supervision. A parent with special dietary concerns should use only a day-care center that serves appropriate meals.

The cost of the center and possible financial aid alternatives should be considered. Day-care costs vary widely, depending on the quality of the center and the range of services offered. Most centers operate on a sliding scale based on the ability to pay. Your parent may qualify for some governmental assistance in meeting day-care costs. In some states, Medicaid may cover the cost of day care (see Chapter 4). Alternatively, you may be able to shoulder day-care costs if your employer offers parent care as an employee benefit. This is a relatively new fringe benefit, but it is expected to become more common, at least among large employers, as the decade progresses and the elder care crisis is felt more acutely in the workplace.

Local day-care centers, like in-home services, can be located by consulting the local telephone directory.

Parents Requiring In-Home Health Care

Medical problems do not automatically mean that a parent can no longer remain at home. An elderly parent requiring medical care may still be able to live at home with the proper assistance. Home care can provide nursing and custodial care on a short-term basis, for example, during periods of recovery from episodes of illness. It can also provide for long-term care (see the discussion in Chapter 4). An agency providing home health care can be located through the local telephone directory or by a referral from a state or local agency.

Be prepared to ask quite a number of key questions, in order to ensure that the home care agency will meet your need:

▶ How long has the agency been in business? If it has a long track record, you might check with the local Better Business Bureau, to learn whether there have been any complaints against it.

▶ Has the agency received Medicare certification? Such certification indicates that the agency has met certain minimum federal standards. Failure to have this certification does not automatically mean that the agency is substandard. It may only mean that the agency has chosen not to participate in the Medicare program. This, of course, can affect the cost of the agency.

▶ Is the agency licensed by the state, if your parent's state has licensing requirements?

▶ Is it accredited by a national association?

▶ How does the agency operate? Does it draw up a written plan for your parent? Are costs spelled out? Have arrangements been made for emergencies? Have reimbursement sources (public and private) been coordinated with the charges levied? Answers to these questions will assure you of some minimum competency. You may wish to ask additional questions, to determine whether the agency's philosophy and sensitivity are consistent with those of your parent and your family.

The National Association of Home Care (519 C Street, N.E., Washington, DC 20002; phone: 202/547-7424) has developed a Bill of Rights for Home Care Patients:

1. You have the right to be fully informed of all your rights and responsibilities by the home care agency.

2. You have the right to appropriate and professional care relating to physician orders.

3. You have the right of choice of care providers.

4. You have the right to receive information necessary to give you informed consent prior to the start of any procedure or treatment.

5. You have the right to refuse treatment within the confines of the law and to be informed of the consequences of your actions.

6. You have the right to privacy.

7. You have the right to receive a timely response from the agency to your request for service.

8. You shall be admitted for service only if the agency has the ability to provide safe and professional care at the level of intensity needed. You have the right to reasonable continuity of care.

9. You have the right to be informed within a reasonable time of anticipated termination of service or plans for transfer to another agency.

10. You have the right to voice grievances and suggest changes in service or staff without fear of restraint or discrimination.

11. You have the right to be fully informed of agency policies and charges for services, including eligibility for third-party reimbursements.

12. If you are denied service solely on your inability to pay, you have the right to be referred elsewhere.

13. You (and the public) have the right to honest, accurate, forthright information regarding the home care industry in general and your agency in particular.

These rights are not binding on care providers. They merely serve as guidelines by which to measure the quality of care provided. If the care falls short of these standards, action can be taken. State and local authorities or the Better Business Bureau should be contacted if problems with care providers cannot be remedied directly. Home health care agencies that fall under the Social Security Administration also have a Bill of Rights for in-home care. (See Chapter 3.)

Safety

If your parent lives alone, you may worry about his or her safety. What if your parent falls in the shower? How can you be sure that your parent can get help? There are two aspects of safety. First, make sure your parent's home is safer and more accessible to diminishing capacities. Second, link your parent to you and the world outside the home, for both social contact and in case of emergency.

───────────────────→ **ACTION ITEM** ←───────────────────

Do a security and safety check of your parent's home regularly. Look over the elder care equipment that home-supply stores stock, to see whether any useful new products have become available. In your parent's home, make sure that necessary safety devices are functioning properly, and do a safety drill with your parents to make sure they know how the devices function.

With the graying of the population, a number of companies are addressing the issues of safety and accessibility in the home. Routine safety protection—smoke detectors, locks, burglar alarms, proper maintenance of furnaces and chimneys—is not to be overlooked. In addition, special aids can make life easier and safer for your parent. Items designed to make a home safer or more accessible for the elderly or infirm include railings inside tubs and near toilets, special toilet seats, ramps at entryways, one-person "elevators" for stairways, and telephones with oversize buttons and automatic dialers. Books are available on elders' safety; special service companies can elderproof your parent's home in the same way that you may have babyproofed your home for your child. Hardware or specialty stores carry the necessary products.

You should be sure that your parent is connected with the outside world, in case of emergency. This can be done without impinging on your parent's privacy or independence.

First, you should have a key to your parent's home. If you live a distance away, it is a good idea for another relative, neighbor, or friend who lives close to your parent to have a key.

Second, you should encourage your parent to institute a "buddy system" for routinely checking in with you or a neighbor. This regular social contact ensures your parent's continued safety. For elderly persons living alone, the U.S. Postal Service has developed a Carrier Alert Program that operates in conjunction with a local agency. A decal on the mailbox signifies that an elderly individual is part of the program. If a person in the program fails to pick up his or her mail within a certain number of days, the local agency is notified.

Finally, you may want to have an emergency program in place. Many local hospitals and several electronics companies offer monitoring devices that your parent can use to call for help, if he or she is unable to reach or dial a phone. A small transmitter worn by the elderly person connects him or her to the outside world when trouble strikes. This system offers a measure of relief to children of the elderly who may not be close at hand.

Local hospitals offering the monitoring service rent out the unit and charge a monthly fee that covers both the unit and the monitoring services. Private companies both rent and sell units.

Lifeline Systems, Inc. (1 Arsenal Market Place, Watertown, MA 02172; phone: 800/451-0525) provides a small electronic device that can be set off in an accident or sudden illness, to summon emergency medical care. A transmitter is worn around the neck or wrist or carried in a pocket. When it is triggered, it operates a self-dialer on the telephone. It automatically calls the local hospital, which then calls back the elderly person. If the person fails to pick up the phone, then, by prearrangement, relatives, neighbors, and friends are called to check up on the person.

Another emergency response product is LifeCall. This is offered by the Emergency Response People, Inc., 1300 Admiral Wilson Blvd., Camden, NJ 08101; phone: 800/322-8377. A third company is Medic Alert Response Service, a division of the Medic Alert Foundation International, P.O. Box 1009, Turlock, CA 95381; phone: 209/668-3333. Medic Alert offers MARS.5000, an emergency response service. In addition to a one-ounce portable transmitter that is worn around the neck, there is a communicator unit that allows for two-way voice contact. The units can be leased or purchased. A monthly charge for the monitoring service runs about a $1 a day.

Keep in mind that these private companies are *not* regulated by government authorities. There have been widespread reports of consumer ripoffs, with companies failing to provide promised services. Therefore, in selecting any of these services, caution is advised.

The Medic Alert Foundation International also has a program called Alzheimer's Links to Life Program, which can help locate individuals with memory lapses who wander off. The program, started in California, is now expanding.

Most homeowners are entitled to a one-time tax exemption of $125,000 from the sale of a home. If your parent is selling a home, when should he or she take advantage of this exclusion?

There is no simple answer to this question; generally, the answer depends on what the parent intends to do *after* the sale of the house. If the plan is to buy another one (at a substantial cost), it may make sense to keep the exclusion for when that new home is sold. In most cases, where the living arrangement after the initial house sale does not involve a home purchase (such as when a parent enters a nursing home or a lifetime care facility), the exclusion should be taken.

When does a reverse mortgage for an elderly homeowner make sense?

The essence of a reverse mortgage is that it frees up equity that has been tied to the ownership of the home—while the parent can make use of it. It is especially sensible when a parent strongly desires to remain in the home, despite a limited budget for taxes and maintenance expenses. It also makes sense when there is an expectation of a sizable financial settlement in the near future (such as a lawsuit settlement) whose proceeds could be used to pay off the mortgage. When arranging for a reverse mortgage, be aware of the payback requirements, which can include a forced sale of the home.

What does it mean when a home care agency has Medicare certification?

This indicates that the agency has met minimum federal standards; however, if the agency lacks the certification, it may simply mean that it chooses not to participate in the Medicare program. Inquire further about state or national licensing or accreditation.

What can be done to make a parent's home more livable?

First, do what you can to make the home easier to use, by investigating, and perhaps investing in, elderproofing housewares such as motorized stairs, easy-to-read telephones, new bathroom fixtures, and the like. Next, check the security of the home: fire and burglar alarms, window gates, etc. Try to set up a buddy system with a neighbor, and check with local government agencies (Postal Service, police and fire departments) for monitoring services. You may also consider a subscription to one of the national monitoring franchises, which will give your parent a communication device to use in case of emergencies.

Should an elderly parent take in a boarder or roommate?

It depends on how comfortable the parent is with nonfamily persons. The up side is that he or she may find companionship and a more comfortable living situation by doing so, aside from the potential financial advantages of charging rent.

DOWNSIZING AND/OR RELOCATING

For some parents, the house they have lived in for these past number of years may seem to have grown too big to manage. For financial or personal reasons, it is time for them to sell out and move on. The decision to sell out and move on requires a parent to make a number of other decisions: where to locate and what type of housing to select. The tax consequences of selling the home should also be taken into account.

Location or Relocation

Your parent may prefer to remain in the same locality. The merits of staying within the community—family, friends, and familiarity—may far outweigh any other considerations. In this case, the sale of a home is solely for the purpose of "downsizing." Downsizing may mean moving to a smaller unit, moving in with the family, or entering an adult community or a care facility. (These latter housing options—residence with family, an adult community, or a care facility—are discussed later in this chapter.)

Some elderly people are forced to move to a new location because of health reasons. The great migration to the Sun Belt, although considerably lessened from the great wave of the 1970s and 1980s, continues to be supported in large measure by retirees. Weather and the health benefits associated with dryer, warmer climates are not the only reasons for a move south or to any other location.

A number of things should be checked out before changing locality:

▶ Health services. What facilities are present in the particular area your parent is considering? Florida, for example, boasts that it is one of the country's best states for skilled medical care.

▶ Public transportation. As people grow older, the wisdom of continuing to drive becomes questionable. It is probably safe to say that more elderly should give up their driver's licenses and stick to public transportation or obtain privately arranged rides. Diminished eyesight may force some elderly to do this, regardless of their personal preference. It is important for the elderly to have access to stores and doctors by means of public transportation.

▶ Other local services for the elderly. The types of services and activities offered vary from locality to locality. Some areas have a wide range of recreational activities geared to the elderly, such as senior-citizen centers and various church-related groups. These activities not only enrich the lives of those who participate, but, for some, they also provide companionship, functioning as surrogate families. Certain localities are particularly sensitive to the needs of the home-bound elderly, with programs such as Meals-on-Wheels and other in-home services.

▶ Taxes. A number of states are attractive for the elderly because they impose low or no *state income taxes*. However, with budgetary problems abounding, some previously tax-free states may begin to levy an income tax.

→ ACTION ITEM ←

Before your parent uproots and moves to another state, consider taking a short vacation together in that region, to explore what facilities are available and how comfortable the life-style there will be if your parent makes the move.

The purchasing power of the elderly is affected by *state sales tax* levied on necessities ranging from various grocery items and clothing to medicine and drugs. Only about a half-dozen states do not have any sales tax.

Although a decision to relocate may not take into account the effect of the move on one's heirs, it is worth noting that it is cheaper to die in some states than in others. The types of *death taxes* vary from state to state. Some states impose an inheritance tax that is levied on one's heirs. Some states have an estate tax, which is paid by the estate before distribution of assets to the heirs. Some states impose what is called a "pick-up" tax: the amount allowed as a credit against the federal estate tax for state death taxes. Pick-up tax allows the federal government to collect estate tax revenue without increasing the total tax payable by the estate or heirs. It only applies when the estate exceeds $600,000 and is therefore subject to federal estate tax. Some states impose both an inheritance and a pick-up tax, or an estate and a pick-up tax.

→ ACTION ITEM ←

If your parent has residences in two states, for death tax purposes it may be advisable to establish domicile in the state with the lower levy. Domicile can be established in several ways: registering to vote, filing a federal income tax return from a particular address, registering a car and, where applicable, filing a homestead claim.

Your parent's domicile determines which state can collect death tax. Domicile has a slightly different meaning than mere residence. It is the place your parent treats as home. Thus, for example, if your mother lives in the same house in New Jersey that she has owned for 30 years, but spends the winters each year in Florida, she is still considered to be domiciled in New Jersey. This is the place where she has her family ties, is registered to vote, has her religious affiliation, and generally considers herself "home."

Housing Options in Downsizing

Your parent may want to continue fully independent living, only with less worry and cost. Purchase of a smaller house or condominium or rental of a smaller unit may be the solution. With age a factor, the maintenance of the unit selected is an important consideration. No- or low-maintenance housing is preferred. Homeowner associations in areas being considered should be checked, to see exactly what is covered by monthly maintenance charges.

Cost may be another consideration. Smaller does not necessarily mean cheaper. The old house that was paid off years ago may be less costly, month to month, than a newer, smaller house, because of the rising cost of housing during the past two decades. Still, with housing in a slump in the early 1990s, it may be an ideal time to pick up a smaller house at a bargain price.

Tax Consequences of Selling the Home

If your parent decides to sell the home, the tax impact should be considered. Your parent may be eligible to claim an exclusion of $125,000 of the gain from the sale of the residence. There are three key requirements for taking advantage of this tax break:

▸ The home must be your parent's principal residence.
▸ Your parent must be age 55 or over on the date of sale.
▸ Your parent must have owned *and* lived in the residence for 3 of the 5 years preceding the date of sale.

Note that if your parent is forced to sell because of a move to a licensed nursing home or other facility, then the ownership and use test drops to 1-out-of-5 years preceding the date of sale.

If all three requirements are met, then the election to use the $125,000 exclusion is permitted, as long as your parent has not made a prior election. This is a once-in-a-lifetime opportunity.

Suppose your parent sold the home 10 years ago, used the exclusion at that time, and moved to a condo. Now your parent is selling the condo and moving to yet another location. Is any other tax break available? Possibly, even though the once-in-a-lifetime exclusion has already been used. Getting another tax break depends on whether your parent buys another home or merely rents a residence. If your parent buys another residence at a price higher than the selling price of the old residence, tax on any amount of gain is deferred.

WEALTH   *Deferring Tax on the Sale of a Home When Down-*
BUILDING   *sizing.* Assume the tax basis of your parent's house
PROFILE   is $60,000 (the original cost plus improvements), and
                that the home is sold for $200,000. This results in a
gain of $140,000 ($200,000 sale proceeds less $60,000 basis). (For purposes of this example, broker's fees and other selling costs are disregarded.) If your parent buys a new home for $200,000 or more, then no gain is recognized in the year of the sale. The gain will be taxed only if your parent later sells the second home and does not buy a new home of sufficient cost.

If, in this example, your parent buys a home costing $175,000, then $25,000 of the gain is currently taxable ($200,000 − $175,000). This gain is treated as capital gain. Assuming that the house was owned for more than 1 year, it would be subject to a top federal income tax rate of 28 percent.

To take advantage of this deferral rule, the home must be your parent's principal residence and not merely a vacation home. The new home must be bought or built within 2 years before or after the date of sale of the old home.

Where sales proceeds are substantial and a reinvestment is made, it is possible to combine both the exclusion and the deferral rules. They will avoid all current tax. The exclusion is taken into account first, in reducing what is treated as the selling price of the old home. Thus, only the net amount (after the exclusion) is considered to be the selling price of the old home, for purposes of the deferral rules. This greatly reduces the amount that must be reinvested to avoid current tax on the balance of the gain.

WEALTH	*Combining the Exclusion with the Deferral, to*
BUILDING	*Minimize Income Tax.* In the profile above, the
PROFILE	house cost $60,000 and it sold for $200,000. If the

exclusion can be used in this case, the reinvestment required to fully avoid all current tax is limited to $15,000 ($140,000 gain less $125,000 exclusion).

If your parent plans to buy a replacement residence, it generally is advisable to use the deferral rules and save the exclusion for a time when no further replacement residence will be purchased. Let's say your parent is downsizing to a smaller house; this move may result in gain. However, a few years down the road, your parent may be forced into a nursing home. At that time, the smaller house may be sold. Because no replacement residence is purchased at that time, the sale is ideal for the exclusion.

The rules for the tax treatment of home sales are spelled out in the instructions to IRS Form 2119. This form must be filed for the year of sale, along with the parent's Form 1040. "Sales price," "cost basis," and other related terms have special tax meaning. They are explained in the instructions to Form 2119. For further information on tax breaks for home sales, see IRS Publication 523, which can be obtained at any IRS service center or by calling 1-800/829-3676.

ADULT COMMUNITIES

Your elderly parent may prefer to move to an adult community. Residence there will allow your parent to be among contemporaries and may permit access to special services and facilities. There is a wide range of characteristics among adult communities. The one that may be right for your parent depends not only on health concerns but also on money. Here are some options that are under the umbrella of the adult community.

Retirement Communities

Throughout the country, there are numerous communities for those who no longer have small children at home. They may take the form of one-family houses, condominium units, or apartment dwellings.

Retirement communities offer social and recreational activities for those over set ages, such as 55+ or 65+. These retirement communities are intended for those in good health. They are for the elderly who prefer to live without the noise and tumult experienced in neighborhoods with children. Restrictions by homeowner associations to keep children out have come under various attacks in recent years. Some associations have won victories upholding the restrictive covenants, but the trend is away from these restrictions. Still, it is not likely that the prevalence of retirement communities will diminish significantly as the population continues to age.

Lifetime Care Facilities

These facilities are also called continuing care retirement communities—CCRCs. Some elderly may require a measure of medical care; others may anticipate a need for access to medical care. For them, a lifetime care facility offers private living arrangements, typically in apartment units. Furnishings can be provided by the resident, to personalize the unit and make it a home.

The facility offers congregant dining as well as social and recreational activities. Meals (typically breakfast and dinner, but sometimes all three meals) are served in a group dining room. Weekly activities are prominently posted and open to all residents. These might include classes, card games, and special events.

The key aspect of the lifetime care facility is the medical services provided. The extent of these services varies from facility to facility. The most extensive care provided is 24-hour nursing care. In determining whether the facility offers the kind of care that your parent requires, its hospital affiliation should be checked.

———————————→ **ACTION ITEM** ←———————————

Lifetime care facilities obviate the need for long-term care insurance, because nursing-home care is part of the services provided by the facilities.

The cost of continuing care facilities is not low. Most require an initial entry fee (also called an entrance fee, accommodation fee, or founder's fee), which can be quite steep—as much as $80,000. In addition, there is a monthly maintenance charge, which rises annually. Some continuing care facilities do not require an initial fee. Instead, they charge only monthly fees to cover the cost of the apartment and meals. In some facilities, there may be an extra charge for limited health care.

A move to a continuing care community is a big commitment. There is, of course, the psychological aspect of acknowledging that this is probably one's home for the remainder of life. The financial considerations are also important. Because the initial fee may be high, a number of factors should be checked out thoroughly before signing any agreement. It is essential to determine the financial soundness of the sponsors and administrators; quite a number of facilities have gone under and their residents lost their initial fees. The fees represented their life savings. Find out whether the fee can be recovered under certain circumstances. Can the fee be recouped if your parent dies within a short time or decides to move for whatever reason?

Tax Aspects

There are tax aspects to consider with respect to the initial entry fee. If your parent has already used the once-in-a-lifetime exclusion to avoid gain on up to $125,000 of profit from the sale of a residence, he or she may not be able to benefit from the deferral rules. The IRS has taken the position that the payment of an initial entry fee is not the same as buying a new residence. An interest in the continuing care community is not the equivalent of the purchase of a residence. The interest in the facility is viewed as a right to future support rather than a legal interest in property. Even where there is a right to transfer the membership obtained by the initial entry fee, the interest does not equate to a fee interest in property.

It may be possible to get a medical expense deduction for a portion of the initial entry fee. Although no deduction is allowed for the prepayment of medical expenses, a deduction may be taken to the extent that there is a current obligation to provide medical care. The facility should allocate the lump-sum payment between health care and rental and other benefits. Remember that medical expenses are only deductible if such expenses exceed 7.5 percent of adjusted gross income and if the standard deduction is not taken.

There is one more tax aspect to the initial fee. Under certain circumstances, the IRS views a partially refundable fee as an interest-free loan that can result in immediate taxation to the elderly person. Whether tax results in this situation depends on the size of the fee and several other factors. It is advisable to ask the facility or a tax adviser about the tax implications of the initial fee.

Assisted Living Projects

These are board and care homes, residential care facilities, sheltered housing, or adult care homes. For an elderly parent requiring greater services, an assisted living facility may be a better choice. This type of facility offers 24-hour care, both nursing and personal. For example, the facility can supervise medications. In view of the extensive nature of services provided, this type of facility is designed for those generally over age 75, whether or not they have immediate medical needs.

Assisted living projects offer private or semiprivate apartment units. Full group meals; daily maid, linen, and laundry services; and regular medical checkups are also included. Some facilities are homey; others have a more institutional look. Their appearance does not necessarily affect the quality of services provided.

Good assisted living facilities strive to help the elderly maintain their independence. Additional services (above and beyond group meals) are offered on a personal basis (when and to the extent needed) rather than according to schedules. These services can include bathing assistance, shopping trips, and doctor visits. Some facilities attempt to keep costs down by offering fewer personal services.

The cost of assisted living varies with the types of accommodations offered. Rents in facilities offering extensive services can run to over $2,000 a month; those offering minimal services can be well under $1,000 a month. The services offered versus the costs required must be balanced when choosing a specific facility for your parent.

Assisted living arrangements can eliminate the need for planning for nursing-home placement. Assisted living can provide the custodial care that would otherwise be obtained from a nursing home. Therefore, there may be no need to ever move from an assisted living arrangement. On the other hand, the type of nursing care available may be very limited. Be sure to investigate and understand fully the extent of nursing coverage provided.

Currently, a significant number of the elderly are already living in assisted living facilities. The concept of assisted living is expected to grow tremendously in the next few years, with the entry of major corporations (e.g., Marriott Corporation) in the field. In some states, assisted living facilities must meet licensing requirements. As this type of living arrangement proliferates, it can be expected that state regulatory action will spread.

MOVING IN WITH FAMILY

Through the ages, the housing alternative of choice for most elderly parents was to move in with their children. Only a few decades ago, it was not uncommon for several generations to be living under the same roof. Then families spread out across the country as a result of job opportunities, divorce disruptions, or other events. The place for Mom and Dad in the home was no longer readily apparent. However, the rising costs of adult living have returned this age-old option to favor for many families.

How can you accommodate your parent in your home? There are a number of alternatives to consider.

Member of the Household

In some families, an elderly parent is given an extra bedroom and is fully incorporated into the household. For some families, this is the method of choice, for personal or financial reasons. Before undertaking this alternative, it is important to understand the impact that this change will have on the family dynamics. Conflicts may arise as to who is the head of the house, you or your parent. Loss of privacy is another change that will affect all members of the household. As difficult as the change may be for you or your children, it is equally if not more difficult for your parent. Great sensitivity is advised.

─────────────→ **ACTION ITEM** ←─────────────
**Be sure that both your parent and you fully under-
stand what is involved in living together. Where
this housing arrangement is desirable but conflicts arise, consider seeking the help of family
therapists or other advisers.**

Granny Flats or ECHOs

Some families endeavor to maintain more privacy for all concerned by devising special housing arrangements. One type of arrangement that has come into vogue is the accessory apartment, also known as the Granny flat or ECHO (elderly cottage housing opportunity). The accessory apartment may be a portion of a home that is converted into a separate unit complete with its own kitchen and bath facilities. Alternatively, the accessory apartment may be a separate cottage on the premises. In some areas of the country, prefabricated units can be installed for this purpose. After a parent dies, the units can be removed. In other parts of the country, strict zoning laws may prevent the construction or erection of a cottage on your property. However, as demand for these types of living arrangements increases, zoning laws may have to give way to political pressure. In one instance, after a number of heated town meetings, a wealthy community just outside New York City recently lifted its ban on accessory apartments, with some restrictions remaining.

OTHER HOUSING OPTIONS

The type of housing arrangement best suited for your parent may be limited only by imagination. If the needs of your parent and the resources available can be well defined, you may be able to devise an arrangement that is suitable to the situation.

Shared Housing

An elderly parent with enough living space can consider sharing the house with others. The television show "Golden Girls" has glorified this living arrangement, which indeed offers many advantages. The parent can remain in his or her own home and enjoy additional income from rentals. The parent may also like the social aspects of having other people around with whom to talk and with whom tasks can be shared. The disadvantage for some is a loss of privacy. Therefore, a parent's personality must be considered before undertaking this type of living arrangement.

If your parent has an interest in house sharing, there are a number of ways to obtain a tenant. The option of placing an ad in the local newspaper, asking for a roommate, requires your parent or you to screen applicants by speaking or meeting with them and checking their references. A second alternative is to use a roommate service. In many areas of the country, there are a number of private, for-profit companies that find roommates. These companies are listed in the local telephone directory. A growing number of nonprofit companies will assist with roommate placement. Local government departments for the elderly should be able to provide referrals to these nonprofit agencies, if the telephone directory is not helpful.

Roommate Arrangements

If your parent does not own a home and is in good health, becoming a roommate may be a way to keep costs down and obtain companionship at the same time. This housing arrangement is the flip side of the homesharing alternative just discussed. Instead of looking for a roommate, your parent is looking to become one. This type of living arrangement is not suitable for everybody. It takes a certain personality to be able to live with relative strangers in close quarters.

For further information on housing alternatives for the elderly, contact the American Association of Homes for the Aging (AAHA), Suite 500, 901 E Street N.W., Washington, DC 20004; phone: 202/296-5960.

─────────────── **POINTS TO REMEMBER** ───────────────

▸ Housing choices for a parent depend on four key factors: health, personal preference, financial resources, and available housing alternatives. Remember that housing choices are not a one-time thing—as needs change, so may appropriate housing options.

▸ If reverse mortgages make financial sense for your parent, examine the repayment terms closely. Some reverse mortgages practically require that a house be sold at the end of the mortgage's life.

▸ There are tax consequences for both parties when you buy your parent's home and rent it back to the seller (a sale-leaseback).

▸ For a parent living at home who may need some caregiving services, look into city, state, and federal agencies; charitable organizations such as churches; and private (nonprofit or for-profit) agencies.

▸ For a stay-at-home parent, make contingency and emergency plans and preparations. Elderproof the home with safe stairs, suitable bathroom fixtures, smoke detectors, and personal conveniences. Consider setting up a monitoring service with a neighbor, the Postal Service, a hospital, or a private agency set up for this purpose.

▸ Be aware of the tax consequences of selling the home when your parent is downsizing or relocating.

▸ Various types of senior-citizen living arrangements range from adult communities to assisted living facilities. Consider the type of service your parent may desire, and look closely at the services provided and their cost.

6

Protecting Health Care Decisions

*M*odern medicine is often miraculous. Through the development of various drugs and procedures, life expectancy has been dramatically extended. Modern medicine also has the ability to keep some people "alive" by means of respirators, feeding tubes, and other extraordinary measures. Although people hooked up to respirators or feeding tubes can eat and breathe, they may be incapable of ever smelling a rose, hearing a song, kissing a loved one, smiling, or otherwise functioning on their own.

An individual can fall into a coma or other state of extreme physical or mental disability that prevents that person from speaking up on his or her own behalf regarding medical treatment. The medical community will use all means available to maintain "life." Ethics committees set up in most hospitals may continue to debate medical responsibility in particular cases, but, by and large, fear of malpractice suits and the counsel of the hospital's attorney may prevent a doctor from "pulling the plug" unless the patient is brain-dead. The patient's family may be forced to endure prolonged mental anguish regarding decisions on life support systems. Family members may be in disagreement over what to do and which relative best understands the wishes of the patient.

In some cases, the family may be confident that the wishes of the patient to do without extraordinary treatment are fully understood. Still, the family may be forced into costly and lengthy litigation in order to get a court decision instructing the hospital to withdraw extraordinary measures of care. In a 1976 landmark case, Karen Ann Quinlan's family wished to have Karen, who was comatose, taken off mechanical respiration. The family had to go through a lengthy, costly, and highly public trial in New Jersey, to obtain court approval for withdrawing the respirator. Eventually, they won the right to remove the respirator.

The whole process of court action, especially during a difficult time, is traumatic for the family of the patient. Even worse is the possibility that a court may ultimately refuse to honor the family's request. This is the outcome when the patient's wishes are unclear. For example, a New York court refused to order the withdrawal of a life-sustaining feeding tube from a man who was in a coma for more than 2 years. He was given no reasonable chance of recovery. According to the court, there was not enough proof that he would have wanted the tube removed. The court noted that it was limited in its action to "effectuating the clearly expressed wishes" of the patient. The court cannot engage in speculation.

In June 1990, the U.S. Supreme Court decided a case called *Cruzan*. At issue was whether there is a constitutional right to the withdrawal of life-sustaining medical treatment. The case focused on a young woman—Nancy Cruzan—who, because of oxygen deprivation after a car crash, was in a permanent vegetative state. Her family wanted to remove the gastrostomy tube that was surgically inserted in her stomach to provide nourishment. It was possible that this woman could have continued in this manner for decades to come.

The Supreme Court endorsed the concept that there is a constitutional right to refuse medical treatment and that a living will can be an expression of that right. Unfortunately, Nancy Cruzan, a woman barely out of her teens, did not have the foresight to have a living will, and the Court refused to order the discontinuance of artificial feeding and hydration for her. (A state court later granted the family its request and ordered the feeding tube removed. Nancy Cruzan died several days later.)

There is a growing awareness of the sophistication of medicine in the area of life support. There is also an increasing attitude, among individuals and organizations, that such care is not wanted. In 1986, the American Medical Association recognized, for the first time, that artificial feeding should be terminated under certain circumstances, if so requested. Several actions can be taken now to protect your parent's decisions regarding medical care, but these actions must occur while he or she is competent to execute legal documents. These measures will ensure that medical care, in the event of coma, terminal illness, or other extreme situation, conforms to your parent's wishes. An elderly person can complete certain documents—collectively referred to as "advance directives"—spelling out decisions on extraordinary care. These documents expressing your parent's wishes will be respected by doctors and hospitals. Your parent should also alert family, close friends, and doctors to health care decisions.

These documents are not limited to the elderly. An individual of any age may fall victim to accident or illness, as the *Cruzan* case clearly demonstrated. Use of these documents can be as beneficial for you as for your parent. Throughout this chapter, we refer to the documents that can be made by your parent, but the discussion applies equally to you. Your awareness of these tools for your parent's benefit should alert you to the need to plan on your own behalf.

Understandably, many people have great reluctance to discuss such delicate subject matters. In many families, any talk related to death is taboo. Avoidance of the issue will not make it go away. If action is taken now, your parent and you can have peace of mind. In the event an accident or illness brings your parent to the brink of death, your parent will be allowed to die with dignity. Your family will be spared from having to make extremely difficult decisions under extremely difficult circumstances.

Not every state recognizes each type of document presented here. You should, therefore, consult an attorney to discuss which form will best serve your parent's purpose and will be acceptable in the state in which your parent lives.

In addition to the documents for expressing health care preferences, the chapter explains hospices as a health care choice for terminally ill individuals. The philosophy behind hospices may be well suited for those who know they are dying and wish to do so with dignity and without prolonging death by extraordinary means.

We will also mention euthanasia. This health care alternative is not legal in this country. Still, it is being used, and relatives who assist a suicide are risking legal consequences for their actions.

Finally, we will discuss certain arrangements that your parent might designate to go into effect at death. These include organ donations and funeral arrangements.

HEALTH CARE DOCUMENTS

Living Wills

According to the highest court in this land, every competent adult has the constitutional right to refuse medical treatment, including life-sustaining treatment. It is believed that, if given the option, as many as 70 percent of the population would refuse life-sustaining treatment for imminent death or terminal conditions. At present, it is estimated that 10 percent of competent adults already have living wills.

Although there is a right to refuse medical treatment, a person may not be able to express his or her position; accident or illness may prevent communication. Family members and doctors would surely want to carry out a person's wishes, but they may not know exactly what those wishes are. To inform relatives and doctors of personal wishes concerning life-sustaining treatment, your parent can make what is known as a *living will*, or health care declaration.

Simply stated, a living will is a short document describing the kind of treatment your parent wishes to refuse and the kind of treatment he or she wishes to receive, in the event of an incurable or irreversible mental or physical condition from which there is no reasonable expectation of recovery. For example, your parent may specify that he or she does not want to receive cardiac resuscitation, mechanical respiration, or artificial feeding by tubes when such treatment merely prolongs dying. Similarly, a living will may state that your parent does not want to undergo operations or receive antibiotics where such treatment cannot reasonably improve the chances of recovery.

By the same token, the living will can be used to request certain treatment. Your parent may ask to receive treatment designed for comfort and the relief of pain. This would include, for example, medication and nursing care. Your parent may also request in a living will that he or she be allowed to die at home, if possible.

A living will's instructions to terminate artificial life support, or not to start such treatment in the first place, is *not* considered suicide in the religious or legal sense. Theologians recognize that refusing extraordinary means of medical care merely allows nature to take its course. In fact, two Jewish organizations in the New York area have drafted versions of living wills that incorporate a religious aspect into medical directives. These living wills state that the decision to terminate life support systems is to be made only after consultation with a rabbi. Legally, a living will has no effect on life insurance policies that refuse payment for death by suicide, during a period of contestability.

Will the Living Will Be Recognized?

The first living will law was passed in California in 1976. Now, most states have laws recognizing the living will (or other types of medical directives discussed later in this chapter). New Jersey, the state in which the *Quinlan* case first drew national attention to the issue in 1976, did not enact a living will statute until 1991. Recognition means that, if a living will complies with state law requirements, the doctor and hospital *must* honor it automatically. Typically, on admission to a hospital, your parent would be asked whether he or she has a living will. If so, the living will is attached to your parent's medical chart so that the terms can be followed.

In those states that do not have a living will law, there is still a good reason to make one. In the event that a family is forced to seek court assistance to carry out a patient's wishes, a judge will use a living will as evidence of that patient's intent. In New York, for example, the living will is not recognized by statute (although a health care proxy is now accepted, as discussed later in this chapter). However, New York's highest court has acknowledged that a living will is an ideal expression of a person's wishes concerning the cessation of treatment in the event of a hopeless condition. If a person named as health care proxy is not available to act, your parent can be assured, with a living will, that his or her wishes ultimately will be respected.

The conditions covering a living will vary in different states. Oklahoma, which has a living will statute, is now considering expansion of its provisions, to allow for the removal of artificial nutrition and hydration.

One question that has not yet been settled is whether a living will made in one state will be recognized in another. For example, a parent living in California makes a living will, which is valid in that state. The parent visits an adult child in Colorado. During the visit, the parent suffers a stroke resulting in irreversible brain damage that deprives the parent of ever regaining cognitive functions. Will the state of Colorado recognize the parent's California living will? In many locations, this remains to be seen.

Making a Living Will

A living will is a simple, one-page document stating decisions on medical care in the event of an incurable or irreversible mental or physical condition with no reasonable expectation of recovery. Consult an attorney in your parent's state to get an example of a living will. The living will must be signed and dated in the presence of two witnesses, who must also sign the document. The witnesses must be adults (over age 18) who are not related to the individual making the living will. They should not be doctors or others concerned with the medical treatment of that person.

Some states require that a living will be resigned at stated intervals. In California, for example, a living will must be renewed every 5 years. If the availability of medical treatment changes or certain decisions have been reconsidered, the old living will can be destroyed and a new one executed.

—————————→ **ACTION ITEM** ←—————————
Review a living will from time to time, and initial and redate it. This will show that the document continues to reflect your most current wishes.

Your parent may wish to consult an attorney to prepare a living will. The attorney will know the status of such a document in your state. The details of preparing the living will vary from state to state. For example, in Oklahoma, the law requires that a living will be signed *after* diagnosis of terminal illness. In Missouri, a living will only applies in the event that death is imminent; it is not valid for merely diagnosed terminal conditions. Requirements also vary on who can act as a witness and whether the living will must be notarized or renewed after a period of time. The document is not complicated, so the attorney's fee should be small.

Alternatively, a living will can be prepared on one's own. Preprinted forms are available from local stationery stores. A living will can also be obtained free of charge from the Society for the Right to Die and Concern for Dying, a nonprofit organization working for nationwide recognition of the right to die with dignity. The type of form to use will depend on the state in which your parent lives. (The Society is located at 250 West 57 Street, New York, NY 10107; phone: 212/246-6973.)

Safekeeping for a Living Will

It is very important to know where a living will is kept. It will not serve your family at all if it is buried underneath a pile of old newspapers. The original form should be stored where other important papers are kept. It is not advisable to put it in a safety deposit box. It becomes inaccessible there. Copies of the living will should be given to your parent's doctor and to you. If the state in which your parent lives requires an original document, then it may be smart to make more than one original, with your parent signing each copy. If a living will is amended or revoked, be sure to get back or destroy all the outstanding copies of the old living will.

It is also helpful to carry a card in a wallet, stating that a living will has been made and describing its location. The existence of a living will can also be noted on a Medic Alert™ bracelet or medallion. Medic Alert Foundation International, a nonprofit organization, is located at P.O. Box 1009, Turlock, CA 95381; phone: 800/432-5378.

Surrogate Decision Makers

There is another way in which your parent can express his or her wishes regarding medical care, even if he or she cannot speak: another individual can speak on your parent's behalf. Your parent can name a surrogate (also called a health care proxy or agent) to speak on your parent's behalf. The document used for this purpose is called a *durable power of attorney for health care* or a *health care proxy*. This document names a person to make medical decisions on your parent's behalf, in the event that your parent becomes unable to communicate instructions for care. The durable power of attorney for health care makes it clear who represents your parent's wishes. It avoids possible conflict among relatives and health care providers.

The durable power of attorney for health care or health care proxy is a more flexible document than a living will. An agent for health care can speak for a principal (your parent) regarding a broad range of medical care in situations not limited to terminal illness or imminent death. For example, a stroke or heart attack can render a person temporarily incapacitated. Eventually, he or she may recover and be able again to communicate personal decisions. For the time when the principal cannot express his or her wishes for medical care, the agent can act in the principal's place.

State laws provide great latitude in the powers that can be delegated to the agent. They also detail what actions *cannot* be taken by an agent through a durable power of attorney for health care. In some states, for example, a durable power of attorney for health care cannot be used to commit the principal to an institution, or to consent to electroconvulsive therapy, psychosurgery, abortion, or sterilization.

States Recognizing Surrogate Decision Making

At present, more than 30 states recognize surrogate decision making; of these, nearly two-thirds have health care proxy laws.

The following states allow health care surrogates as part of their living will statutes: Arkansas, Delaware, Florida, Iowa, Louisiana, Minnesota, Texas, Virginia, and Wyoming. The designation of an agent for health care decision making in a living will is more limited than a separate document for this purpose. The designation in the living will simply provides that, should the patient become unable to communicate instructions contained in the living will, the agent designated in the living will can act on the patient's behalf. The agent may not make other decisions on the principal's behalf. For example, if new technology is created after a living will is executed, the agent in this case would not be able to act with respect to the new technology because it was not specifically referred to in the living will.

What happens if a person has both a living will and a surrogate for health care decision making, and there is a conflict? The rules in states recognizing both are not uniform. In Texas, for example, the living will takes precedence over the durable power of attorney for health care. In Utah, the opposite is true. An agent's decisions control, despite a validly executed living will. In California, a court has held that neither document is the exclusive means for an incompetent to express legally cognizable wishes about withholding life-sustaining measures and that, in the absence of either document, a conservator can seek court permission to act. In Illinois, however, if a person has both a living will and a durable power of attorney for health care, both of which are allowed under state law, the agent named in the power of attorney supersedes any instructions in the living will.

In some states, there is no living will statute. The only means for communicating health care decisions is through a durable power of attorney for health care. This is so, for example, in New York and Rhode Island. However, the ability to use surrogate decision making does not eliminate the need or advisability of a living will. For example, in New York, a health care proxy is permitted, although there is no state law specifically authorizing a living will. Still, legal experts encourage a person to have both documents. Why? As mentioned earlier, in case the agent named in the health care proxy is not available to act, the living will can serve as a fallback position for the family. Should a family be forced to go to court on the basis of a constitutional right to determine medical treatment, then there will be evidence of a parent's intent about treatment (or the withholding of treatment). The living will can provide guidance to the health care proxy on what treatments are (or are not) desired.

Even in states that do not yet specifically recognize the durable power of attorney for health care or health care proxy, there is nothing to lose in naming a surrogate. The laws may eventually catch up to your parent's intentions, and the preexisting designations may then be honored.

Because the laws on durable powers of attorney for health care or health care proxy vary greatly from state to state, it is advisable to consult an attorney. The attorney can tell your parent whether the laws of your state recognize surrogate decision making for medical treatment. He or she can also explain the powers that can be granted to an agent (and what the agent cannot do). Finally, the attorney can advise on the requirements for making the document conform to state requirements, such as the form of the document to use and who can act as witnesses. In New York, for example, the only type of form sanctioned is a health care proxy (although no set form of this proxy is required); a durable power of attorney for health care is not recognized. An attorney can also inform your parent about when a document must be executed or reexecuted. In California, for example, the power is valid only for 7 years. Thereafter, a new form must be signed. In Virginia, a health care power of attorney can only be effective if made *after* a diagnosis of terminal illness.

─────────────────→ **ACTION ITEM** ←───────────────

Even if your parent has a general durable power of attorney for property management (see Chapter 8), there should be a separate durable power of attorney for health care. The first type of power of attorney is a financial document; the other is for health care matters only.

Your parent may choose to name a different agent for each power of attorney. After all, the person whom your parent wishes to manage his or her property in the event of disability or incompetence may not be the same person of choice for making decisions on medical care. For example, assume a parent has a daughter who is an accountant. She may be given a general durable power of attorney over property. However, she lives some distance away. A son lives in the same city as the parent. In this case, it may be preferable to name the son to act as health care agent on the parent's behalf.

Alternatively, it may be possible to use one document to name an agent for both property management and health care decisions. Check with state law on this point.

Making the Documents

The durable power of attorney for health care or health care proxy is a one- or two-page form in which the parent (the principal) names the agent (the attorney in fact) and indicates the agent's address and telephone number. In some forms, the agent is also called a surrogate. An alternate agent or surrogate can also be named. The agent or surrogate is authorized to carry out the principal's general and specific instructions and desires with respect to medical care. The principal acknowledges in the form that the agent or surrogate has been told about the principal's wishes regarding medical treatment, including views on withholding or withdrawing all forms of life-sustaining treatment, such as tubal feeding and medication. It is essential that a principal does, in fact, discuss his or her wishes with the person named as agent or surrogate. That person is not required to sign the durable power of attorney for medical care document. Therefore, the principal should learn whether the person named as agent or surrogate is comfortable in acting in that role and whether he or she fully understands the principal's wishes concerning medical treatment.

The document must be signed in the presence of two adult witnesses. Each state has different laws on who can and cannot act as a witness. For example, a spouse or an agent named in the document may *not* act as a witness. The document may have to be notarized by a notary public.

The durable power of attorney for health care or health care proxy becomes effective only when the principal can no longer make his or her own medical decisions. The document remains in effect throughout the period of disability or incompetence. Unless otherwise specified, the power terminates if a spouse is named as the agent and then divorce ensues. In some states, the document must be renewed at specified times (e.g., every 7 years) in order to remain in effect.

Where to Keep the Documents

Like the living will (discussed above), the durable power of attorney for health care should be kept in a convenient location so that it can be accessed by the family in time of need. Be sure that the family and the person named as attorney-in-fact know the whereabouts of the completed form or have signed copies of the form.

Surrogate Decision Making Without a Document

What if your parent has not made a durable power of attorney for health care and becomes unable to communicate? There are limited circumstances in some states in which surrogate decision making is still possible. In New York, it is possible to get a surrogate decision on behalf of residents in mental health facilities who cannot consent to treatment because they lack capacity and do not have a guardian or conservator.

Under New York's procedure, a public panel of 12 or more persons can make decisions on major medical treatment. They are precluded from deciding on the withdrawal or termination of treatment (e.g., ending life supports).

If a family wants to use these alternate surrogate decision-making courses, time and expense are involved. It is better, for all concerned, to provide for surrogate decision making in advance.

Do-Not-Resuscitate Orders

When a person stops breathing or suffers cardiac arrest, medical personnel will automatically begin a procedure called cardiopulmonary resuscitation (CPR). This procedure tries to restore normal breathing and heartbeat. CPR encompasses a variety of techniques: mouth-to-mouth breathing, injection of adrenalin into the heart, use of electric shock to stimulate the heart, and massage of the heart after surgically opening the chest cavity. Some of these techniques are benign; others are invasive and painful. There is no guarantee of CPR's success. Even if breathing and heartbeat are restored, the person may have suffered brain damage.

In a medical emergency, everyone is presumed to consent to receive CPR. However, there may be circumstances under which your parent would prefer not to receive such treatment. For example, if your parent is terminally ill or brain-damaged, he or she may wish to forego CPR. By doing so, your parent has chosen to let nature take its course. A natural death will result. In New York, your parent has the right to refuse CPR by making a *do-not-resuscitate order* (DNR order).

A DNR order is a notation on a patient's medical charts that, in the event the patient stops breathing or his or her heart stops beating, the doctors, nurses, and other medical personnel will *not* administer emergency procedures. Such procedures include the full range of CPR techniques, including mouth-to-mouth resuscitation, external chest massage, electric shock, a tracheotomy to open the airway, injection of medication into the heart, and open-chest heart massage.

The DNR order also provides directions for a patient in a nursing home. In the event that breathing or heartbeat has stopped, the nursing home staff will neither administer emergency resuscitation nor transfer the patient to a hospital in order to receive such treatment.

The DNR order can be tailored to include or exclude specific treatment. For example, it is permissible to request mouth-to-mouth resuscitation but forbid open heart massage.

If your parent has a DNR order, the doctor must enter it in your parent's medical charts and honor it. If the doctor's conscience prevents him or her from doing so, the doctor must transfer responsibility of your parent's medical care to another doctor who will honor it. There are also rules for referring your parent's case to mediation if there is a dispute.

The DNR order does *not* apply to other forms of medical treatment; it is confined to a refusal of CPR techniques. How does a DNR order fit in with a living will or other health care directives? A DNR order is not mutually exclusive with a living will. It is advisable, where desired, to have all such medical directives. The DNR order covers a limited situation of breathing cessation or cardiac arrest, and takes effect in an emergency situation. The living will applies to terminal conditions, emergency or otherwise. It applies to a wide range of both short-term and long-term treatments, such as respirators and feeding/hydration tubes. It may be possible to incorporate a DNR into a living will. Check the laws in your state.

Making a DNR Order

It is simple to make a DNR order. There are several choices on how to go about it:

▶ Your parent can make a DNR order merely by telling hospital or nursing-home personnel in the presence of two witnesses that he or she consents to the DNR order. One of the witnesses must be a doctor.

▶ Your parent can make a written DNR order. Again, it must be witnessed by two adults who sign the document after your parent does.

▶ Your parent can use a living will to cover DNR situations.

Your parent can change his or her mind and withdraw consent to the DNR order. This is done merely by informing the doctor or nurses of the new decision in writing or in the presence of two witnesses.

DNR Order by Someone Else

Under certain circumstances, another person can enter a DNR order on your parent's behalf. Your parent can appoint someone to act in his or her stead. This person is referred to as a surrogate. If your parent is a patient in a hospital or nursing home, your parent can name someone in the presence of two witnesses. Your parent can also name someone to decide for him or her, before entering a hospital, by putting the necessary instructions in writing. The written instructions must be witnessed by two adults who must also sign the statement.

Even if your parent does not name an agent, a DNR order may be entered in your parent's medical files. In the absence of a person named by your parent to decide about resuscitation, the following people can decide for your parent: a court-appointed guardian, your parent's closest relative (spouse, child, parent, adult sibling), or a close friend. A close friend, for this purpose, is a person over 18 who can swear in an affidavit that he or she knows the patient and is familiar with the patient's health and religious beliefs. Thus, a live-in companion may be permitted to act as surrogate if there are no family members to do so. A surrogate can agree to a DNR order under the following conditions:

▸ Your parent becomes unable to decide for himself or herself, *and*

▸ Your parent has a terminal condition or is permanently unconscious, or CPR would be either medically futile or an extraordinary burden on your parent, in light of the medical condition and the expected outcome of resuscitation. Someone deciding on your parent's behalf is supposed to take your parent's wishes into account, including your parent's religious views and moral beliefs. If a relative or friend does not know your parent's beliefs, then the decision must be made in your parent's best interest. If there is a conflict among relatives, the matter can be put before mediation.

Even if there is no guardian, relative, or friend to act on your parent's behalf, a DNR order can still be entered if two doctors decide that CPR would be medically useless or if a court approves a DNR.

Before consenting to a DNR order, your parent and you should discuss the medical condition with the attending doctor. Your parent should also explain his or her feelings regarding CPR under extreme medical emergencies.

The DNR order is a new creature of law. New York was the first state to enact a DNR order, in 1987. Consult an attorney in your parent's state, to learn whether a DNR order is recognized where your parent lives.

Patient Self-Determination Act

Beginning in December 1991, nursing homes, hospitals, and other health care providers in the Medicare/Medicaid system are required, under a federal law called the Patient Self-Determination Act of 1990, to inform patients in writing of their rights under state law to refuse medical treatment to prolong life and other health care decision-making rights. In effect, the law requires that patients receive "Miranda-type warnings" about their rights on artificial life support. This law affords patients the opportunity to take actions under state law to ensure that their wishes are followed. They can sign living wills, health care proxies, or whatever other documents are applicable. This information is then noted in their medical records.

HOSPICE CARE

The concept of hospice care began in Europe several hundred years ago. It was not put into action in the United States until 1971, when the first hospice was organized in Connecticut. Hospice care can be thought of as a philosophy of care for the terminally ill. Essentially, those who endorse hospices believe that an individual who is terminally ill should be allowed to die with dignity and with the support of family and friends. Toward this end, a hospice team—doctors, nurses, social workers, and volunteers—enables a terminally ill individual to spend the balance of his or her life at home, in familiar surroundings, amid the people and the possessions most cherished. Medical treatment is limited to supporting this purpose rather than to prolonging life. Medication to ease pain and suffering is consistent with hospice care; artificial life support systems are not.

→ **ACTION ITEM** ←

Hospice care is a decision that requires the understanding not only of a parent but also of his or her family. A medical team will help the family to see all the ramifications of a commitment to hospice care.

Where there is no family to undertake hospice care, a terminally ill individual may consider hospital-type centers that provide hospice care. To create a home-like environment, a hospice resident can bring his or her belongings to the hospice center.

Individuals who choose hospice care are protected by a Bill of
Rights that provides guarantees similar to those given to nursing-
home residents, as explained in Chapter 3.

Hospice care can be financed through the Medicare program. For
further details on Medicare's coverage for hospice care, see Chapter 2.

For a listing of hospice programs near you, contact your local hospital or the National Hospice Organization, 1901 North Fort Myer,
Rosslyn, VA 22201; phone: 804/243-5900.

EUTHANASIA

Euthanasia—mercy killing—is a form of health care decision that is
not recognized in this country. (In November 1991, people in the
state of Washington defeated an initiative that would have legalized
an "aid in dying" measure.) Unlike living wills, which prevent or
terminate certain types of care that artificially prolong life, euthanasia is an affirmative act to end life. It is treated as murder by
state authorities. In some states, individuals who assist in euthanasia can be prosecuted for murder. Numerous cases have attracted public attention on this issue. An elderly spouse might kill
the other spouse to end pain and suffering; children might help their
parents to die. Betty Rollin, a noted writer, admitted in her book,
Last Wish, to helping her terminally ill mother take pills that ended
her life. On rare occasions, a doctor is charged with assisting a
patient in dying. There are a great many moral and legal ramifications to such actions.

In June 1990, a 54-year-old Michigan woman named Jane Adkins,
who was diagnosed with Alzheimer's disease, committed suicide
using a device that triggered a lethal dose of potassium chloride.
The doctor who created the device and gave it to this woman was
charged with murder, although a state court threw out the murder
charge on the grounds that the doctor had not planned and carried
out the death of Mrs. Adkins. Mrs. Adkins carried out her own death
alone. Michigan has no law against assisting a suicide; most other
states do.

More recently, a book on techniques for suicide, *Final Exit: The
Practicalities of Self-Deliverance and Assisted Suicide for the Dying*, by
Derek Humphrey, rocketed to the top of the best-seller list. Other
books on the topic can be anticipated.

For further information on euthanasia in this country, contact the
nonprofit organization called Society for the Right to Die and Concern for Dying (250 West 57th Street, Suite 323, New York, NY 10107;

phone 212/246-6962) or the Hemlock Society (204 West 20th Street, New York, NY 10011; phone: 212/807-5548).

ORGAN DONATIONS

Thanks to medical advances, some people may be given new leases on life through organ transplants. To use organs for this purpose, time is of the essence. The organs must be retrieved almost immediately following the death of the organ donor. Your parent may be in a position to provide a miracle for someone and, in more than just a religious sense, live on after death. Your parent can become an organ donor when he or she dies.

Not everyone wants to become an organ donor. Your parent may already know how he or she feels on the subject. If those feelings are unclear, your parent may wish to discuss the issue of organ donations with family, friends, and religious advisers. Your parent should be aware that age or illness is no bar to donating certain organs. For example, an elderly person who dies from liver cancer may still be an ideal candidate to donate much needed corneas. Organs, even afflicted ones, are also needed for medical research.

If your parent decides to act as an organ donor, the appropriate steps must be taken. Every state and the District of Columbia has enacted the Uniform Anatomical Gifts Act, which prescribes the conditions under which organs can be donated. All that is required is to complete a Uniform Donor Card and sign it in the presence of two witnesses. On the card, your parent may explain the gift. For example, your parent can donate his or her whole body or limit the gift to certain body parts.

The card should be carried in a wallet.

—————————→ ACTION ITEM ←—————————

Your parent should let you and other family members know that he or she has elected to become an organ donor. This will spare the family from having to deal with painful questions in their time of grief.

Many states allow organ donor information to be entered directly on a driver's license. Find out whether your state has this procedure.

If your parent still drives and wishes to become an organ donor, ask
the local motor vehicle department how the information can be entered on the driver's license.

   To obtain a free Uniform Donor Card, contact the National Institute
of Health, 9000 Rockville Pike, Bethesda, MD 20014, or the National
Society for Medical Research, 1000 Vermont Avenue, Washington, DC
20005; phone: 301/496-4000.

FUNERALS

Many people prefer to let their families worry about funeral arrangements after their death. Others choose to have a hand in their own
funeral arrangements. If your parent wishes to take an active role in
the final arrangements, your parent should know what arrangements
to make and how to communicate his or her wishes.

Rights on Funeral Rites

Funeral costs today average $5,000. This is a large expenditure. For
many people, it is the third largest purchase of their lifetime, following
a home and a car. People would not buy a $500 TV without shopping
around, yet they readily pay ten times that amount for a funeral. In the
past, it was difficult to comparison shop. However, several years ago,
the Federal Trade Commission adopted a rule that protects against
misrepresentation of funeral pricing and requirements, and unwanted
funeral purchases. As a result of this rule, a person may obtain price
and service information over the telephone. A person is also entitled to
receive itemized price lists for general services, caskets, and outer
burial containers.

   A funeral home may not represent that embalming is required,
when state or local law does not require it. For example, New York does
not require embalming. Similarly, a funeral home may not represent
that a casket or other container is required for cremation, when state
law does not require it.

   Instead of making burial arrangements, which require the purchase
of a cemetery plot if one is not already owned, there are two alternatives. These alternatives merely eliminate the need for burial; they do
not preclude a memorial service.

   The first alternative is cremation, which is being used increasingly
in this country. Religious opposition to the practice by some faiths
may preclude this alternative for your parent. A second alternative is

donation of one's body to a medical school or other research center, as discussed above.

Communicating Your Parent's Wishes

Your parent can communicate his or her wishes to family members or close friends informally or through a *letter of instruction.* Your parent can, for example, state a desire to be cremated or describe in detail the type of burial arrangements that are preferred. *Final instructions* can also be included in a person's last will and testament. It is not advisable to state one's wishes *only* in a will, because it may take some time before a will is located and read.

Prepaying for Funerals

Some individuals not only arrange their funerals before their death, but they also pay for them. In 1988, it is estimated, 800,000 prepaid funeral contracts were sold.

In general, prepayment of funerals is *not* recommended before the time of need. There is an opportunity for fraud, unless the state has laws protecting prepayments. For example, a funeral home might be required to deposit prepayments into a trust fund account until the money is to be used. If the depositor requests it at any time before the funds are used, the funds must be returned, with interest.

How many people have living wills today?

About 10 percent of competent adults, according to estimates. It is becoming more and more common to have a living will, and most states have incorporated laws pertaining to this document (or a proxy equivalent). If desired, get one drawn up not only for your parent, but also for yourself.

Where should a living will or power-of-attorney document be kept?

In a safe place, but not in a safety deposit box at a bank, which generally is inaccessible when a person becomes ill or incompetent.

What is a durable power of attorney for health care?

This is a legal document that assigns health care decisions to a designated individual, who can then make certain medical decisions on behalf of an incapacitated patient. In some states, it is superseded by a living will; in others, the opposite occurs.

What do funerals cost?

On average, about $5,000. For many people, a funeral may be the third highest single expenditure in their lives. It is possible to make prior arrangements for a funeral, specifying such things as cremation or the type of funeral services desired. These wishes can be recorded by a letter of instruction; putting them in a will may not be suitable because of the length of time between a death and the reading of the will.

—————— POINTS TO REMEMBER ——————

▶ Because of advances in medical care, it is now frequently possible to maintain life in an essentially vegetative state. By documenting one's wishes (a parent's, or yours) before any such crisis arises, the legal rights of the patient can be preserved. In many (but not all) cases, living wills or other documents can control.

▶ Look into the specific state laws pertaining to living wills and related powers of attorney in the state where your parent resides. Each state has its own laws.

▶ Many religious faiths have approved the concept of living wills as a moral decision; it is not considered suicide.

▶ Hospices are places where the terminally ill can go to obtain sufficient medical care to maintain a quality of life, even when the outcome is certain. Medicare provides coverage for hospice care.

▶ To be an organ donor, the desires of the individual must be identified on a witnessed document. The states have made this possible through the Uniform Anatomical Gifts Act. Fill one out, if it is your wish or your parent's wish.

7

Maximizing Income

*I*f the elderly as a group were polled, their main concern would probably be whether their resources will last for as long as they live. This concern is very real, for several reasons. First, assets accumulated during working years may have to last many years longer than had been originally anticipated. Preretirement planning may have projected only a few years of retirement. With longevity as it is, many people will enjoy more than a few postworking years. Not too long ago, statistics gave a person who retired at age 65 a maximum of 10 more years to live. A 65-year-old can now expect 20 or more years, and the longevity figure continues to grow! The ranks of the centenarians are growing, and people in this group have enjoyed more than 35 years beyond the normal retirement age.

Another reason for concern is inflation. The specter of inflation is never far away. Although the double-digit inflation of the late 1970s and early 1980s has subsided considerably, inflation still exists. Even mild inflation seriously erodes the buying power of a dollar. A 4 percent annual inflation rate means that, after 10 years, a dollar buys only half of what it did a decade before. With a 4 percent inflation rate, if someone receiving a fixed income lives 20 years beyond retirement, the buying power of that person's income is only a quarter of what it once was. Put another way, a person need four times the original income to buy the identical items purchased 20 years ago. More severe inflation—say, at the rate of 12 percent—results in an erosion of buying power of 50 percent after only 6 years.

A third reason for concern is the high cost of health care, particularly long-term health care. As individuals live longer, there is an increasing utilization of medical treatment. A person may have saved for a lifetime, figuring to provide basic living expenses—housing, food, recreation, and routine medical care. Unfortunately, if a person lives long enough, he or she is virtually assured of needing additional funds for help in doing ordinary personal tasks, such as cooking, cleaning, shopping, banking, or even bathing and toileting. An elderly person may eventually require long-term care in a nursing home. Accumulated savings will dwindle quickly.

These three critical factors—the long length of time that money must last, the erosion of the purchasing power of that money by inflation and the increased need for money to cover health care—combine to make money management for an aging parent critical. Funds must be maximized and made inflation-proof as much as possible.

What can be done to ensure that your parent does not outlive his or her savings, continues to beat inflation, and has enough capital to meet the added costs that result from increased longevity?

▸ Ensure that your parent is getting all benefits to which he or she is entitled.

▸ Review your parent's investments to see that optimum returns are being achieved.

Social security (or other government programs) and pensions that were earned during working years are the two primary sources of income to which your parent may be entitled. These sources are more or less "fixed income," although they may be adjusted periodically for inflation. It is important to see that they are fully utilized.

A secondary source of income is not based on entitlement but rather reflects a lifetime of savings. This source of income is composed of IRAs and personal investments. Because these investments are readily within a parent's control, they can be monitored to achieve two key investment goals: bringing in maximum income without sacrificing the safety of one's principal, and keeping pace with inflation.

To achieve these goals, it is necessary to assess a parent's personal financial picture and make changes where appropriate. Naturally, by the time a person becomes elderly, his or her financial status is fairly well established. Social security benefits and pensions have already been earned. Investments have already been acquired. Money has already been saved. It is difficult to add meaningfully to this financial picture, but it is never too late to initiate improved financial planning. Property can be bought and sold. New investments can be made. The lessons of this chapter may be helpful to those who are not yet elderly. Such individuals can see the importance of taking a long-term approach to personal finances.

GOVERNMENT SOURCES
OF INCOME

Social Security Benefits

The social security system is a federal program for providing retirement and other benefits to workers and their survivors. Workers, employers, and self-employed individuals pay into the system through Federal Insurance Contribution Act (FICA) taxes and self-employment taxes. Money paid into the system is used to pay benefits to those who are currently collecting. The system is not set up like a bank, with a worker paying in, saving, and eventually withdrawing his or her own contributions. Rather, it is essentially intended to be a pay-as-you-go system, with current collections generally used for current payments.

Payments into social security are not used solely to fund retirement benefits. They also go toward hospital insurance (Medicare Part A; see Chapter 2).

Benefits under the system are paid to those who are at least age 62 or over and who paid into the system. Benefits typically begin at "normal retirement age"—currently, age 65. At the beginning of the next century, the normal retirement age will begin to increase, in phases. When the increase is fully phased in by 2025, the normal retirement age will be 67. Here is how the normal retirement age is set to increase:

Year of Birth	*Year of Age 65*	*Age for Full Benefits*
Before 1938	Before 2002	65 years
1938	2003	65 years, 2 months
1939	2004	65 years, 4 months
1940	2005	65 years, 6 months
1941	2006	65 years, 8 months
1942	2007	65 years, 10 months
1943 to 1954	2008 to 2019	66 years
1955	2020	66 years, 2 months
1956	2021	66 years, 4 months
1957	2022	66 years, 6 months
1958	2023	66 years, 8 months
1959	2024	66 years, 10 months
1960 and later	2025 and later	67 years

Those who begin to draw benefits before normal retirement age receive a reduced monthly benefit. For those who delay retirement past 65, there is an increase in monthly benefits.

Benefits for a spouse are calculated in one of two ways. If the spouse worked, then the spouse collects on the basis of his or her earnings, unless higher income can be realized on the basis of the other spouse's earnings. Alternatively, a spouse who hasn't worked, or who can realize higher benefits, claims benefits on the basis of the other spouse's earnings and is entitled to 50 percent of the amount paid to the spouse. The 50 percent allowance is paid if the couple was married at least a year and the nonworking spouse waited until age 65 to begin collecting benefits. If the spouse begins to collect benefits at age 62, the benefits are fixed at $37^1/_2$ percent of the other spouse's benefits.

→ **ACTION ITEM** ←

A spouse who has worked and paid into the social security system should have benefits figured under both methods. Such a spouse is entitled to receive benefits under the more favorable method.

Benefits are also paid to "survivors." Survivors include widows and widowers who are age 60 (50, if disabled; any age, with a child under 16). Survivors also include parents who are at least 62 and who were dependent on a worker who died.

What about divorced persons? A claimant/ex-spouse can claim benefits based on the earnings of a worker/ex-spouse, if the couple was married for at least 10 years. If the spouses have been divorced for at least 2 years, a claimant/ex-spouse may be able to begin retirement benefits at age 62, if the worker/ex-spouse is *eligible* to draw benefits. (It is not necessary that the benefits are actually being drawn.)

Figuring Benefits

A complicated formula is used to compute a person's monthly benefits. This computation is made by the Social Security Administration (SSA); it is not necessary for an individual to figure the amount of benefits to which he or she is entitled. If there is any question about whether the maximum benefits are being paid, it is advisable to make a computation. The local SSA office can provide the necessary information to assist in this computation.

If your parent has not yet begun to collect social security benefits, he or she may request an estimate of benefits. The request is made on

Form SSA-7004. You can get this form by calling 1-800/772-1213, or by writing to the SSA Consumer Information Center, Department 55, Pueblo, CO 81009.

Benefits may be adjusted annually to keep up with inflation. Cost-of-living adjustments (COLAs) have been as high as 14.3 percent in 1980 and as low as 1.3 percent in 1986. In 1990, the COLA was 4.7 percent; in 1991, it was 5.4 percent; in 1992, it was 3.7 percent. For political reasons, Congress has been reluctant to abandon COLAs, but it must be cautioned that, as budget crises loom, nothing in the fiscal domain is "sacred."

To claim benefits, a person must be "fully insured." This means that a person must have worked 40 quarters during his or her lifetime. As a rule of thumb, someone who worked for 10 years is fully insured.

What is required to earn a quarter of coverage? For work prior to 1978, earnings of at least $50 in any calendar quarter earned one quarter of credit. A calendar quarter is January 1 through March 31; April 1 through June 30; July 1 through September 30; or October 1 through December 31. After 1977, the number of quarters of coverage depends on earnings in the year. A quarter of coverage in 1978 is $250 in earnings. Each $1,000 earned in 1978 entitles the person to four quarters of coverage. In 1979 and later years, a quarter of coverage depends on the following earnings:

Year	Earnings	Year	Earnings
1979	$260	1986	$440
1980	290	1987	460
1981	310	1988	470
1982	340	1989	500
1983	370	1990	520
1984	390	1991	540
1985	410	1992	540

Quarters of coverage are credited regardless of when in the year the money was earned. For example, a person who earned $1,000 in January and February of 1978 and didn't work for the rest of the year still earned four quarters of coverage for 1978.

Receiving Benefits

Payment of benefits is not automatic. A person must apply to the SSA to start benefit payments. Application for benefits may be made in person or over the telephone. It may also be possible to have a social security representative visit a home or hospital, if an individual cannot venture out. Certain documents must be presented in order to qualify. A social security card establishing the social security number is helpful. W-2 forms can be used to show FICA contributions and earnings just prior to retirement. If someone is qualifying as a spouse or widow/widower, a marriage license is required.

Once benefits begin, they continue to be made by check on a monthly basis until death. If no other instructions are given to the SSA, the check is mailed to the individual's home. For convenience, it is possible to arrange to have benefits paid directly into an individual's bank account. This direct deposit alleviates the problem of having to retrieve the check from the mail and then make the bank deposit, and it prevents the possibility that the check will be stolen. It also can be a financial benefit. If the check is deposited into an interest-bearing account, direct deposit may earn a day or more of additional interest. This additional interest may seem inconsequential but, when compounded over the months and years of collecting benefits, the interest can add up to a considerable amount.

Tax on Social Security Benefits

Elderly who receive social security benefits may have to pay tax on a portion of them. For low-income individuals, the benefits are entirely tax-free. For those whose income exceeds a threshold amount, up to half of the benefits is included in gross income.

The starting point for figuring the taxable portion of social security benefits is "adjusted gross income" (which is essentially income less expenses, *not* counting itemized deductions). To this are added tax-free interest and half of the social security benefits (the amount reported on Form SSA-1099, divided by two). If the sum of these three items exceeds $25,000 for single individuals or $32,000 on a joint return, then as much as half of the social security benefits must be included along with other income. (Married persons filing separate returns have a zero threshold amount; automatically, half of their benefits is subject to tax.) The IRS provides a worksheet in the instructions to the federal tax return. This worksheet, reproduced in Figure 7–1, is used for figuring the taxable portion of social security benefits.

Continuing to Work While Collecting Social Security

A person can have *any* amount of investment income or pension income without having social security benefits reduced. But benefits may be

If you are married filing a separate return and you did **not** live with your spouse at any time in 1991, enter "D" on the dotted line next to line 21a.

1. Enter the total amount from **Box 5** of **all** your **Forms SSA-1099** and **Forms RRB-1099** (if applicable) . . . .   **1.** _____

Note: *If line 1 is zero or less, stop here; none of your benefits are taxable. Otherwise, go to line 2.*

2. Divide line 1 above by 2 . . . .   **2.** _____

3. Add the amounts on Form 1040, lines 7, 8a, 8b, 9 through 15, 16b, 17b, 18 through 20, and line 22. Do not include here any amounts from Box 5 of Forms SSA-1099 or RRB-1099   .   **3.** _____

4. Add lines 2 and 3 . . . .   **4.** _____

5. Enter the total adjustments from Form 1040, line 30 . .   **5.** _____

6. Subtract line 5 from line 4. . . . .   **6.** _____

7. Enter on line 7 the amount shown below for your filing status:

   • Single, Head of household, or Qualifying widow(er) with dependent child, enter $25,000

   • Married filing a joint return, enter $32,000   **7.** _____

   • Married filing a separate return, enter -0- ($25,000 if you did **not** live with your spouse at any time in 1991)

8. Subtract line 7 from line 6. Enter the result but not less than zero . . . .   **8.** _____

   • If line 8 is zero, stop here. None of your benefits are taxable. Do not enter any amounts on lines 21a or 21b. **But** if you are married filing a separate return and you did **not** live with your spouse at any time in 1991, enter -0- on line 21b. Be sure you entered "D" on the dotted line next to line 21a.

   • If line 8 is more than zero, go to line 9.

9. Divide line 8 above by 2 . . . .   **9.** _____

10. **Taxable social security benefits.**

   • First, enter on Form 1040, line 21a, the amount from line 1 above.

   • Then, enter the **smaller** of line 2 or line 9 here and on Form 1040, line 21b. . . . .   **10.** _____

Note: *If part of your benefits are taxable for 1991 and they include benefits paid in 1991 that were for an earlier year, you may be able to reduce the taxable amount shown on the worksheet. Get Pub. 915 for details.*

————————————— Figure 7-1 —————————————

Social security benefits worksheet from instructions to Form 1040.

reduced if a person continues to work while collecting social security. Your parent need not be an employee to be affected by this rule. Even self-employment income, such as compensation under a consulting contract, can result in a cut in benefits. Whether benefits are reduced depends on age and the amount of wages or self-employment income received. In 1992, those under age 65 can earn $7,440 without loss of benefits; $1 is lost for every $2 earned over this dollar limit. Those ages 65 through 69 can earn $10,200 without loss of benefits; $1 is lost for every $3 earned over this limit. Those age 70 or older can earn *any* amount without loss of benefits.

As long as one works, earnings are subject to social security tax. Thus, a parent who works must still pay into the social security system even if he or she is also collecting benefits.

?

What are the usual sources of income during one's retirement?

Social security or other government programs; pensions; and savings and investments.

How is a spouse's social security benefit figured?

If the spouse has never been employed and made no contributions, benefits are based on the wage earner's contributions. A spouse who has worked may claim benefits on the basis of his or her contributions. The choice between the two situations is made on the basis of which claim provides greater benefits for the spouse.

Are social security benefits taxable?

Yes! If adjusted gross income exceeds certain limits, up to half of the benefits are subject to tax.

Do earnings from continued work after applying for social security affect benefits?

Yes. If earnings are above an amount set each year. In 1992, the limit is $7,440 for those under 65, and $10,200 for those ages 65 to 69. Those 70 and over can earn any amount without loss of benefits.

Railroad Retirement Benefits

Former railroad employees may be entitled to monthly retirement benefits that are similar to social security benefits.

Two types of monthly benefits are payable to retired railroad employees. Tier I benefits are paid to former railroad employees who have worked for a railroad for at least 10 years and have reached normal retirement age under the social security system (currently, age 65). Tier II benefits provide a supplemental monthly amount to those who have completed 25 years of service as of the social security retirement age, or 30 years of service by the age of 60. Benefits are payable to divorced and surviving spouses of former railroad employees in the same manner in which social security benefits are paid to divorced and surviving spouses.

Railroad retirement benefits are taxable in the same manner as social security benefits. Because Tier I benefits are treated as social security benefits, up to half of the benefits may be includible in gross income if other income, including tax-exempt income, exceeds threshold amounts. The social security benefits worksheet shown in Figure 7–1 can be used to calculate the taxable portion. Tier II benefits, which are treated as payments from an employer's qualified retirement plan, are taxed as pension distributions.

An elderly person may, under certain circumstances, collect both railroad retirement benefits and social security benefits. This can happen if an individual works for a sufficient period of time for both the railroad and a nonrailroad employer, or spends some years working for the railroad and others self-employed. Alternatively, an elderly person may have contributed to the social security system while also being a surviving spouse of a former railroad employee.

Supplemental Security Income (SSI)

It is a sad fact that, although most of the wealth in this country is now in the hands of the elderly, many elderly individuals are poor. In 1987, 3.5 million seniors lived below the poverty line—defined at that time as an income of $5,447 for singles and $6,872 for couples. It was estimated in 1987 that 9.8 percent of those between the ages of 65 and 74 were below the poverty line. Of those age 85 and over, 19.2 percent had income below the poverty line.

Various explanations have been offered as to why this is so. One reason for the large number of elderly poor is the fact that many of these are single women. When these women were younger, they may not have worked. Typically, they were married and now are widowed. Now, they are only able to collect a small social security check. Any pensions to which their husbands may have been entitled either ended with the husbands' death or were greatly reduced.

Fortunately, there is a federal program to provide some income assistance. This program is called Supplemental Security Income (SSI). In 1988, about 2 million elderly individuals received monthly supplemental income under this program.

SSI is run by the Social Security Administration. It provides a monthly income for those who are poor. It is intended to bring an individual's monthly income up to 75 percent of the federal poverty level and a couple's monthly income up to 90 percent of the federal poverty level.

Even though this program is run by the Social Security Administration, it is not the same as social security benefits. The program is financed by general revenue and not by worker contributions. Benefits from SSI are dependent on need; they do not relate to earnings or contributions into the social security system.

As a practical matter, SSI is not a panacea for enabling the elderly poor to live comfortably. The monetary definition of the federal poverty level is painfully low to begin with, and SSI brings income up to only a percentage of that amount. It pays only the difference between the SSI ceiling amount and a person's income.

SSI is not automatic; an individual must apply for benefits. There may be a natural reluctance to apply among many older individuals who view SSI as "welfare." It is estimated that well over 1 million elderly individuals could qualify for SSI if they only made an application for it.

As a general rule, eligibility for SSI mirrors that for Medicaid (see Chapter 4). There are income limits, asset limits, and rules on asset transfers. Application is made through a local social security office. As with social security benefits, there is an administrative review process if SSI is turned down. After reconsideration by the Social Security Administration, an appeal to an Administrative Law Judge, and a final review by the Appeals Council of the Social Security Administration, a suit may be brought in a U.S. District Court.

Disability Income

Suppose a person becomes disabled *before* retirement age. For example, a parent may suffer from Alzheimer's disease at age 55 and become fully disabled. Although that parent is too young for retirement benefits, government assistance may be forthcoming in the form of disability benefits. The social security system pays disability benefits to those who are eligible.

Eligibility is based on two factors: having paid enough into the social security system, and being sufficiently disabled.

To qualify, an individual must be so severely disabled that he or she is prevented from substantial gainful employment as a result of a disability expected to last at least 12 months or to result in death. There is a 5-month waiting period. Thereafter, disability benefits under the social security system are similar to retirement benefits.

Widows, widowers, and surviving divorced spouses may also be entitled to disability benefits. If such surviving spouses of deceased workers are disabled within 7 years of the workers' deaths, then they may collect at age 50 or later. The definition of disability is stricter for surviving spouses than for workers themselves. However, if a widow, widower, or surviving divorced spouse is blind, a different definition if disability is used. If its conditions can be met, then benefits may begin at age 55.

If disability benefits are paid under workers' compensation or another federal, state, or local disability program, social security disability payments are reduced accordingly. There is no reduction if disability payments are made by private insurance carriers or former employers.

Disability benefits from social security are taxed in the same way as social security benefits. If disability income and other income, including tax-exempt interest, exceeds a threshold amount, then up to half of social security benefits are included in income and taxed accordingly. You can use the social security benefits worksheet in Figure 7–1 to calculate the taxable portion of disability benefits.

EMPLOYER RETIREMENT PLANS

Pensions

Many employers set up qualified retirement plans for their employees. They are called pension plans, profit-sharing plans, money-purchase plans, ESOPs, 401(k) plans, and 403(b) annuities.

Pensions vary greatly from employer to employer. Some parents may have earned pensions yielding monthly benefits nearly equal to their salary in their working years. Others may receive only what amounts to a token benefit. Some pensions were funded entirely through employer contributions, others solely from employee contributions, and many others through a combination of employer and employee contributions.

Some plans pay out benefits in a lump sum at retirement. Other plans continue to pay out monthly benefits for life. The latter type of plan can be thought of as an annuity that provides regular income in monthly installments. Some retiring employees have the option of choosing whether to take benefits in a lump sum or to have them paid out as a monthly annuity. Where the choice exists, there are several factors that impact a decision:

▶ Is the employer's plan enjoying a good rate of return, or could the retired employee do better on an individual basis?
▶ Is there an immediate need for the funds?
▶ Is a lump sum needed to buy a retirement home?
▶ Would it be wise to delay the receipt of income for tax planning purposes?

—————————————▶ ACTION ITEM ◀—————————————

Tax can be deferred if the benefits are received in a lump sum and then rolled over into an IRA. However, benefits cannot be kept in the IRA indefinitely. They must begin to be withdrawn no later than April 1 of the year following the year when your parent is 70$^{1}/_{2}$.

Tax Considerations

Taxes play a major role in timing the receipt of pensions. They also are important in assessing how much pension benefits add to your parent's income. To make a meaningful assessment, benefits should be figured on an after-tax basis: take the annual pension and subtract the federal income taxes that must be paid on that pension.

How are retirement benefits taxed? The answer depends on two key factors: the method in which they are paid (lump sum versus annuity-type payments), and whether your parent contributed to the pension on an after-tax basis. Lump-sum distributions enjoy special tax treatment under the Internal Revenue Code. They may be taxed using a special averaging method, provided certain conditions are met. A limited portion of the distribution may be taxed as capital gains, under certain circumstances. Alternatively, as mentioned previously, a lump-sum distribution can be rolled over into an IRA. In a rollover, tax is postponed until withdrawals from the IRA begin.

If retirement benefits are paid as an annuity, all or a portion of each monthly amount is subject to tax. If the employer contributed the entire amount or if employee contributions were made on a pretax basis (such as under a salary reduction arrangement), then *all* amounts received are fully taxable. If the employee contributed to the retirement plan on an after-tax basis, a portion of the benefits is excluded from tax. This portion is the amount treated as a return of the employee's own contributions. This excludable amount cannot be recovered up front but must be spread out over the life expectancy of the retired employee. Special rules apply on how to figure this excludable amount. The breakdown of contributions is reported on an information return (Form 1099R).

If your parent lives in a state that charges an income tax, the after-tax amount of the pension is further reduced. The rules in various states, governing retirement benefits, do not necessarily mirror the federal rules. Some states, for example, provide special exclusions for certain benefits.

Some states tax pensions *earned* in those states, even though the recipients no longer live in the state and the pensions are *paid* out of state. These states are: California, Iowa, Kansas, New Jersey, New York, and Oregon. Connecticut is considering similar legislation. The ability to tax people who are no longer state residents is sure to be challenged in the courts.

Other Benefits

In addition to qualified plans, employers may offer other important benefits to former employees. These include:

▶ Health insurance for retirees (discussed in Chapter 2).

▶ Continued payment of group term life insurance.

▶ Deferred compensation plans. An elderly person may have contracted with an employer to have current income deferred until retirement. At that point, periodic payments (monthly or annually) may begin and can continue for many years. The payout is taxable when it is received. It is important to note that the payout may affect social security benefits: the payout is treated as current earnings under FICA, even though it was actually earned many years ago. Thus, depending on a parent's age and the amount of the deferred compensation received, social security benefits may be reduced.

▶ Stock option plans. An elderly person may have received stock options from the employer corporation. Generally, such options are required to be exercised within a period of time after employment. However, in privately held companies, there may be other stock option arrangements.

▶ Nonqualified retirement plans. These plans include deferred compensation plans or other plans that do not meet qualified retirement plan requirements. Nonqualified plans can provide for payment in a lump sum or monthly installments.

INDIVIDUAL SAVINGS

Because individual savings are within a person's control, they can be managed to suit personal needs. There are two subcategories of individual savings: IRAs and personal investments.

IRAs

In addition to employer-sponsored pensions, many individuals have set up their own qualified retirement plans. These are called individual retirement accounts or individual retirement annuities—IRAs, for short. IRA funds may be invested in a variety of places—banks, insurance companies, brokerage firms, or mutual funds. Sizable sums may have accumulated over the years, through tax-deferred interest compounding.

IRA funds may be used at any time, but early withdrawal carries a penalty. There is no premature withdrawal penalty for using IRA funds after age 59½. (It is even possible to use IRA funds without penalty at an earlier age, if withdrawals are properly structured or are taken on account of disability.) It is important to remember that IRA investments need *not* be tapped at retirement, if there are other income sources. However, the Internal Revenue Code requires that IRA funds *begin to be withdrawn* once a certain age is reached. The key date is when your parent turns age 70½.

A hefty 50 percent penalty is levied on the failure to take "minimum distributions" from IRAs. The first such distribution must be taken no later than April 1 of the year following the year the account holder reaches age 70½. Successive minimum distributions are required each year thereafter. They must be taken no later than December 31st of each year.

WEALTH BUILDING PROFILE   *Timing Required for Minimum Distributions.* Although the first required minimum distribution can be delayed until April 1 of the year following the year of attaining age 70½, it might be advisable to take that first distribution at the end of the year of attaining age 70½. If the first distribution is postponed until April 1, it will mean that *two* distributions will have to be taken in that year: one by April 1 and the second required distribution by December 31.

For example, Mary turns 70½ in 1991. She can delay the first required distribution until April 1, 1992. However, if she does so, she will have two distributions to report in 1992: one taken on April 1, 1992, and the second required distribution taken no later than December 31, 1992.

What are minimum distributions? Essentially, they are amounts that are designed to exhaust the IRA over the life of the owner or over the joint lives of the owner and beneficiary. In reality, the IRA may never be fully exhausted, because life expectancy is taken from IRS tables. Under the tables, a person of any age (even someone who is 115!) has a life expectancy. Therefore, a final balance need never be withdrawn during the owner's lifetime.

The account balance in an IRA may even continue to grow over the years, depending on investment return, even as minimum distributions are being taken out of the IRA. This is because the percentage that must be withdrawn in one's early 70s may be lower than the rate of return on the IRA investment. For example, assume that an account is earning 8 percent interest on an existing bank CD. The percentage that must be withdrawn that first year (assuming the minimum withdrawal is figured on only the owner's life) is only 6.25 percent. The account will grow, even though the required withdrawal is made. The minimum withdrawal percentage does not reach 10 percent until age 79. It is only 20 percent of the remaining balance at age 90.

→ **ACTION ITEM** ←

As a general rule, it is better to take income from taxable sources rather than from the IRA. This will allow the IRA to continue to grow free from current taxation.

Special rules are available to keep minimum distributions as low as possible by naming certain beneficiaries. The scope of tax planning

for IRAs is too extensive for adequate treatment here. It is advisable
for those with IRAs to consult a tax specialist.

IRAs offer great flexibility in income planning. As long as minimum distribution requirements are satisfied, the IRA owner can take
as little or as much from the account as desired.

When income is needed, it can be withdrawn as often as necessary—for example, annually, semiannually, or monthly. The only restrictions would come from the type of investment used for the IRA.
Thus, for example, if the IRA is an annuity with an insurance company, the terms of the annuity may dictate the amount and frequency
of withdrawals.

Personal Investments

This section explains some investment alternatives that may be particularly attractive for the elderly. Any investment decision must take
into account a great many factors: a person's wealth, risk tolerance,
income needs, demands for liquidity, and market opportunities. Considered below are the main types of investments. The list is not ex-
haustive. Rather, emphasis is placed on those investments geared
toward producing income for old age.

Stocks

Stocks represent ownership in the corporation issuing the stock certificates. The price of a stock rises and falls according to the fortunes
of the company and the variants in the market. Stocks can be issued by
public corporations—those whose shares are traded on regular ex-
changes, such as the New York Stock Exchange, the American Stock
Exchange, and the Over-the-Counter (OTC) Exchange. Stocks can also
be issued by privately owned corporations. For these stocks, there is no
ready market.

There are two main types of stock: common stock and preferred
stock. Common stock generally looks for appreciation; preferred stock
provides for a fixed income, called a dividend. Many common stocks
pay dividends, and preferred stocks may not pay regular dividends, but
may accumulate dividends for the future instead.

In old age, investment emphasis generally is on income and
safety. This limits the choices to quality stocks. Certain categories of
companies merit more serious consideration than others. For example, utilities typically yield a good return while providing necessary
safety. Within this category of stock, some utilities are better than
others.

Bonds

A bond is essentially an IOU. The issuer promises the bondholder to repay principal *and* pay interest on that principal on specified dates.

There are a variety of bonds: corporate, state, municipal, and Treasury bonds. When investing in bonds, consider safety and yield. Bonds issued by corporations, states, and municipalities are rated by rating services such as Moody's and Standard & Poor's. The highest (and safest) rating is AAA by Standard & Poor's (Moody's has a comparable alphabetic rating system). Investment grade bonds include those with a rating of B or better. A rating lower than B is applied to a bond that is already in default or, if not in default, one that is a "high yield bond"— another term for "junk bond." It is possible to buy insured bonds. The insurance gives the bond an automatic AAA rating and an added measure of safety that is as good as the company giving the insurance. Bonds issued by the federal government are the safest form of investment. They are backed by the full faith and credit of the U.S. government.

There are several types of federal securities to consider. Short-term obligations of the federal government are Treasury bills (T-bills). They are sold at a discount and redeemed at face value at maturity. For example, a $10,000 T-bill may sell for $9,600. Six months later, when the T-bill comes due, the holder receives $10,000. The $400 represents interest.

The federal government also issues longer-term obligations— Treasury notes and Treasury bonds. Obligations with a maturity between 1 and 5 years are Treasury notes; obligations with longer maturities—up to 30 years—are Treasury bonds. These obligations pay interest twice a year.

Another type of federal obligation is U.S. savings bonds. Like T-bills, these are discount obligations. They are sold for half their face value. Thus, a $200 bond can be bought for $100. At maturity, the bond is redeemed for $200. The difference between the redemption amount and the initial cost represents interest that the government pays on the bond.

In the past, Series E bonds were issued. Many of these bonds have begun to reach maturity. It is important to note the maturity date because they will not pay interest beyond maturity. Many elderly individuals bought savings bonds over the years and put them away for safekeeping. These bonds should be reviewed to make sure that they are still earning interest. Matured bonds can be turned into sources of income by redeeming them and investing in income-producing securities. Alternatively, the accrued interest on the matured bonds need not be reported at redemption, if they are rolled over into Series HH bonds. These bonds pay interest semiannually for as long as 20 years. However, the interest on these bonds is not tax-deferred and must be reported currently.

Today, Series EE is used. Like E bonds, Series EE bonds offer special tax advantages. Interest is exempt from state and local income tax. Federal tax on the interest can be deferred until maturity and, as in the case of E bonds, matured EE bonds can be rolled over into HH bonds to continue the tax deferral of the EE bond interest. EE bonds also offer another advantage: the deferred interest is *not* taken into account for purposes of figuring the tax on social security benefits. In contrast, the tax-exempt interest on municipal bonds can adversely affect the tax on social security benefits.

Safety has a direct impact on yield. Junk bonds have high yields because there is an element of risk. The bonds may default, in which case principal could be lost.

Yield should be figured not only on the actual amount of interest paid on the bond (the coupon rate) but also on the after-tax impact of that rate. Treasury bonds are exempt from state and local income taxes but fully taxable for federal income tax purposes. Corporate bonds are fully taxable. State and municipal bonds (other than certain private activity bonds) are exempt from federal income taxation. They are also exempt from income tax for bondholders living in the state of the issuer. However, the interest on these bonds is taken into account in figuring the taxable portion of social security benefits.

Some bonds are sold as "zero coupon" bonds. This means that they are sold at a deep discount from the face of the bond and pay no interest from the time of purchase until the time of maturity. In the interim, interest is accruing but nothing is paid out. Whether such accrued interest is taxable depends on the issuer of the bond. When municipalities issue zero coupon bonds, the accrued interest is tax-free. In contrast, the accrued interest on corporate bonds and Treasury instruments that are sold as zero coupon bonds must be reported currently, even though no actual interest is received.

Annuities

Commercial annuities can be purchased from insurance companies to provide regular income. During working years, these annuities may have served as tax-deferred investment vehicles. Lump-sum or periodic contributions to the annuities generated earnings that compounded tax-free. Now, when income is needed, the funds can be "annuitized" for income. Because the earnings were not taxed before, they are subject to tax when withdrawn. Essentially, each payment represents a return of principal as well as earnings. The extent of each portion (earnings or return of principal) depends on the payout period (a term of years, or life) and the investment in the contract (the contributions made to the annuity).

Annuities, like bonds, vary in terms of safety and yield. The insurance companies issuing the annuities are rated for safety just as bonds are rated. A widely respected rating service for insurance companies is A. M. Best and Company. In today's economic climate, where the fiscal soundness of several insurance companies has been called into question, it is more important than ever to check a particular company's ratings. If your parent bought an annuity several years ago and now it seems that the insurer's soundness is questionable, it may be advisable to switch to another company.

→ ACTION ITEM ←

An annuity from one company can be exchanged tax-free for the annuity of another company, as long as the annuitant is the same in both policies.

Annuities can serve helpful functions for the elderly by eliminating investment decisions and providing an income stream. Check with insurance companies to learn about age limits on annuity investments.

Ginnie Maes

In this type of government security, issued by the Government National Mortgage Association, the investor acts like a mortgage lender. The investor can buy a Ginnie Mae or an interest in a Ginnie Mae fund. Each month, there is a payment of interest as well as a return of principal. This type of investment is suitable for the elderly, for several reasons. First, it is safe; it is an obligation of a federal agency. Second, it provides a steady flow of income. Checks are paid each month. Third, there is the opportunity to stay current with market trends. Because there is a constant return of principal, there can be reinvestment in other instruments at current market prices.

Mutual Funds

There is a vast array of mutual funds offering all types of investments. The underlying investments of the funds, the fund managers, the fees charged, and many other factors contribute to the return that can be realized from an investment in mutual funds. The funds offer a particular advantage for income-planning purposes: they can pay out income at chosen regular intervals (monthly, quarterly, semiannually, or annually).

Certificates of Deposit (CDs)

These are savings accounts with a fixed maturity ranging from 3 months to as long as 5 years or more. CDs offer liquidity (although banks may charge early withdrawal penalties for cashing in CDs prior to maturity), certainty of return (interest is stated at the outset), and safety (an FDIC-type agency guarantees them up to $100,000). In light of the savings and loan crisis, it is important to see that the bank carries federal insurance and that the funds in the account have not passed the $100,000 mark.

Collateralized Mortgage Obligations (CMOs)

These rather complicated investments can yield a greater return than CDs or Treasuries, without incurring much more risk. Essentially, CMOs are mortgage-backed bonds where the mortgages themselves are backed by government agencies (e.g., Ginnie Mae, Fannie Mae, and Federal Home Loan Mortgage Corporation) or private corporations. With CMOs, the cash flow of the mortgage pool is put into short-, medium-, and long-term securities, called tranches. Each tranch is paid a fixed rate of interest at regular intervals. The yield increases with the length of maturity.

ASSESSING INCOME RESOURCES

Many elderly individuals have saved up sizable sums during their working years. Their nest egg generally was accomplished the old-fashioned way—through regular and systematic savings. Their investment goals during their working years were usually appreciation and growth; the emphasis now, for many individuals, is on producing income for old age.

However, the emphasis on income-producing securities—such as Treasury bills; municipal, corporate, and federal bonds; and money market instruments—is shifting. These investments do have safety of principal and an assurance of income flow designed to meet living expenses. However, the overemphasis on income-producing securities is being challenged as unwise today. The reason is simple: *inflation*. As mentioned earlier, inflation, no matter how mild, continually eats away at the buying power of the dollar. At a 4 percent annual inflation rate, a person would need twice the capital at the end of 10 years just to be in the same financial position. Those who live 20 years past retirement age would need four times the capital they started with at retirement, to retain the same purchasing power. Therefore, it becomes essential to continue to grow at least some portion of capital during retirement years. As a general rule, this can only be done effectively with equities—namely, common stocks.

In reviewing holdings to determine how to maximize income, take a simple three-step approach to investments:

▶ Consider the many types of investments available. Different investments serve different objectives—income or growth. Some investments may be more suitable for old age than others. These investments have been discussed earlier in this chapter.

▶ Formulate what proportion of assets should be invested in various types of investments—stocks, bonds, CDs, annuities, and so on. In making this determination, tax considerations come into play. Taxes naturally determine how much is left to spend or reinvest after income taxes (federal and, possibly, state and local). For example, taxes affect the decision to buy a taxable versus a tax-exempt bond. Once a person's tax bracket is taken into account, a true comparison of the yield from the bond can be made. In making tax projections, keep in mind that two special tax breaks apply for those age 65 and older. First, an additional standard deduction (in 1992, $900 for singles and $700 for married individuals filing joint returns) may be claimed. This tax break provides no benefit if a taxpayer itemizes deductions. Second, a tax credit for the elderly of up to $750 for singles and $1,125 for a married couple is allowed. This credit is designed primarily for lower-income individuals who do not receive social security benefits and certain pensions. The credit may also be claimed by someone under 65 who is permanently and totally disabled and receives disability income. Another consideration in determining optimum investments is the level of personal involvement required for them. An elderly parent may not want to be bothered with investment decisions on a day-to-day basis. For example, your parent may invest in 6-month CDs. However, as each CD matures, it is necessary to shop around again for the best rates, possibly requiring yet another visit to a bank or several banks.

▶ Examine current holdings to see whether changes should be made, and then make them. To maximize income, it is necessary to review individual income resources as well as potential sources of income. To do this effectively, it may be helpful to complete the financial data pages in Chapter 11.

Making Changes in Investments

The types of investments that were appropriate during working years or even at the outset of retirement may no longer suit investment objectives for old age. Look for these key points:

▶ Some stocks may be too speculative for later years. With old age, the swings in the stock market may make this type of investment too risky. During working years, it may have been wise to load up on stocks with great growth potential; now, it may be better to shift toward income-producing stocks. They may promise less spectacular growth but offer not only current income but also greater safety of principal.

▶ Rental property may have been ideal at one time as an income-producing investment. However, with old age, the management responsibilities may be too heavy. The property can be sold and the proceeds used to buy income-producing assets. Alternatively, if it is advisable to continue holding the property, then it may be better to transfer it into a trust and shift management responsibilities to a trustee.

▶ Raw land may have been acquired with appreciation in mind. Later in life, it may be better to turn that land into some income-producing asset.

⟶ ACTION ITEM ⟵

In making changes in investment holdings, do not overlook the tax implications. The current income tax cost of selling assets may outweigh the additional income sought.

For further assistance in income planning, it may be helpful to consult with a tax attorney, an accountant, a stock broker, or a financial planner. For a referral to a professional who can assist in income planning, see page 245.

————— POINTS TO REMEMBER —————

▶ Money management for the elderly is critical because: life expectancy after retirement is increasing every year; medical expenses increase as one ages; inflation erodes fixed income.

▶ Rule of thumb: If someone has worked for 10 years (not necessarily consecutively), then he or she is fully insured by the social security system.

▶ As a general rule, eligibility for Supplemental Security Income (SSI) mirrors that of Medicaid. There are income and asset limits, and rules on asset transfers.

▶ Generally, the focus of personal savings and investments shifts from growth, during one's working years, to income production, during one's retirement years. The vehicles for income production (bonds, Treasury bills, certificates of deposit, and so on) should be evaluated in light of the effects of inflation, which erodes the value of fixed investments over many years.

8

Ensuring Money Management for Declining Capacity

Your elderly parent may have worked a lifetime with the expectation of attaining a measure of financial comfort in retirement. Savings were squirreled away. Pensions were earned. Social security taxes were paid and benefits earned. Your elderly parent may also have seen to it that postretirement expenses match financial resources. Adequate insurance for health care may have been maintained. However, despite the best laid financial plans, a catastrophic illness or accident may strike. What are the consequences for financial well-being?

Catastrophic illness or accident adversely impacts finances in two ways. First, accident or illness may place enormous strain on available resources. Expenses for medical or custodial care not covered by insurance can easily outstrip one's income *and* savings. Medical costs, Medicare rules, and insurance policies designed for catastrophic illnesses were discussed in earlier chapters.

The second major consequence faced as a result of a health-related catastrophe is that an elderly person may no longer be able to personally manage his or her finances. Others—relatives, or even strangers— will be called on to make financial decisions for that elderly person. However, this situation need not occur. Your parent may make those financial decisions by taking certain actions before accident or illness strikes.

There are both personal and practical considerations involved in handling money. Parents' range of experience with managing money varies greatly. Your parent may have spent the better part of life managing a business, making investment decisions, and handling personal finances. It is not pleasant to face the possibility that, at some point, he or she may be unable to continue to manage personal finances. Understandably, there may be a natural reluctance to part with control.

Some parents may not ever have concerned themselves with money. Perhaps all financial decisions were handled by a spouse. When the spouse is deceased or unable to oversee finances, the task of managing finances falls to the financially inexperienced surviving spouse. This person must make plans for the future management of his or her money as well. The fact that there is little or no financial sophistication does not prevent your parent from taking action now.

Whatever the tie to finances has been until now, your parent should begin to recognize that it might change in the future. With the coming of old age, many people have a diminished capacity to take an active role in managing assets and making financial decisions. Illness, accident, or simple aging may make it difficult or impossible to write a check, get to a bank, collect rent from a tenant, or decide when to buy or sell securities. If no arrangements are made before experiencing diminished capacity, then a court may be called on to decide that an elderly person is no longer able to run his or her own affairs. This can be a humiliating experience for a parent. What is more, it can turn family members into adversaries and cause rifts that never heal. The court may also decide who will manage the finances of the elderly person.

With advance planning, your parent can be assured that a trusted person will manage his or her money and act according to expressed wishes. Moreover, this planning will save your family the pain and expense of having to take the matter to court. Without planning, the state may decide the fate of your parent.

A child's role in money management for a parent should also be considered, although it is a particularly difficult subject for a child to raise with a parent. It is vital to make plans that can assure a parent of continued protection. Sometimes, all that is needed to motivate a parent to act is an explanation of what would happen if no plans were made.

It is also important to understand what happens to the management of a person's money in the event that no prior arrangements have been made. The types of arrangements that must be undertaken when there has been no prior planning fall under the umbrella of *protective services*. These require court intervention. Examination of various types of protective services serves a double purpose: it shows what can be avoided with some planning, and it remedies a situation in which your parent may already be incapable of managing finances but failed to do any planning. You may have no choice but to take some of the steps that are outlined below and begin managing your parent's finances.

Finally, there are steps that your parent can take, while still competent, that will ensure the management of his or her money in a way that is consistent with lifelong aims and objectives. These steps, which for the most part are quite simple, will protect your parent's money management if catastrophe strikes. These simple alternatives include: a durable power of attorney, fiduciary designation, joint ownership, and trusts.

These planning alternatives are directed at an elderly person, but they serve with equal weight for younger individuals. Regardless of age, disability can always strike unexpectedly. In reviewing the options for a parent, consider putting them into practice for yourself, even if you are not yet elderly.

PROTECTIVE SERVICES

Guardianships

When a person is no longer capable of managing his or her own affairs because of a physical or mental illness, then a court may be called on to declare that person incapable of providing for himself or herself and, therefore, incompetent. As such, every aspect of that person's life can come under court supervision. Some states say that a person's civil rights are not jeopardized. Yet, as a practical matter, it is possible for a person adjudicated incompetent to lose virtually all civil rights: the ability to marry or divorce, the right to vote, the capacity to buy or sell property and sign contracts, and the capacity to make a will. A person may even lose the right to make other personal decisions, such as where to live. Guardians may be able to arrange nursing-home placement. All money decisions are placed in someone else's hands. When a person is still able to make personal decisions but can no longer deal with monetary issues, only financial independence is taken from an individual and given to a fiduciary.

According to some figures, about a half-million Americans are wards or conservatees; their lives are controlled through the guardianship system. Each state has its own rules and regulations, as well as its own name for the guardian. Some of the names used to describe a person who functions as a guardian are conservator, committee, fiduciary, tutor, or curator. In some states, more than one title is in use; the different titles can mean that different standards are applied for proving incompetency. It may have to be shown that a person is no longer able to provide for personal needs. Substantial impairment in the ability to care for oneself must be proven. Alternatively, it may have to be shown that a person is incompetent to manage his or her affairs.

The guardianship system has come under increasing criticism, for a number of reasons. The proceedings have a number of shortcomings:

▶ The process is time-consuming. Numerous procedures must be followed in bringing the court action. Pleadings must be served and filed. Medical testimony must be obtained.

▶ By and large, the elderly are too easily declared incompetent. The system is supposed to protect the alleged incompetent, but there do not appear to be sufficient safeguards. Even with a trial by jury, the interests of the person who is supposed to be protected may not in fact be protected.

▶ The process of guardianship may be started by anyone, very easily. A relative or neighbor can begin the process merely by submitting a court petition. The petition only has to allege that the proposed ward is unable to manage his or her money and, in many cases, his or her personal affairs.

▶ In most but not all states, the proposed ward has a right to counsel. This attorney is referred to as the "guardian ad litem." The problem of such representation is that it may conflict with the elderly person's own wishes. The guardian ad litem may adopt an "I know best what's good for you" attitude.

▶ The proceedings typically are a short affair, lasting only a matter of minutes. It is often questionable how well the counsel serves the elderly person.

▶ Each state has its own grounds for declaring someone incompetent and appointing a guardian. More than half the states do not require medical evidence of incompetency. In the past, advanced age alone was grounds for appointment of a guardian. The trend is away from an automatic finding of incompetency, but almost half the states will still set up a guardianship where there is a finding of senility or advanced age, as interpreted by the judge in the particular case.

The operation of the guardianship system, in many instances, does more harm than good for the person the system is supposed to protect. Those named as fiduciaries may not necessarily protect the ward. Typically, spouses and then adult children are appointed as guardians. These relatives may very well not act in the best interests of the elderly person.

▸ A person appointed as fiduciary by a court may not have a personal interest in the elderly person. Where there are no relatives who qualify under the laws of the state, a stranger may be appointed. This may be a "professional" guardian—typically, a lawyer who is named by the court to act. Some states allow organizations, such as banks, to be named. In some states, there are public guardianships for elderly persons who are poor and whose property management will not generate sufficient fees to induce a private guardian (person or organization) to act. A state agency then assumes the role of guardian. For example, in California, the Board of Supervisors in any county can file a petition on behalf of an elderly person who is in need of a guardian and has no relative or other person available to act.

▸ There is potential for abuse. There is scant policing of guardians. Many guardians are political appointees. Guardians are "fiduciaries" who are supposed to exercise a high degree of integrity. Nonetheless, cases of abuse of that fiduciary position are numerous. A handful of states do not require any financial reporting by guardians; other states do not enforce financial accounting rules. Some guardians are required to post a bond to protect the incompetent from the guardians' financial misconduct. Unfortunately, the bond may be inadequate.

▸ The system may not serve the interests of the elderly. The powers of the guardian may be limited by law, and these limits may not be the best for the elderly. For example, in New York, a guardian may spend for "necessities" and make "legal" investments. However, other expenses and investments, such as a sale of real property or invasion of principal, require a court order. The fiduciary must return to court, and time and expenses are wasted.

▸ The system is costly to the elderly. This is so even where guardians act in the best interests of the elderly. Guardians are entitled to fees set by the court. The amount varies in different states. The fees may be on an hourly basis. In some places, the fees are determined with reference to the assets spent on behalf of the incompetent. In other states, the fee may be set by the guardian as long as it is "reasonable."

There are procedures for removing fiduciaries where there has been incompetency or misconduct. In general, an "interested party" may start a removal proceeding.

Guardianships serve a legitimate function in providing certain care for the elderly when there has been no advance planning. However, the guardianship process in general is expensive and time-consuming, and may not serve the best interests of the elderly. It is preferable to seek alternatives. Advance planning, regardless of the size of a parent's wealth, is strongly advised. At a minimum, it may be possible in some states to influence the choice of guardian where there is no spouse or adult child to act. The court may ask for the ward's choice and give serious merit to that choice. In some states, advance designations of fiduciaries will be respected. (This planning tool is discussed later in this chapter.)

It should be remembered that advance planning does not rule out the use of guardianships.

WEALTH BUILDING PROFILE *Court Action Despite Advance Planning.* Having a durable power of attorney does not prevent the appointment of a guardian. This may be a good thing for some individuals. For example, an attorney-in-fact named in a durable power of attorney may not be acting in the best interests of the elderly person who is now incompetent. A guardian can be named. That guardian can seek court action to remove the attorney-in-fact.

Limited Guardianships

Some states permit limited forms of guardianship. For example, in California, it is possible to name a one-time decision maker to take steps for Medicaid (Medi-Cal) qualification. In Maine and Washington, a court may appoint a guardian to do only certain tasks that the person cannot perform independently, such as check writing and banking.

→ ACTION ITEM ←

The less expansive the court determination, the better it is for the elderly person. Autonomy should be maintained for as long as possible.

Other Protective Services

Appointment of a guardian for an incompetent is an extreme measure. In some cases, lesser forms of intervention may serve as well.

▶ In California, where it is possible to seek court approval for a surrogate one-time decision maker, the court must find that the ward lacks the ability to act for himself or herself, but grants the fiduciary the power to act in only one instance. This instance is clearly spelled out in a court order.

▶ To avoid problems of neglect, the use of in-home support services (homemaker and chore services) may be enough. Such services may help an elderly person with diminished capacity to manage day-to-day living.

It is a great tragedy when elderly individuals fall victim to physical, emotional, and/or financial abuse. Often this abuse comes from those closest to the elderly, such as their adult children. In the extreme, these children may beat their parents and steal their money.

Protective services are available to end abuse of the elderly. These include domestic protective orders issued by a court and enforceable by the police. Unfortunately, many elderly abuse victims are more than a little reluctant to cooperate with authorities. Even if they do cooperate and obtain protective orders, the orders are short-lived and are difficult to enforce.

DURABLE POWER
OF ATTORNEY

Planning for money management can save money, time, and inconvenience while ensuring that a parent's wishes are respected. There are several alternatives in planning for property management: durable power of attorney, fiduciary designation, joint ownership, and trusts. They are not mutually exclusive. All can be used to some advantage in ensuring good management of your parent's finances.

Perhaps the simplest and least expensive alternative for money management is to have a document called a *durable power of attorney*. In the past, a power of attorney was only operational for as long as the person granting it remained competent. A court order stating that a person was incompetent acted as an automatic termination of the power of the agent to act. Gradually, states came to recognize the inability of a person to direct activities after he or she is no longer competent. The durable power of attorney came into being. It got its name because the powers granted by the document remained in effect even after the person granting them became incompetent. Now, all states and the District of Columbia recognize this format.

A durable power of attorney typically is a one- or two-page document that names someone to act as your parent's agent in certain circumstances. The agent is called an attorney-in-fact. The document must be made while your parent is still legally competent. The legal standard for competence varies from state to state, but it generally means that your parent must understand the nature of the document and what it means to sign it. Even if your parent is suffering from a mental disability, there may be days on which your parent is lucid enough to have legal competency. A doctor familiar with legal standards and your parent's condition may be consulted to assure that this is so.

The document is simple but it is extremely powerful. The durable power of attorney may avoid the need for a guardian or conservator. It also takes care of the practical day-to-day problems. Bills can be paid, services arranged, and other matters seen to without court intervention. Even where a durable power of attorney is properly executed, it does not prevent other action. If the document fails to provide some necessary power, the family can always commence a guardianship procedure. Often, the agent will be named by the court to act as guardian.

The person granting the power (your parent) is called the principal. The person given the power to act for the principal (you, or someone else named by your parent) is the agent. This agent is given the authority to handle your parent's money. The agent may be given as much or as little power as your parent considers appropriate. The document is a notice to other parties that the agent has the legal right to make money decisions on behalf of your parent.

To ensure that the document remains effective even *after* your parent becomes incompetent, it must specifically state that the powers survive the incompetency of the principal.

→ **ACTION ITEM** ←

Review any power of attorney that was drawn up some years ago, to be sure that it is a *durable* power of attorney. Otherwise, it will not be of any help if and when your parent becomes incompetent or disabled.

The form of the durable power of attorney varies from place to place. In most places, you may use a preprinted form available at many stationery stores. Alternatively, you may have an attorney draw up the document for you. Because the document is not complicated, the fee for preparation should be reasonable. The attorney will also know what the law of your state requires for proper execution of the document. The number of witnesses required may vary from state to state. Different states have different rules about whether the document has to be notarized. Again, although the document is simple, its powers are great. It may be advisable to consult an attorney so that the power of attorney conforms to your parent's overall planning needs. In some states, it may be absolutely necessary to use an attorney. In Oklahoma, for example, a durable power of attorney requires court approval.

Who Should Be Named as Agent?

There are two basic requirements for an attorney-in-fact. First, and most important, the person named should be someone your parent trusts. This cannot be overemphasized. Because the agent has great power, the opportunity for abuse of that power exists. The agent should understand your parent's attitudes toward money and agree to act in harmony with them. Your parent may name a relative, or an attorney, or someone else.

WEALTH BUILDING PROFILE

Naming Multiple Agents. Grace, an elderly woman, has two sons, one who lives near her and one who lives in the next town. She is concerned that her arthritis may soon prevent her from getting around like she used to. She wants to give her sons power of attorney to handle her financial affairs. She names the son living near her as her agent. But she is concerned that, if that son has the power to make gifts, the other son will be jealous and concerned that he and his family are not receiving an equal share. So, for purposes of the power to make gifts up to the annual gift tax exclusion, she names both sons as coagents and states that they must act jointly. This will ensure that Grace will not create any jealousy between her sons.

When an elderly parent has more than one child, there is a possibility of family discord if only one is named as agent. Two or more individuals can be named as coagents. They can be required to act in concert ("jointly"). Alternatively, each agent named may be given full powers to act independently ("severally"). In some cases, it may be advisable to use a single agent for the routine matters but require two agents to act jointly for more important actions.

The use of multiple agents is not without problems. Agents may disagree about the proper actions to take. Fights may ensue. It may be preferable to discuss the possibilities with all concerned, and then reach a consensus on who should be named as sole agent. Another adult child can be named as a successor agent, in case the first one is unable to act or chooses not to act.

The second basic requirement is that the person named should be someone who is capable of exercising the powers conferred on him or her. Check state law regarding any restrictions on who can be named. In some states, it may be necessary to name a state resident as agent, or the agent may have to be a certain age. The powers to be exercised may require special skill. For example, if your parent owns an interest in a business, it may be important to name an accountant or someone who has the necessary financial expertise to act in your parent's stead. A close relative may be trustworthy but may not necessarily be capable. It is important to name someone who is physically able to act in all given powers. If your parent lives in one state and you live in another, it may be impractical for you to be named as agent. Even if state law does not prohibit it, the choice is not good, for practical reasons. You cannot readily get to your parent's bank to make deposits and withdrawals, pay monthly bills, complete your parent's tax returns, or do other chores for which your parent requires assistance.

Powers in the Power of Attorney

Each state has its own standard form for the durable power of attorney. In these forms, the attorney-in-fact is granted a variety of powers. In addition to the stated powers, any other powers (unless illegal) may be added. The powers included in a power of attorney are as follows:

▸ Conduct real estate transactions. The agent can enter into a mortgage or buy and sell a house for the principal. This power is very important if a parent owns a house, condominium, or other realty. For example, assume a parent owns a home outright. This represents a valuable asset. It may be possible to tap into that asset by means of a reverse mortgage. The funds can be used for a parent's living expenses or health care needs. Without the power of attorney, it would be necessary to go through the formality of a court petition. A guardian of a parent's property would have to be named, as discussed earlier in the chapter. Guardianship entails cost as well as time.

▶ Complete transactions for goods and services. This includes, for example, buying appliances on credit.

▶ Buy and sell stocks, bonds, securities, and commodities. If a parent has a brokerage account, it may be necessary to complete a special power of attorney form provided by the brokerage firm. For some reason, brokerage firms prefer their own durable power of attorney forms, and may refuse to honor a parent's document or, at best, may create hassles and delays if their form is not used.

▶ Conduct banking transactions. This power includes making deposits and withdrawals, signing checks from your parent's account, taking out bank loans, and paying off loans. Like brokerage firms, banks generally prefer their own durable power of attorney forms. Even where the banks may be subject to penalty for refusing to honor a valid durable power of attorney (e.g., New York), it may still be necessary to use the bank form. The bank may simply pay the fine and insist on the use of its own form.

▶ Handle business operations transactions. If your parent owns a business interest, it is essential that an agent be empowered to continue running that business. As already pointed out, it is important that the agent be qualified to act in this capacity. There is no requirement that the agent named to handle business transactions be the same person designated for other purposes. A separate power of attorney for this function may be used, if one person is not able to perform all appointed tasks.

▶ Act for the estate. This power allows an agent to act in estate and probate matters. For example, when a person dies with a will, a person who would inherit property if that will did not exist must consent to allow the will to be probated. Alternatively, that person can contest the will.

▶ Handle claims and litigation. If your parent is involved in a legal dispute, the agent would be empowered to start a lawsuit, settle the claim, and file an appeal.

▶ Handle personal relationships and affairs. In some states, it is possible to name a person to act as surrogate in health care matters in the same document used for financial affairs (see Chapter 6). State law may permit a durable power of attorney for financial matters to include this health care proxy designation. Some states (such as New York) prohibit the naming of an agent for health care in the power of attorney used for financial matters. Even where it may be permissible to use a durable power of attorney for health care, it may be better to use separate documents for financial matters and health care matters. This is especially advised if different agents are assigned for the different functions.

▸ Collect benefits from military service on a parent's behalf. If a parent was a veteran, he or she may be entitled to certain benefits from the Veterans Administration. Naming an agent to act on a parent's behalf will facilitate collection of these benefits.

▸ Obtain all records, reports, and statements to which a parent is entitled. For example, this power may allow an agent to process Medicare claims without any questions or difficulties.

▸ Delegate any of these powers to another person. If the person named as agent does not have the skill to perform a certain job, the agent can hire a professional.

▸ Gain access to safe deposit boxes. Opening a safe deposit box requires the signature of the box owner. Naming an agent will allow someone other than the owner to gain entry. Some banks are very cautious about allowing an agent to get into a safe deposit box. However, it may be possible to ultimately prevail. In New York, for example, banks are specifically prohibited from refusing to honor a power of attorney and are subject to penalty if they so refuse. Some banks still prefer to pay the relatively small fine for violating the law rather than be exposed to greater liability for honoring a power of attorney that may later be contested. As a practical matter, it may be advisable to have a safe deposit box placed in joint name with a parent, so that a child is automatically a signatory to the box.

▸ Complete and sign tax returns and IRS powers of attorney. The agent may be given the power to sign tax returns, endorse refund checks, and settle tax disputes. The IRS has its own power of attorney form, Form 2848, and, in general, bureaucratically refuses to accept other power of attorney documents. Recently, however, the IRS made it easier to handle federal tax matters. The IRS will now permit an agent named in a non-IRS form to execute the IRS power of attorney form, as long as the non-IRS form specifically authorizes the agent to handle tax matters. The agent then merely attaches to the IRS form a statement that the non-IRS power of attorney is still in effect.

▶ Deal with retirement plans, including IRAs, 401(k) plans, and rollovers. For example, the agent may decide whether to take a lump-sum distribution in lieu of monthly pension benefits. If a lump-sum distribution is selected, the agent can decide whether to pay tax currently or make a tax-free rollover.

▶ Fund inter vivos trusts. If a parent has set up a lifetime trust (as explained in Chapter 9), the agent may be given the authority to transfer money or other property to the trust.

▶ Borrow funds to avoid a forced liquidation of assets. If a parent owns a business, it may be necessary to routinely take out a loan.

▶ Deal with life and other insurance. The agent may be given the power to cancel an existing life insurance policy, to borrow against its cash value, or to convert a term policy to whole life. If a parent is the beneficiary of a life insurance policy, the agent can decide whether to take the proceeds in a lump sum or in installments. The agent can also settle insurance claims.

▶ Enter into buy–sell agreements. If a parent owns a business interest, an agent may be permitted to contract with the business or other owners on buyout arrangements.

▶ Forgive and collect debts. An agent may hire a collection agency to track down delinquent debtors.

▶ Complete charitable pledges. A parent may have promised to make a gift to a charity but then became incompetent before completing the transfer. An agent may be empowered to complete such gifts.

▶ Make statutory elections and disclaimers. This power relates primarily to elections that arise when a person dies. For example, assume that there is an elderly couple and one spouse dies. The decedent's will leaves all property to the surviving spouse. For estate tax reasons, it may be preferable for the surviving spouse to disclaim all or a portion of the inheritance; however, if the surviving spouse is incompetent, no disclaimer can be made. If the surviving spouse has given this power to an agent prior to incompetency, then the agent may disclaim on behalf of the surviving spouse.

▶ Pay salaries of employees. With this power, a parent's business can continue functioning despite his or her disability.

▶ Make gifts. This power allows the agent to continue estate tax planning on the parent's behalf. For instance, over the past several years, your parent may have given you and the grandchildren a set amount of money each year. This gift was not only a way to express generosity, it was also meant to aid in estate planning. The typical form of the durable power of attorney is silent on the matter of gifts. Still, the attorney-in-fact may be given the power to make gifts, and this power can include the ability to make gifts to the agent and the family of the agent. The size of gifts can be limited to a monetary amount, or general limits can be set. The annual gift tax exclusion ($10,000 annually to each donee) is a typical limit. It is important to specify that the agent can make gifts to himself or herself and to the agent's family, if the parent so desires. The potential for abuse of this power is great. It is essential that the parent understand the scope of this power and grant it judiciously. An unlimited gift-giving power that can be exercised in favor of the agent can create estate-planning problems for the agent. This power may be viewed as a general power of appointment that could result in the agent's being taxed on all the principal's property, if the agent dies before the principal. This gift power can also be used for Medicaid planning purposes. For example, in New Mexico and Washington, the law specifically authorizes agents to transfer property or income to a principal's spouse for the purpose of qualifying for government assistance.

▶ Exercise other powers. In some states, it is possible to use a general umbrella clause to give the agent power in all other matters. Washington, however, precludes any powers not specifically stated in the document.

A parent is free to tailor the document to suit particular needs. Any of the powers may be limited. For example, a parent may allow the agent to buy and sell stocks and bonds but not to transfer real estate.

The durable power of attorney becomes effective as soon as it is signed and notarized. Some people may feel uncomfortable in granting financial power to another while still exercising control over their money. The document can be given to a third party (such as the attorney who drafted the durable power of attorney) for safekeeping until the time when disability or incompetence strikes. At that time, the third party can give the document to the attorney-in-fact, who can begin to assume his or her role as overseer of the disabled person's finances.

The durable power of attorney continues in force until it is revoked or the principal dies. It may be necessary to notify a bank, brokerage firm, or other third party that the power of attorney has been terminated. The power may no longer be terminated when the principal becomes incompetent. The power is *durable;* it outlasts the princi-pal's disability and continues in effect until the principal's death.

As mentioned earlier, banks, brokerages, and insurance compa-nies may have their own forms for a power of attorney and may resist honoring another type of form. If a parent typically deals with cer-tain companies, get their forms and sign them. This is just a way to save time and money. When a company's forms are not used and an agent wants to act, there can be delays and it may even become necessary to take legal action. An attorney may have to intercede and even fight the company. The simplest solution is to use the com-pany form.

Springing Durable Power of Attorney

Instead of having the power of attorney become effective immedi-ately upon signing, it is possible to postpone its effectiveness until the time when it is really needed—when disability strikes. This can be accomplished in some states by means of a *springing durable power of attorney.*

The springing durable power of attorney comes into effect *only* upon the principal's disability or some other triggering event speci-fied in the document. Some states provide the specific instances when the document will be considered to become effective. In other states, the document must describe the circumstances under which disability will be judged. For example, the document may provide that it is necessary for two doctors to agree about disability. The docu-ment may even name the two doctors your parent wishes to act in this regard.

More than 20 states have statutes recognizing the springing durable power of attorney; 2 states specifically prohibit this type of document.

The regular power of attorney immediately entrusts financial au-thority in someone else; the springing power of attorney may backfire. Disputes may arise between relatives, over whether the disability has occurred. It may even become necessary to seek court assistance to determine whether the triggering event has taken place.

There is another potential problem with the springing power of at-torney. Banks, brokerage firms, and other institutions may be hesitant to act on a power of attorney executed several years earlier. A question of "staleness" may prevent these institutions from acting promptly, even though state law does not limit the power of attorney by date. As a practical matter, it might be more workable to opt for the regular durable power of attorney.

FIDUCIARY DESIGNATION

Naming a Guardian

In some circumstances, a durable power of attorney may not be broad enough to deal with all contingencies. It may be necessary to seek court assistance to act on behalf of an elderly person. A guardianship or other similar proceeding may have to be commenced. The elderly person may be able to influence the choice of guardian. In 20 states, it is possible to name a guardian (or other fiduciary title) in advance.

The method of designation varies from state to state. In Washington, for example, the designation can be made in a durable power of attorney. In contrast, New York requires that the designation be made with all the formalities required for a will.

──────────── ➤ ACTION ITEM ◄ ────────────

Check with an attorney to determine the steps necessary for your parent to designate a guardian or other fiduciary.

Representative Payees

If a person is incapable of handling his or her finances, the Social Security Administration may no longer mail social security checks to that person. It is necessary for the incompetent to have a representative payee. Checks are then mailed to the representative payee for the benefit of the incompetent. The Veterans' Administration and the Civil Service Commission also use representative payees.

Typically, a representative payee is a relative of the incompetent. Friends can also act as representative payees. Some elderly have no relatives or friends to act for them in that capacity. The Social Security Administration estimates that about 250,000 elderly have representative payees who are strangers to them.

There has been a move to change the rules regarding representative payees. First, there is sentiment that checks should not be stopped when the SSA suspects incompetency. The checks should be allowed to continue until a representative payee is in place. Second, there should be greater policing of representative payees. At present, the SSA asks annually for an accounting by the representative payee. The representative payee must list, under penalty of perjury, how the money received has been used.

JOINT OWNERSHIP

Some financial problems can be overcome by a simple arrangement known as joint ownership. An elderly individual can have a bank account over which another person is given joint ownership. In the event that the elderly person is no longer able to get to the bank, the joint owner may act.

There are three basic forms of joint ownership: joint tenancy with rights of survivorship, tenants by the entirety, and tenants in common. Under a joint tenancy with rights of survivorship, each tenant has an undivided interest in the entire property. When one tenant dies, the other tenant becomes the owner of the entire property. This creation of ownership is automatic; it happens by what is called "operation of law." This means that the very nature of joint tenancy confers an inheritance on the tenants. Any two or more people or entities may become joint tenants. There is no requirement that joint tenants be related to one another. Only one person need create the tenancy. The other tenant does not even have to know about the arrangement or consent to it. This is the type of joint ownership form that would be used by an elderly parent and adult child for a bank account, brokerage account, or other property interests. It allows the adult child to have full access to the funds and, presumably, to use them to meet the parent's needs. When the parent dies, the child inherits whatever remains.

Tenants by the entirety is the same arrangement as joint tenancy with rights of survivorship, with one special requirement: it can only be made between spouses. As with joint tenancy, the entire property becomes the property of the surviving spouse upon the death of the other spouse.

Tenants in common may be thought of as "partners." Each tenant, in this arrangement, owns a share of the whole property. That share is his or hers alone. The share can be sold, given away, or bequeathed to heirs. This kind of joint ownership arrangement is typically used in financial arrangements with nonfamily members. Throughout the balance of this chapter, when joint ownership is discussed, it refers to joint tenancy or tenancy by the entirety, not to tenants in common.

Joint ownership has several advantages:

▸ It is simple to create. A joint ownership is set up merely by doing so: opening a joint bank account or brokerage firm account, or putting title to property in joint name. In general, there is no need for a lawyer or other professional to create a joint tenancy. However, the use of a lawyer's services may be necessary when a deed to solely owned real estate is transferred to joint name.

────────────── ➤ **ACTION ITEM** ◀ ──────────────

When transferring title of a parent's home to joint name, it is advisable to check with the title insurance company to see the effect, if any, on the title insurance.

──

▸ It allows someone other than the elderly parent to deal with the property. Without any documents or forms, a joint owner is able to use jointly owned property for the benefit of the other owner. Where there is a feeling of trust, the joint tenancy can be used between friends who have taken it upon each other to care for one another. Not all elderly parents are married nor do they have children available to help out. A joint tenancy can permit either tenant to look after the interests of the other tenant.

───────────────

WEALTH BUILDING PROFILE *Using a Joint Bank Account.* Robert, an elderly father, sets up a joint checking account with his son, John. When Robert is no longer able to write monthly checks, get to the bank to make deposits, or otherwise handle routine financial chores, John can do so. John does not have to notify the bank or any other party about his right to use the money in the account. The very fact that John is a joint tenant on the checking account is sufficient to confer the necessary authority to act.

───────────────

▸ There are no special costs. The joint owner who uses jointly owned property to support an elderly person does not receive any compensation for doing so. Unlike a trustee in a trust, who is entitled to fees, a joint tenant is not paid for acting. However, nothing prevents that tenant from withdrawing funds for his or her own use, as payment for services rendered.

▸ Some estate-planning goals can be served by a joint tenancy. Because the property passes automatically to the surviving tenant, there are no hassles about ownership. This may be especially helpful if the elderly person wants the property to pass to someone to whom other family members may object. For example, an elderly person may have a long-time companion, as well as brothers, sisters, and children. If property is placed in joint name with the companion, then siblings and children cannot deprive the companion of that property. Joint property passes to the surviving tenant directly; it does not have to go through the probate process. Therefore, savings on administrative costs may be realized.

A joint ownership arrangement may be simple to create, but it is tricky in operation. Consider its many disadvantages:

▸ There is nothing to bar the joint owner from withdrawing all the funds. The joint owner is legally able to assume complete ownership over the account, with no accountability. Therefore, it is critical that, if joint ownership is used, the person given the joint interest is someone who is trusted. An elderly person should understand fully the ramifications of putting property in the form of a joint tenancy.

▸ Joint ownership does not solve all financial problems. Although joint ownership may be suitable for bank accounts and certain property, it does not empower the joint owner to act. The joint owner may have access to bank funds. There is nothing that tells the owner to use the funds for the co-owner's benefit or to do other financial tasks, such as filing tax returns on behalf of the co-owner. There is no way to require the joint owner to apply the assets in the joint account for the other owner's benefit.

▸ Joint ownership may create gift tax problems. In some instances, the creation of a joint tenancy results in a gift to the co-owner. Although transfers between spouses are tax-free, transfers between parents and children or other persons may result in gift tax. For example, a parent changes the title to the family home to joint ownership with his adult child. Because the half-interest in the home is a gift to the joint tenant, gift tax may be due. Creating a joint bank account generally does not result in a gift, because the creators of the account still have the right to withdraw all the funds. Thus, there has not been a completed gift.

▸ Joint ownership may not resolve ownership problems. Sometimes a joint bank account is set up for the convenience of the depositor: the joint tenant can use the depositor's funds to pay the depositor's bills. A joint tenancy passes automatically by operation of law, but it can still be contested. For example, in one New York court case, the relatives who would inherit under the will of a deceased person successfully brought an action against the joint tenant. The court included the funds remaining in the account at death in the decedent's probate estate, on the grounds that the joint bank account was merely a convenience account and not a true joint tenancy. The court deprived the joint tenant of these funds.

▸ Joint ownership may do a disservice to estate planning. There is a common perception that joint ownership by itself is an estate plan. It is true that jointly owned property passes directly to the joint owner. Jointly owned property is not part of the probate estate and, therefore, saves on administrative costs. However, putting property in joint name does not eliminate the need to go through the probate process. In addition, because joint property passes outside the probate estate does not mean that it passes outside the taxable estate. The deceased tenant's interest is included in the gross estate, and there may be tax due as a result of that interest. Whether the joint tenant is liable for any portion of that tax depends on the deceased tenant's will. If there was no will, then state law may dictate who pays that portion of estate tax.

▸ Joint ownership may actually prevent estate tax savings, in certain circumstances. Each person is entitled to pass to heirs up to $600,000 free from federal estate tax. When a married couple's estate exceeds $600,000 and they own everything jointly, their joint ownership prevents utilizing this $600,000 allowance to the fullest. There will not be any estate tax on the estate of the first spouse to die, because of the unlimited marital deduction. However, when the surviving spouse dies, that estate will be needlessly burdened with additional estate tax. What is more, joint tenancy may prevent postmortem planning. Even when a spouse leaves everything to the other spouse, it is possible to benefit from the $600,000 allowance by refusing to accept any amount in excess of $600,000. A disclaimer may be made to take advantage of the $600,000 allowance. However, a joint owner cannot disclaim jointly owned property upon the death of the cotenant. (The estate planning drawbacks of joint tenancy are discussed in further detail in Chapter 10.)

?

Who is the "principal" in a power of attorney document?

The principal is the person, such as your elderly parent, who may desire to have a power of attorney document drawn up to handle financial or other concerns, in the event that the elderly person becomes disabled or mentally incompetent.

What is the difference among a conservator, a guardian, a fiduciary, or a curator?

It depends on the state—all of these titles are involved with retaining control over an incompetent person's finances. Different states use different labels. You should investigate the practices and titles used in your parent's state.

When does a durable power of attorney "spring"?

This term is used to describe a procedure under which the power of attorney does not commence until the principal becomes disabled. It is not available in every state.

What is joint ownership?

Joint ownership is created when two people (such as a parent and a child) share ownership of something (such as a bank account). In a joint tenancy, one "tenant" (one of the owners) generally can act to execute issues on behalf of both. There are various types of joint ownership, and there are limitations on its usefulness.

TRUSTS

For people who have sizable assets, there is another planning strategy to consider: using a trust for asset management. A trust is a separate entity. It has its own tax identification number, it may have to file its own tax return, and it can sue or be sued.

The person who owns the assets creates the trust. This person is called the "grantor" or "settlor." Assets placed in the trust are then owned by the trust. Title to property is held by the trustee, but the benefits of property ownership do not inure to the trustee. The trustee is merely a fiduciary who holds the property for the benefit of the "beneficiary" named in the trust. This can be the grantor and/or other parties.

The trustee—the person named by the grantor to carry out the terms of the trust—is given certain powers. These may be as broad or as limited as the grantor decides.

There are several reasons why a person may consider establishing a trust:

▸ Management of assets can be placed in capable hands. For example, when a person is no longer able to see to the day-to-day chores of handling property, this job can be given to a trustee. That trustee should be someone who is qualified to manage property. The property involved may consist of rental real estate for which the trustee must collect rents, obtain tenants, negotiate leases, and oversee repairs and capital improvements. Or, the property might be an unincorporated business. The trustee in this case would need expertise in running that type of business or the ability to hire people who do. The property might be a large portfolio of stocks and securities. The trustee in this instance should be well-versed in stock market transactions. If the property is a combination of business interests, real estate, and securities, the trustee would probably have to rely in part on the assistance of several experts.

▸ Estate-planning objectives can be served. "Living trusts" have become popularly known as devices to beat the cost of dying. Because the property in trust can pass directly to heirs under the terms of the trust, the trust is kept out of the probate estate. In turn, there are savings on administrative costs. Living trusts generally do not save estate taxes. (The use of trusts in estate planning is discussed in Chapter 9.)

───────────────→ **ACTION ITEM** ◆───────────────

There are no minimum money requirements for setting up a trust. However, as a practical matter, it is not worth the bother for a few thousand dollars' worth of assets. There are legal fees for setting up a trust and, in some cases, a charge for managing the trust. Use of a trust is primarily designed for wealthy individuals.

───────────────────────────────────

A variety of trust forms can be used to meet lifetime and estate-planning objectives. Trusts are discussed in greater detail in Chapter 9.

For legal assistance with various mechanisms for money management, contact the National Academy of Elder Law Attorneys (655 North Alvernon Way, Tucson, AZ 85711; phone: 602 881-4005), the American Bar Association (750 North Lake Shore Drive, Chicago, IL 60611; phone: 312 988-5000), or your state or local bar association.

—————— POINTS TO REMEMBER ——————

▸ The government, or even complete strangers, may be called in to make financial decisions for an elderly person who is declared incompetent. For this reason, it is strongly advisable to work out a plan, and a designated guardian, for that person.

▸ A durable power of attorney is a legal document that extends beyond the time when a person is physically or mentally competent. Even when this document is drawn up, family members can seek guardianship status, to review decisions made by the attorney-in-fact.

▸ Joint ownership of financial assets can be helpful in cases where one of the owners ("tenants") becomes disabled. It has the advantage of being simple to institute, but the disadvantage of being potentially costly or troublesome when ownership is being transferred.

9

Using Trusts and Other Special Arrangements

*E*lderly parents with sizable fortunes may not be able to rely on traditional investment tools to manage their finances. With size comes complexity. More structure may be needed to make investment decisions and to handle assets on a day-to-day basis. This need for management assistance for wealthier individuals becomes even more pronounced when old age interferes with management and investment abilities. Concerned relatives may fear that elderly parents will foolishly dissipate assets or become overly indebted to creditors. There may also be a desire to achieve tax savings.

Fortunately, to address these concerns, there is a straightforward mechanism for money management, called a *trust*. In simplest terms, assets are placed in a trust by transferring their legal title to the person who will run the trust. This person (or company) is called a *trustee*. The assets placed in the trust are then managed by the trustee. The benefits from the trust—income and principal—are enjoyed by one or more *beneficiaries*. Assets in the trust may in some cases be protected from the claims of the creditors of the trust beneficiaries. Trusts can also be used for tax-saving purposes.

There are many types of trusts, and they may be tailored in a variety of ways, to suit the needs of an individual. This chapter explains the various types of trusts and considers their advantages and disadvantages. Emphasis is placed on the types of trusts best suited to meet the objectives of an elderly parent. Trusts designed primarily for estate tax planning rather than lifetime money management are discussed in Chapter 10.

Also considered are special trusts designed to meet special tax-saving or other objectives.

There are alternate arrangements for sophisticated money management, besides trusts. These include private annuities, installment sales, sale–leasebacks, and life income plans.

All of these arrangements are quite complex. It is advisable to discuss them with an attorney. (The Appendix listings will aid in obtaining a referral for an attorney in your parent's area.)

WHAT IS A TRUST?

Before considering the role of a trust in managing the assets of an elderly parent, it is important to understand the nature of a trust. A trust is an entity created by a person to hold assets and use the income and principal for stated purposes. The trust becomes a separate unit. It can hold title to property in the name of the trustee. It can have a bank account. Some trusts need to file a tax return and may have to pay income taxes. Such trusts must have a taxpayer identification number.

Like a corporation, a trust has an existence separate and apart from the person who creates it. It may not feel separate to a person who sets up a trust and then acts as trustee. Little will seem to have changed. Control over the property continues to be exercised in the same way; income is still taxed to the owner. However, a separate entity has been created.

A trust can outlast the life of the person who sets it up. It can outlast the next generation as well. A trust can run for many years, subject to limits set by state law. A trust terminates when its purposes have been fulfilled. Typically, termination occurs when the person entitled to trust income for life dies and the balance of trust property is distributed to the named beneficiaries.

The requirements for setting up a trust vary according to state law. A number of trust forms are available in stationery stores or in libraries. However, because a trust is a highly personal and important document, it is strongly advised that it be drafted by an attorney who is familiar with the goals and finances of the elderly parent as well as state law requirements.

There is no dollar requirement for setting up a trust. Whether a person is wealthy or of modest means, the use of a trust is available. As a practical matter, however, it may not be advisable to go through the bother, inconvenience, and expense of a trust unless there are significant assets at stake.

Trust Terminology

A number of words used in connection with trusts have special meaning. It is helpful to understand these terms so that they can be discussed with an attorney if a trust is to be drawn up.

The Person Creating the Trust

The person setting up the trust is called the *grantor*. He or she may also be referred to as a settlor, creator, or trustor.

Those Benefiting from the Trust: The Nature of Their Interests

As noted earlier, the persons for whom the trust is created and who will derive benefit are called beneficiaries. The grantor may also be a beneficiary of the trust.

A beneficiary may be entitled to receive income produced by the trust. This right to income can be for life or it may be only for a stated number of years. If it is for life, the beneficiary's interest is called a *life estate*. If it is for a number of years, it is called a *term interest*. The beneficiary may have no right to income. The beneficiary may be named to receive only principal, after the income beneficiary's interest has ended. The interest of a beneficiary entitled only to principal after the end of the income interest is called a *remainder*. If the beneficiary entitled to receive the principal after the end of the income interest is the same person who set up the trust in the first place, then the remainder interest is referred to as a *reversion*.

There is no limit on the number of persons who can be named as beneficiaries of a trust. A grantor may include his or her entire family. Alternatively, the trust can be used to benefit only one person, such as the grantor's spouse. A trust can also be used to benefit charitable institutions. (There are tax advantages for doing so.) Most importantly for purposes of money management for the elderly, the grantor may be a beneficiary under the trust. An elderly person may set up a trust and be entitled under the trust to receive the income from the property for the rest of his or her life.

The Person Managing the Trust

The trustee, the person who manages the trust, is a fiduciary. As the name implies, the trustee has a position of trust: the trustee is held to a certain level of conduct by state law. Each state has its own list of duties and powers of a fiduciary. The trust instrument may impose limits on these powers or may grant other powers not specified in state law (as long as they are legal).

▶ *Duties.* In general, the trustee has the duty to take possession of trust property and to use reasonable care and skill in managing it. This duty includes preserving trust assets and making them productive. The trustee may also be required to make periodic accountings of trust activities. The trustee must keep trust property separate from his or her own property. The trustee may not delegate fiduciary responsibilities.

▶ *Powers.* State law grants certain general powers. These may include, for example, the power to invest and reinvest in accordance with the terms of the trust instrument. This includes the power to vote securities, exercise stock options, buy and sell property, make repairs, take out property insurance, and contest, compromise, or settle claims with respect to trust property. In addition, the trustee has all other powers granted by the trust instrument. These may include, for example, the power to borrow or lend funds, make capital improvements, run a business, employ agents, and even keep funds uninvested or nonproductive.

The trustee can be an individual or it can be an institution. Banks and trust companies may act as trustees, if the trust assets are large enough. A trustee may be the person setting up the trust (although a co-trustee may be required in this case), or a family member.

→ **ACTION ITEM** ←

If the purpose of the trust for an elderly parent is to alleviate management responsibilities, the grantor will not want to act as sole trustee. It may be preferable to name an adult child to be the trustee.

The trust instrument may name more than one trustee. These trustees may be required to act in concert. They must agree to investment choices and other decisions. No one can be forced to act as a trustee. A person named as trustee must agree to serve in that role. Banks and trust companies generally set a minimum dollar requirement before they will agree to act as trustees.

The trust instrument may name a backup to the trustee, called a *successor trustee*. A successor trustee assumes the duties of trustee when the original trustee is no longer able to act or chooses not to do so. For example, the trustee may resign. A successor trustee is given all the powers of the original trustee.

A trustee may be required to post a bond or other security, as a means of protecting the assets of the trust from any trustee misconduct. However, it is more usual for a trust instrument to waive bond or security requirements, especially if a relative is named as trustee. If an institution serves as trustee, bond or security requirements may be retained.

A trustee typically is paid a fee for services. This fee may be any reasonable amount provided in the trust instrument. If the instrument is silent on the issue, the fee may be fixed according to a fee schedule set by state law. Typically, the schedule is fixed in relation to the size of the trust. Alternatively, the trust can provide that the trustee waives all fees to which he or she may be entitled. This waiver may be used where the trustee is a family member willing to serve without compensation.

Trust Property

Assets transferred to the trust are called the *trust fund, principal,* or *corpus*. Any earnings on the assets are called *income*. State law or the terms of the trust control when additions to the trust are income or principal. For example, in certain cases, capital gain earned on trust property is treated as additional principal and added to the trust fund; in other cases, it may be disbursed as income.

Types of Trusts

There are two main categories of trusts: *inter vivos* and *testamentary*. Inter vivos trusts are created by a person during life. They are also called lifetime trusts or living trusts. Testamentary trusts, as the name implies, are created by a person in a will. Testamentary trusts do not become effective until the person creating them dies. Because testamentary trusts do not come into existence until after the death of the grantor, they are not suitable for managing the finances of an elderly person. They do serve an important role in estate planning, and are discussed in Chapter 10.

Within the category of inter vivos or living trusts are two variations: *revocable trusts* and *irrevocable trusts*. With a revocable trust, the person creating the trust can decide to end it. An irrevocable trust is a permanent trust. The person setting it up cannot change his or her mind at a later time and end the trust. A revocable trust can become irrevocable upon the happening of a specified event. This event may be the death of the person creating the trust or the disability or incapacity of that person.

Trust Document

A trust comes into existence by a *trust document*. It is also called a *deed of trust* or a *trust instrument*. On this piece of paper, all the terms of the trust are spelled out. The document names the trustee. It can also name an alternate or successor trustee to act in the event that the original trustee can no longer act or chooses not to act as trustee. The document specifies the powers granted to the trustee and names the beneficiaries. The property to be held in trust may be listed in the document.

Trust Requirements and Special Trust Clauses

Importance of State Law

State law defines the requirements to create a valid trust. In general, the grantor must have the legal capacity to set up a trust. Precisely what this legal capacity is may be hard to define. In New York, for example, it is the same level of capacity required of a person to make a will. At the time the trust is created, the grantor must be of sound mind and understand the nature of what he or she is doing. Generally, this means understanding the extent of his or her property holdings and the relationship of the persons named to benefit under the trust.

Likewise, the person named as trustee must be competent. If the trustee is a natural person (as opposed to a bank or trust company), he or she must be of legal age and sound mind. Again, state law may specify who is not able to be named as a trustee. For example, a foreigner residing out of the country may not be qualified to act as a trustee. As a practical matter, even if such a person were permitted to act, the choice would be questionable, given the distance involved.

Spendthrift Provisions

As mentioned earlier, a trust set up on behalf of another person may be used to protect assets from creditor claims (e.g., a son can set up a trust for his mother and assets are protected from the mother's creditors). This is referred to as *spendthrift protection*. The nature and extent of this protection varies from state to state. In most jurisdictions, the trust document must include language specifying spendthrift protection. In some jurisdictions, however, automatic spendthrift protection is given to the income interest *unless* there is language in the trust document authorizing a transfer, voluntarily or involuntarily, of the income interest.

Invasion of Principal for Income Beneficiary

It is possible to set up a trust that allows principal to be used for the benefit of the income beneficiary under certain circumstances. The trustee can be given total discretion on when to use principal ("invade principal") for the income beneficiary. Alternatively, a trustee may be permitted to invade principal, subject to a specific standard. This standard typically is limited to the support and maintenance of the income beneficiary according to that person's standard of living.

Utmost care must be exercised when including invasion clauses in trusts. Typically, trustees are given liberal invasion powers with the intent of protecting the beneficiaries against unforeseen changes in circumstances. However, in some instances, the best intentions may result in the worst consequences. For example, if a trust is designed to protect assets from Medicaid, an invasion power geared to the support and maintenance of the income beneficiary could render the entire trust worthless for asset protection purposes. Medicaid may be able to bring suit to compel the trustee to use trust assets for the support of the income beneficiary. This would prevent or delay Medicaid eligibility.

WEALTH BUILDING PROFILE *Using Trust Clauses with Medicaid in Mind.* Steven sets up, in his will, a trust for his wife, Gloria. The trust provides for liberal invasion of principal. Steven dies.

Sometime later, Gloria develops a chronic condition that requires placement in a nursing home. If Gloria applies for Medicaid eligibility, the principal of the trust can be counted as a resource of Gloria's, because the trustee has the power to invade the principal for her medical care.

Steven might have *wanted* the principal used for Gloria's care in a nursing home; in this case, the clause permitting the liberal invasion of principal was appropriate.

Withdrawal Clauses

Trusts may give the income beneficiary certain invasion powers. The purpose of these clauses is to ensure advantageous gift tax treatment. More specifically, such clauses allow additions to the trust to be treated as current interests rather than future interests, so as to qualify for the $10,000 annual gift tax exclusion.

One invasion clause gives the income beneficiary the right to withdraw as much as $5,000 or 5 percent of the value of the trust, whichever is greater. This is called a *5 and 5 power*. Another invasion clause comes into play when the trust does not require distribution of income. Instead, income may be accumulated and added to principal. This invasion clause allows the income beneficiary to demand the withdrawal of income and principal up to a set amount (typically, the amount of the annual gift tax exclusion). This invasion power is called a *Crummey power* and is named after the case in which the power was given effect. More specifically, the Crummey power says that the income beneficiary may demand to be paid a set amount. There is a window of time in which this demand must be made. If no demand is made within this time, the right to demand payment expires (lapses). It is important for an elderly person to know about the 5 and 5 and Crummey powers, if a trust is being created, for estate planning purposes, to benefit others. These powers are not used in trusts in which the grantor is named as income beneficiary.

REVOCABLE TRUSTS

An elderly parent may not want to give up all control over property. An alternative for solving financial management requirements without immediate loss of control is a revocable trust. Property is transferred to the trust. The trust is managed by the trustee named by the elderly parent. The elderly parent can act as trustee and/or can name some other relative if so desired.

A trust generally is made irrevocable. If an elderly parent wants to create a revocable trust, this might be clearly stated in the trust document. More specifically, the document should state that the grantor reserves the power to revoke, alter, or amend the trust.

In recent years, there has been a great deal of publicity surrounding "living trusts." Living trusts are not new. They have been around for hundreds of years. The term simply means inter vivos trusts. They are old devices that have become more popular because of growing awareness of the benefits they can produce.

Standby Trusts

One type of revocable trust useful for elder care planning is called a *standby trust* or an *unfunded trust*. The trust is set up, but assets other than a token amount are not transferred to the trust at the time of creation. The trust stands idle until needed. This need could arise when the elderly person becomes incompetent and can no longer manage assets. At that time, assets are transferred to the trust and used in accordance with the terms of the trust.

WEALTH   *Combining a Trust with a Durable Power of At-*
BUILDING   *torney.* Harry is still able to manage his money but
PROFILE   is concerned that this ability might diminish in the
                 future. He wants to have a trust used only at such
time as he is no longer able to handle his affairs. He sets up an unfunded trust. At the same time, he makes a durable power of attorney under which the agent is authorized to transfer assets to the trust when Harry is no longer able to manage his own affairs. When this occurs, the agent acts under the power of attorney to fund the trust.

When a grantor sets up a revocable trust but then becomes mentally incapacitated, the trust automatically becomes irrevocable because the grantor lacks the competency to exercise the revocation power under the trust instrument.

The grantor can act as the trustee of the trust while the trust stands idle (essentially unfunded) and while competent to do so. If the grantor becomes incompetent, the trust is funded and another trustee previously named by the grantor can be substituted.

Directions on what is to happen to the property after the grantor's death can be conveyed in one of two ways. The trust instrument can say who gets the remainder. Alternatively, the trust instrument can state that the remainder "pours over" to the grantor's estate. The remainder in this case gets distributed as part of the grantor's testamentary estate. This is not the usual procedure, because it creates additional probate costs and delays; these are avoided when trust assets are distributed directly under the terms of a trust rather than according to a will.

The key to a standby trust is an event of incompetency that brings the trust to life. Therefore, the trust should be very clear on what constitutes incompetency. There are a number of choices for a definition of incompetency:

▸ The definition of disability in the Internal Revenue Code;
▸ An insurance industry definition from a disability policy;
▸ A Social Security Administration definition of disability;
▸ A definition specially created by the trust itself.

The definition referred to in the trust may require the opinion of one or more doctors, who must then certify the grantor's condition. Specific doctors can be named in the trust. If names are given, alternative doctors should be designated, in case the named ones die or are unable to act at the required time.

It may not be a good idea to allow a relative to decide on incompetency. This could lead to family disputes.

A grantor may prefer to have a court adjudication of incompetency. This is costly and time-consuming but may be appropriate in some instances.

→ ACTION ITEM ←

There is an important point to consider with standby trusts. If the grantor dies suddenly, rather than after a period of incompetency, the trust will remain unfunded. At the grantor's death, the assets will still be in the grantor's probate estate; there will be no probate cost savings. This factor alone may work against using a standby trust.

Pros and Cons of Revocable Trusts for Lifetime Money Management

Advantages

There are a number of reasons favoring the use of revocable trusts for money management purposes. Revocable trusts provide a great deal of flexibility. They can give trustees great discretion—more than can be given to an agent under a durable power of attorney.

Use of revocable trusts can avoid court costs and delays in deciding whether a person is incompetent and who should manage his or her money. Their use also maintains the privacy of an elderly parent and eliminates the need for an adjudication of incompetency, which becomes a matter of public record.

Revocable trusts can help to ease the emotional stress involved with getting older and having to face increasing physical or mental limitations. With the trusts in place, there is a smooth transition of management over assets, without further emotional strain.

Revocable trusts have relatively low maintenance costs. As long as the elderly parent functions as trustee, there are no additional costs. Once another person takes over as trustee, there may be some trustee fees. However, if an adult child takes on this role, fees can be waived and costs minimized.

Disadvantages

Despite the many positive reasons for using a trust for asset management, there are several drawbacks to consider. First, a trust adds a layer of complexity to financial affairs. Some people are just not comfortable with having their property titled to a trust and having to turn to a trustee for the distribution of income and/or principal. There are many formalities with a trust that may be troublesome or confusing. It takes time and trouble to change the title to property. For example, if a residence is transferred to the trust, a special deed (called a *quitclaim deed, a correction deed,* or some other name, depending on the state) must be filed and then recorded. If there is still a mortgage on the property, a transfer of the residence to the trust can trigger a demand by the bank for payment. Title insurance should also be checked, to see whether such insurance protection will continue after the residence is transferred to the trust.

Second, cost and trouble are involved in setting up a trust. Stationery stores and numerous books in libraries and bookstores have forms available for setting up trusts, but generally it is not a do-it-yourself project. It is a good idea to consult an attorney before taking any action. The rules governing trusts vary from state to state. Because there is a great deal at stake, it is advisable to have an attorney draw up a trust and oversee its execution. This service can be costly, running up to $1,000 or even more, depending on the terms of the trust and the time required to draft it.

Third, special problems may arise with respect to a personal residence. Refinancing a mortgage on the residence may be difficult when the house is titled to the trust. Homestead protection against the claims of creditors may be lost once the house is titled to the trust. In some states, this loss of protection may be minimal; in other states—such as Florida, which offers unlimited protection for the full value of the residence—the loss of protection is great.

Totten Trusts

In New York, there is a special type of revocable trust called a *Totten trust*. This is a bank account in which the person making a deposit names another as beneficiary of the account. The title of the account is, for example, "Mary Smith, in Trust for Jim Johnson." The account remains revocable for the life of the owner, even if the owner gives the bank book to the beneficiary. The beneficiary has no claim on the account. Upon the death of the owner, whatever remains in the account passes automatically to the named beneficiary. If the owner of the bank account becomes incompetent, funds cannot be withdrawn without court authorization.

Tax Consequences of Revocable Trusts

Gift Taxes

There are no gift taxes on the creation of a revocable trust, because the grantor has not parted with control over the property. He or she may recover the property simply by revoking the trust. The transfer to the trust is viewed for tax purposes as an incomplete gift. If the trust becomes irrevocable upon the incompetency of the grantor, there may be a gift tax at that point (see Irrevocable Trusts, below).

Income Taxes

The income is taxed to the income beneficiary who receives it. In a trust created by an elderly parent who retains the income interest, trust income is taxed to the creator of the trust. In fact, no special tax forms are required; the income from the trust is reported directly on the grantor's Form 1040.

If a trust allows a trustee an *accumulation power*, (a permission to keep and reinvest the income rather than distribute it to the income beneficiary) different tax rules apply. The trust becomes a taxpayer in this case. A separate tax return, Form 1041, must be filed by the trustee. The trust may have to pay taxes as well, including estimated taxes, if the amount of income warrants it.

Estate Taxes

The property in a revocable trust is includible in the estate of the grantor, for federal estate tax purposes. The grantor is treated as having owned the entire trust, because he or she had the power until death to reclaim trust property.

IRREVOCABLE TRUSTS

Before an elderly parent sets up an irrevocable trust, the nature of this trust must be carefully understood. Once this type of trust is created, the grantor cannot change his or her mind and recoup the assets transferred to the trust. There is a natural reluctance to part with control over property, and this feeling may be justified. The grantor is parting with all decision making about investments, income distributions, and bequests of the property placed in the trust.

These decisions are set forth in the trust instrument. A great deal of power is given to the trustee. Therefore, the terms of the trust should be carefully spelled out. All contingencies should be anticipated as far in the future as possible.

Pros and Cons of Irrevocable Trusts for Lifetime Money Management

Advantages

Irrevocable trusts offer the same advantages as revocable trusts, for lifetime management purposes. Decision making can be shifted to another person, to alleviate the elderly parent's responsibility for this chore. The need for court intervention, when and if an elderly parent becomes unable to manage his or her affairs, is avoided. The trust is already in place for asset management purposes. The costs of maintaining the trust are relatively low compared with the costs that would result if it became necessary to go to court each time action on property had to be taken.

Disadvantages

As with revocable trusts, disadvantages must be considered. Again, there are the formalities and complexities of the trust itself. The cost of setting up and maintaining the trust is high. Finally, homestead protection is lost when a personal residence is transferred to the trust.

Tax Consequences of Irrevocable Trusts

Although the pros and cons of revocable trusts and irrevocable trusts are quite similar, the tax consequences of these two types of trusts are *very* different.

Gift Tax

Because the transfer of property to the trust is permanent, it is viewed as a gift for gift tax purposes. The grantor is making a gift of the income interest to the person named as the income beneficiary (if that person is someone other than the grantor). The grantor is also making a gift of the principal to the person named as the remainderman. Where the grantor retains the income interest, then the gift is limited to the value of the remainder interest. The amounts are figured using IRS tables. These tables set a factor for valuing the life interest retained by the grantor, based on life expectancy and certain interest rate assumptions. The factor is multiplied by the value of the trust property at the time the trust is created. The product is then subtracted from the total value of the trust property. The older the grantor, the shorter the life expectancy; therefore, the less value assigned to the grantor's life interest and the greater value given to the gift of the remainder interest. The present value of the remainder interest is determined by reference to IRS tables. Here is a sample of the values assigned to varying ages. A 10 percent interest factor is assumed, on a $100,000 irrevocable trust.

Age of Grantor at Trust Creation	Value of Gift of Remainder
55	$17,450
60	22,674
65	28,787
70	35,907
75	43,856
80	52,705
85	61,392

WEALTH　　*Figuring the Gift Tax Cost of Setting Up an Irrevo-*
BUILDING　*cable Trust.* Anna transfers $100,000 to an irrevoca-
PROFILE　　ble trust under which she has the income interest for
　　　　　　　the rest of her life. On her death, the property will
pass to her son, Richard. Anna is 70 years old at the time the trust is
created. The value of the remainder interest that will go to Richard
on her death for gift tax purposes is $35,907. Anna must figure her
gift tax liability for federal (and, if applicable, state) based on this
amount.

A gift of a remainder interest does not qualify for the annual gift tax
exclusion. The remainder interest is a *future interest* (an interest that
comes into effect in the future) and the annual exclusion applies only
to gifts of *present interests* (interests that are immediately effective).
However, the transfer is not necessarily taxable. The unified credit
may be used to offset the tax on the gift. Up to $600,000 in property
may be transferred free of any federal gift tax.

Income Tax

The income beneficiary is taxed on the income received from the
trust. A word should be said here about *grantor trusts*. In the past, it
was possible for an individual to set up a short-term irrevocable trust,
called a *Clifford trust*, to last for at least 10 years and a day. The
income from the trust could be shifted to another person for that
interim. At the end of the trust term, the property would be returned
to the grantor. Trusts in existence before March 2, 1986, continue to
be treated in this way. However, trusts that were created after March
1, 1986, and that give the grantor an interest in the reversion of more
than 5 percent of the value of the property in the trust, are subject to
different rules. They are grantor trusts and the grantor remains taxable on the income.

Estate Tax

The assets that will pass to the remainderman upon the death of the
elderly parent/income beneficiary are still included in the estate of
the elderly parent for tax purposes. It is true that the assets are not
included in the probate estate. Like life insurance proceeds, they
pass automatically to the remainderman. However, because the

elderly parent retained a life estate in the trust, the value of the trust is includible in the gross estate. The gift taxes paid by the grantor would, of course, be taken into account. The details of estate taxes are explained in the next chapter. Suffice it to say that the federal estate tax can run to a hefty 55 percent. In addition, if the assets of the trust are very substantial and the assets pass to beneficiaries in later generations, there may be a generation-skipping transfer tax as well.

Irrevocable trusts can be used for estate tax savings. If the grantor transfers *all* interests and powers in the property to a trust (and does not keep the right to receive income or principal), then the property is not includible in the grantor's estate for tax purposes.

A Revocable or Irrevocable Living Trust?

When a trust is set up during one's life but the terms of the trust cannot be changed and the grantor cannot recover the property, it is called an irrevocable living trust. This trust can be used for the same purposes as the living trust, described earlier. The only difference is that, once an irrevocable living trust is set up, the property cannot be recovered.

Why should an individual irrevocably transfer property into a trust rather than retain the option of reacquiring the property? Many factors should go into such a decision. First, a person may want to put only certain property into that type of trust. Transfer of rental real estate, an interest in a closely held business, or other property requiring a degree of management may be appropriate. Use of the trust relieves the owner of such management responsibilities. Irrevocable living trusts are also used for savings on estate taxes. For example, an elderly parent owns a life insurance policy. If an irrevocable trust is set up and the policy is transferred to the trust, the proceeds can be removed from that parent's estate for tax savings, provided the parent outlives the transfer by more than 3 years.

SPECIAL TRUST VARIATIONS

Different individuals have different needs. Each of these needs may require a different type of trust. Fortunately, trusts offer a great many options. The following sections describe some specialized trusts designed to meet specific objectives.

Grantor Retained Income Trust (GRIT)

A grantor retained income trust (GRIT) is an irrevocable trust in which the grantor keeps (retains) an income interest for a specified number of years. At the end of that term, the property passes to someone else, such as the grantor's child. The grantor pays gift tax on the transfer of the remainder interest. If the grantor outlives the income term, then the grantor or his or her estate will realize transfer tax savings. This is because the gift tax is paid only on the remainder interest, which is the value of the whole property reduced by the value of the grantor's term interest (figured using IRS tables and formulas). The child ultimately receives the entire property and no additional transfer taxes are imposed.

Unfortunately, Congress changed the rules on the tax treatment of GRITs set up after October 8, 1990. GRITs set up earlier can enjoy the tax benefits outlined above. However, GRITs set up after that date are subject to special valuation rules that essentially make GRITs prohibitive from a tax point of view. There are, however, special rules that make certain types of GRITs—specifically, grantor retained annuity trusts and grantor retained unitrusts—still viable.

It is still possible to use a specially structured GRIT for a personal residence of a parent. To repeat the benefit from the use of this device: the entire property eventually passes to the child, but the transfer tax is imposed on only a portion of the property (the entire value of the property less the value of the retained interest). The trust must place restrictions on holding any property other than the residence and cash for certain limited purposes.

Anyone seeking tax-advantaged ways to transfer property should consult an adviser who is knowledgeable in this constantly changing and highly complex area. Such an adviser can assess whether the overall tax savings make sense. For example, use of a GRIT to transfer a residence may well save on transfer taxes, but it may ultimately cost the child more in income taxes than if the residence had been transferred by inheritance. The adviser can ensure that, if a GRIT is desirable, all IRS requirements are satisfied.

Medicaid Trust

If your elderly parent may, in the foreseeable future, have a need to resort to Medicaid to pay for long-term care, asset transfers may be necessary. A parent who may not want to part entirely with his or her assets by means of outright gifts may be amenable to transfers into a trust in which the parent continues to have an interest.

By creating a Medicaid trust, it may be possible to protect the assets of an elderly person without preventing Medicaid eligibility. The assets are protected from spend down requirements and can be passed to the next generation. The trust must be carefully structured to conform to certain requirements, in order to be treated as a Medicaid trust. Before the terms of a Medicaid trust are explained, it should be emphasized that there is *no guarantee* that use of the trust will protect assets. In New York, for example, there is great doubt whether such a trust can accomplish the intended goals of asset protection without jeopardizing Medicaid eligibility. A 1990 court case in New York has lawyers questioning the viability of Medicaid trusts.

In jurisdictions where trusts can be used to protect assets without preventing Medicaid eligibility, there are several key points that the trust should follow. First, the trust must be irrevocable. The elderly person must understand that he or she cannot get the property back from the trust.

Second, the grantor must be entitled to the income from the trust for life. The trust should carefully define this interest: it should not extend beyond the right to the income from the property held by the trust. If the trust permits use of principal for the benefit of the grantor (called an *invasion of principal*), then Medicaid would also be entitled to this amount.

If someone else (such as an adult child) sets up a trust for the benefit of an elderly parent, it may be possible to give the trustee unfettered discretion to invade principal for the benefit of the grantor. Medicaid would not, in this case, be able to compel the trustee to exercise this discretion. However, if the elderly parent or spouse sets up the trust for his or her own benefit or the benefit of a spouse, the trustee cannot refuse to exercise discretion in order to permit Medicaid to step in and cover medical expenses.

All the income paid from the trust continues to be available to pay for medical costs that would otherwise be covered under Medicaid. However, assets in the trust cannot be tapped if they were transferred to the trust more than 30 months prior to the Medicaid application. This feature preserves the assets for the remainderman and ensures that the income from the trust can be used to benefit the elderly person in the event of discharge from a nursing home.

What happens if the trust is set up within the 30-month period? In this case, Medicaid would not have to cover any expenses during a period of ineligibility (up to 30 months). The assets transferred to the trust would be taken into account, and the elderly person would have to pay the entire cost of the nursing-home bill. How can this be done? The trust did not have an invasion power, so the only money available to the elderly person is the income from the trust. To pay the balance of the nursing-home bill, some other avenue would have to be found. In all likelihood, the adult child would have to use his or her own assets to make up the shortfall. When netted against what is ultimately received from the trust, this outlay seriously diminishes the value of the inheritance.

WEALTH BUILDING PROFILE   *Using Medicaid Trusts.* Gregory, an elderly man, has assets of $250,000. He transfers all of his assets to an irrevocable trust. Gregory's former business associate and long-time friend, Stanley, is named as trustee. The grantor's child, Julie, is named as remainderman. The trust is invested in income-producing property yielding 8 percent. The annual income from the trust is $20,000. Gregory is confined to a nursing home costing $30,000 a year. Assume that the trust was set up more than 30 months prior to confinement and that, under state law, this type of trust will not prevent Medicaid eligibility. Gregory may receive help from Medicaid in paying the nursing-home bill. The $20,000 income from the trust is applied toward the cost of the nursing home. Medicaid will pay the rest. The assets in the trust remain safe. They continue to produce income. They will pass undiluted to the named remainderman, the grantor's child, Julie. If Gregory is discharged from the nursing home, he can continue to receive the $20,000 annual income.

There is a way to combine long-term care insurance with a Medicaid trust for protection of family assets, when a trust is not set up before the 30-month period. An elderly person who is still competent to act can set up a Medicaid trust within the 30-month period, as long as he or she has maintained nursing-home insurance. The long-term care insurance need only run for a period of 30 months. (A parent may be required to take a 36-month policy, because such policies typically run in yearly multiples.) The insurance would cover the cost of the nursing home. Alternatively, the insurance proceeds may be combined with the trust income to pay the nursing-home bill.

Charitable Remainder Trusts

Wealthy individuals may want to take advantage of tax deductions while enjoying the income from their property for life. They may have already provided for their children. Their children may be wealthy in their own right and may have no great need of additional capital. For individuals in this enviable position, there is a special type of trust—the charitable remainder trust.

Under a charitable remainder trust, the grantor can retain an interest in the income for life or for a term of a maximum of 20 years. When the income interest ends, the property passes to charity.

The trust can be set up to provide income to the grantor primarily in one of two ways. Income can be paid as an annuity (a fixed income determined when the trust is set up). This type of arrangement is called a *charitable remainder annuity trust*. Alternatively, the trust can pay out an income based on a percentage of the trust principal. This type of arrangement is called a *charitable remainder unitrust*.

The trust must be set up to meet certain requirements. The income interest retained by the grantor must be guaranteed under an annuity trust or a unitrust. The IRS has provided special trust forms which, if used, guarantee that the charitable remainder interest qualifies for a tax deduction. The amount of the tax deduction is figured under IRS tables.

There is no gift tax or estate tax on charitable remainder trusts.

──────────────────▶ ACTION ITEM ◀──────────────────

A charitable remainder trust is a highly compli- cated arrangement that should be undertaken only after a thorough understanding of the implica- tions. It is important to consult an attorney before opting for a charitable remainder trust.

?

Do trusts have to pay taxes?

In some cases, yes. A trust is a legal entity separate from an individual. Although it may be controlled by and may benefit that individual, it must comply with different legal and financial rules.

What does a trustee have to do?

The exact duties depend on the terms of the trust. In general, the trustee must use reasonable care and skill in managing the trust; in return, the trustee may be paid a fee out of the trust's assets.

What is the difference between inter vivos trusts and testamentary trusts?

The first is a "living" trust: it is in force while the grantor is alive. The second becomes effective when the grantor dies.

Medicaid trusts provide ironclad protection of assets: true or false?

False. The protection afforded by such trusts depends on the jurisdiction where they are in effect, and the terms under which they are written. For instance, trusts that provide for invasion of principal are not protected.

How can a parent convert a nonperforming asset (such as land) into an income producer, while minimizing taxes on the transfer?

The possibilities include a private annuity, an installment sale, and a sale–leaseback. Another is a life income plan arranged with a charity.

OTHER PROPERTY
MANAGEMENT ARRANGEMENTS

Private Annuities

A private annuity is an arrangement between two non-insurance-company people. One person (called the *transferor* and *annuitant*) transfers property to the other person (called the *transferee* and *obligor*) in exchange for a promise to pay a stated sum over a set period (such as the remainder of the transferor's life). The size of the payments is figured with regard to the length of the obligation to pay, including interest on the payments.

Typically, the property transferred is property that is currently yielding no income or only minimal income. For example, a parent may transfer a piece of land to an adult child.

Use of a private annuity can increase an individual's monthly income, provide other lifetime benefits, save income taxes, and reduce estate taxes without gift tax cost. This seems like a lot to accomplish. Indeed, there are many benefits, but there are also drawbacks to consider. Let's run down the various features of private annuities.

Lifetime Benefits

The two key reasons, aside from taxes, for making a private annuity are to increase cash flow and to be relieved of management responsibilities. An elderly person may be sitting with an asset that does not produce sufficient income, such as raw land. The value of that asset may be enough to warrant reasonable annuity payments. Thus, the private annuity arrangement can convert an otherwise non-income-producing asset into a cash machine for the parent. The parent may be able to sell the property, take the proceeds, and buy a commercial annuity. However, in this alternative, the income tax on gain from the sale of the land is paid out in one lump sum. After tax, less money is available for the purchase of the commercial annuity. This translates into smaller monthly payments.

Management or investment responsibilities are the other key factor. An elderly person may no longer wish to be involved in decision making or administrative chores. These responsibilities are shifted to the obligor. The obligor may retain the transferred property or convert it into other property.

Income Tax Savings

Gain on the property transferred is not immediately recognized. Instead, it is spread out over the life expectancy of the annuitant, which means the tax on that gain is also spread out. Less tax may also be due on the income from the annuity than on income from the property.

Gift Tax Savings

As long as the property has the same value as the annuity (based on present value), there is full consideration for the exchange and no gift has occurred. If the value of the property is greater than the value of the annuity, then the difference is a gift. Valuation of the annuity is figured by reference to IRS tables.

Estate Tax Savings

The property is removed from the annuitant's estate. Because the annuity ends at death, the annuitant does not own something that must be included in his estate.

The income from the annuity can be used up during the annuitant's lifetime, leaving nothing more to be included in the estate. Alternatively, if the annuitant does not need the money to live on, such sums can be transferred as tax-free gifts. However, if the annuitant merely accumulates the annuity payments, the amount remaining in the estate may well be equal to the property originally transferred, with no net estate tax savings.

It is essential that a professional draw up the documents reflecting the private annuity arrangement. Failure to draft them properly can result in the IRS's treating the arrangement as a transfer with a retained life income interest. This treatment will subject the arrangement to estate tax. It is imperative that the property transferred be accurately valued. Failure to do so may leave the whole arrangement open to IRS attack. Valuation is not difficult if the property is publicly traded stocks or securities. For other properties, qualified appraisals by experts must be used to establish value.

Drawbacks to Private Annuities

If a private annuity is such a wonderful arrangement, why isn't everyone doing it? Because there are several drawbacks to consider. The chief drawback is the risk that the annuitant (the elderly parent) must take. The promise to pay the annuity cannot be secured if tax benefits are to be enjoyed. This means that the annuity is only as good as the person making the promise.

If the obligor dies before the annuitant, it must be hoped that the obligor's estate will continue to make good on the promise. This is another risk to consider.

Yet another drawback is the size of the annuity payments required, if the arrangement is made when the annuitant is elderly. Because life expectancy is shorter, payments must be larger. It may not be easy for the obligor to make these payments. It may be especially difficult if the obligor wants to retain the transferred property intact and the property is not producing sufficient income to make the required payments.

The impact of inflation is another negative factor for private annuities. One of the reasons for making the arrangement in the first place is to provide for cash flow. The erosion of the buying power of that cash flow must therefore be taken into account.

Installment Sales

An elderly parent may have property that can be transferred to an adult child by way of sale. If the sale is structured as an installment sale, it will spread out the income tax on any gain over the period of time for which payments will be received. This is another means of generating an income over a period of time.

WEALTH BUILDING PROFILE   *Using Installment Sales to Provide an Income Stream.* Arnold, an elderly parent, owns a coin collection. He can sell the collection to Harold, his adult child, who agrees to pay for it over a period of 10 years. Arnold receives an income for 10 years. Arnold's tax on the gain from the sale of the collection is also spread over those 10 years.

A word of caution: special valuation rules apply to certain transfers after October 8, 1990; they can subject even sales for full consideration to gift tax. It is important to consult a tax expert before undertaking any transfer between an elderly parent and members of the family.

Sale-Leasebacks

An elderly parent may be able to transfer certain assets by means of a sale, and still retain the use of the property under a lease. This transfer can be used to convert a nonproductive asset into a steady income producer, without losing the use of the property.

WEALTH BUILDING PROFILE   *Using a Sale–Leaseback to Obtain an Income Stream.* Anna, an elderly parent, has a house with no mortgage on it. She can sell the house to Carla, her adult child (assuming Carla has the necessary funds or can obtain a mortgage on the property). Depending on her costs and the sale price of the house, Anna may be able to avoid all tax on the gain. Anna can retain residence in the house under a lease. As long as the rent charged Anna is a fair rent (a rent that would be charged to a stranger), then the arrangement will be recognized for tax purposes. Anna can use part of the income received from the sale to pay the rent.

The sale of a residence to a child is discussed in Chapter 5. In addition to the income and tax aspects of a transfer of a residence, there are other considerations. For example, some states offer homestead protection against creditors. Medicaid laws provide for homestead exemptions. These other considerations must be taken into account.

Life Income Plans

Many charities offer the opportunity to make special donations that will ensure that the donor receives an income interest for life. A person transfers assets to the charity's pooled income fund. Income is fixed and guaranteed for life. The amount of income depends on the size of the transfer to the charity.

The donor is entitled to a charitable deduction for the value of the gift. Individual charities can provide information about their pooled income funds and the guaranteed income and tax advantages they offer.

POINTS TO REMEMBER

▶ A trust is a legal mechanism for transferring control of the financial assets of one person to another person.

▶ Definitions: the person who is giving up control of the assets is the *grantor*. The person assuming control is the *trustee*. The person who gets the benefits of the trust is the *beneficiary* (who may also be the grantor).

▶ There is no minimum dollar amount for setting up a trust. However, because legal assistance is usually desirable in setting it up, it makes little sense to create a trust for small amounts of money (and high fees).

▶ Living trusts can be of two types: revocable and irrevocable. There are tax and management consequences to each type.

▶ A charitable remainder trust provides income tax benefits to the grantor while the grantor is still alive and can take advantage of the benefit.

10

Estate Planning

Some people refuse to deal with their own mortality. They figure that whatever happens after their death will no longer be their concern. Others prefer to take an active role in planning what will happen after their death. There are good reasons for their doing so. They may have spouses, children, grandchildren, or others whom they want to protect. They may have charities they wish to endow. They may own property, accumulated over a lifetime, that they want to pass along with the minimum of estate taxes. Without protective planning, a person's property can be left to decisions by the state in which the person lived. The state and federal government will dictate how much tax is due. With planning, a person can exercise a measure of control over both the disposition of property and the amount of taxes that will be paid.

This chapter examines the consequences of lack of planning. Its primary goal is to encourage estate-planning initiatives. The various mechanisms for estate planning are explained. They include wills, trusts, life insurance, joint ownership, and gifts for estate-planning purposes.

An overview of death taxes is presented, and strategies for avoiding or minimizing them are discussed. It is impossible to present every facet of estate planning within this chapter. Factors that are especially of interest to elderly parents and their families are emphasized.

DEATH WITHOUT PLANNING

When a person dies, his or her property is lumped together in what is called an *estate*. An estate can be *intestate* or *testate*. When a person dies without a will, the estate is intestate. If there is a will, the estate is testate. Each state has its own rules governing the treatment of an intestate estate. These rules say who will be responsible for managing the estate (collecting and distributing assets, filing tax returns, and settling all affairs). These rules also say who inherits the property and who will be guardian of any minor children.

─────────────→ **ACTION ITEM** ←─────────────

The word *estate* has several different meanings for different purposes. The probate estate includes all property subject to the probate process. The gross estate, used for estate tax purposes, encompasses all property in which a decedent had an interest at the time of death.

It is important to thoroughly understand the different types of estates. The probate estate is most easily defined by what it is not. The probate estate is all property that does *not* pass to someone else automatically. Property that passes automatically is transferred by what is called *operation of law*. Property that passes in this manner includes:

▶ Joint bank accounts and brokerage accounts;
▶ Real estate held by tenants of the entirety or joint tenancy with rights of survivorship;
▶ Life insurance proceeds;
▶ Survivorship annuities;
▶ Certain trusts;
▶ Pension benefits.

Property that does not pass by operation of law must go through a court process called *probate*. Some states have probate courts or surrogate's courts especially for this purpose.

Another meaning of an estate applies for tax purposes. Under federal estate tax law, the gross estate includes all property in which a deceased person had an interest at the time of death. This includes probate property and nonprobate property. Here are some examples of property included in the gross estate: interests in jointly owned property (a share in a joint bank account, a joint brokerage account, and jointly owned realty); life insurance proceeds, if they are payable to the person's estate or if the person owned the policy or possessed certain rights in the policy; pension benefits, including IRAs; and property held in a trust set up by the decedent, if he or she retained a life interest in the trust or had the power to alter, amend, revoke, or terminate the trust. Strategies for avoiding or reducing estate taxes are discussed later in this chapter.

Some rules of intestacy are not far off from what most people would want in the first place. However, reliance on these rules would leave too much to chance. To see what happens without planning, let's see how property would be distributed under the laws of intestacy in one state, New York. If a New Yorker dies without a will, his or her property included in the probate estate, regardless of the size of that estate, would be distributed as shown in the following table:

New York Intestacy Rules

Decedent's Survivors	Inheritance
Spouse, no children or parent(s)	100% to spouse
Spouse, one child	$4,000 plus 1/2 of estate to spouse, balance to child
Spouse, two or more children	$4,000 plus 1/3 of estate to spouse, balance to children
Spouse, no children but parent(s)	$25,000 plus 1/2 to spouse, balance to parent(s)
No spouse, but children or their issue, and parent(s)	100% to children or their issue
No spouse, no issue, but parent(s) and siblings	100% to parent(s)
No spouse, no issue, no parent(s), but siblings	100% to siblings or their issue

If a person has no spouse, no children or issue, no parents, and no siblings, then other relatives inherit. These may be grandparents, uncles, aunts, or first cousins. When there are no relatives, the property passes to the state. (More distant relatives are permitted to inherit if the decedent had been declared an incompetent.)

Some individuals may want their property to be distributed roughly in the ways set up under the rules of intestacy. For many others, these rules do not accurately reflect their preferences. For example, they may want their spouses to get everything and their children nothing. Without a will or some other planning, this cannot happen.

Under the rules of intestacy, there is no provision for inheritance by friends or charities. A person may have lived with another person for 40 years. They were not related by blood and were not married. Under state law, the friend has no right of inheritance.

Intestacy only says what portion of an estate should go to which class of survivors. It does not specify which asset should go to which relative.

Without a will, there may be long delays in transferring property from the decedent to the heirs. Conflicts may develop, among relatives, over who should be in charge of distributing property.

Will Substitutes

As already mentioned, there are some property arrangements that can be used to short-circuit the probate process. These include jointly owned property, trusts, life insurance, certain annuities, and pension plans. There is a misconception that if these arrangements are used, then no will is necessary. It is true that property under these special arrangements will pass automatically and does not require a will to say who inherits it and who distributes it to the heirs. It is not true that a will should be dispensed with.

WEALTH   *Using a Will to Avert Family Conflict over Property.*
BUILDING   Norma, a widow with no children, had all her money
PROFILE   in bank accounts owned jointly with her sisters and
brothers. She also had some jewelry that was much admired over the years by various nieces and nephews. She wanted to prevent these relatives from fighting over who gets what piece of jewelry, but she wasn't certain how to distribute these and other personal items. She solved her problem by making a will and naming an executor. She gave the executor the authority to distribute this property to her nieces and nephews in substantially equal shares. However, she also gave the executor the discretion to sell the property and distribute the cash. This allowed her executor to handle the jewelry and personal assets without causing bad feelings among her relatives.

There is one very good reason for having a will, even where special arrangements are made: it is virtually impossible to ensure that all property conforms to one of the special arrangements available. A person may have personal property, or a car, or even a basis for a lawsuit that is not jointly owned or placed in a trust. It is still necessary for a court to confer authority on one person to oversee the estate and supervise the distribution of the estate's property, the filing of tax returns, and other matters. With a will, the person charged with overseeing the estate can be handpicked; without a will, relatives and friends may fight for the privilege (and the fees to which personal representatives are entitled).

There are other reasons for having a will. A will can be tailored to an individual's needs and desires. A will can be used to *prevent* certain individuals from getting property (e.g., to disinherit certain children, if so desired). A will can also be used to name a guardian for a minor child. Most elderly parents are not responsible for minors, but instances of such responsibility do exist, and plans for the minor should be made in a will.

WILLS

A will—or last will and testament, as it is sometimes called—is a legal document in which a *testator* (the person making the will) can decide who gets his or her property.

A will is also used to name certain fiduciaries, such as executors (sometimes called personal representatives) to oversee the estate, trustees to manage trusts set up in the will, and guardians to take care of minors for whom the testator has legal custody or minors who are inheriting property from the testator.

The Executor

One of the key aspects of a will is the naming of an executor (or personal representative). An executor is the person charged with the responsibility of collecting the assets of the estate and distributing them according to the terms of the will. In addition, the executor is responsible for filing tax returns.

The executor may be a relative, a friend, a trusted adviser, or a bank or trust company willing to accept the job. State law may place certain restrictions on who can act as executor (for example, whether nonrelatives must live in the state in which the testator lived).

The executor should be someone knowledgeable about financial affairs and willing to assume the estate's responsibilities. Typically, people name their spouses or children as executors. If an elderly person has no spouse, then children are the next likely choice.

When an elderly parent has two or more children, there may be concern that naming one as executor will offend the others. This is a delicate matter. It is possible to name more than one person to act as executor, and some parents choose to do so. However, pluses and minuses follow from this choice. On the plus side, such a move can maintain family harmony. It can also spread responsibility (and the related chores) among more than one person. On the minus side, the procedure is cumbersome and may in fact lead to more discord. For example, where the choice of assets to be distributed is left to the executor and there is more than one executor, conflict may arise between the executors, over who is to receive specific assets—Mom's favorite painting, Dad's coin collection. When fights ensue, it may become necessary to sell a cherished object in order to fairly split the proceeds.

In addition to naming an executor, it is generally advisable to name a successor executor. This person assumes responsibility only when and if the original executor is unable to act because of death, disability, or choice, or if the original executor resigns.

A Trustee

If a will calls for a trust to be set up, then a trustee should be named in the will. The trustee can be the same person as the executor or it can be someone else.

As with executors, it is generally advisable to name a successor trustee who can act if the original trustee is unable to do so.

The person named as trustee should have familiarity with handling financial matters, because he or she will be called on to make investment decisions, handle rental properties, file tax returns, make distributions to trust beneficiaries, and generally oversee the property held in trust.

Making a Will Legal

A will is a legal document that requires certain formalities if it is to be recognized in court. It must be signed and witnessed. Each state has its own rules on these formalities (for example, the number of witnesses required). It is advisable to see an attorney for the preparation and execution of a will.

Self-Planning

Although it is important that an attorney help with a will, the time
and expense involved can be greatly reduced if your parent knows his
or her estate-planning goals. To organize these goals, it may be helpful to complete the following estate planning data worksheet. The
worksheet contains only the *minimum* information necessary to
complete a will. Additional information should be included, if applicable: out-of-state property, whether fiduciaries should post bonds
and/or serve without compensation, and any funeral arrangements
that are to be included in a will (a separate statement on arrangements is recommended). All of this information can then be presented to an attorney who can help your parent fine-tune estate plans
and translate the data into a legal will.

━━━━━━━━ Wealth Building Worksheet ━━━━━━━━

Estate Planning Data

My name is: _____ I live in the state of: _____

My estate is worth today approximately $_____

I already have a will: Yes _____   No _____

My executor is: _____

My successor executor is: _____

I want to leave my property to the following individuals or charities in
the amounts or percentages specified:

_____   _____

_____   _____

_____   _____

_____   _____

_____   _____

I want to set up a trust in my will for:

_____

_____

_____

My trustee is: _____

My successor trustee is: _____

Other special instructions: _____

_____

_____

_____

Codicils

A codicil is a separate document that changes a portion of the original will. The change can be simple, like naming a new executor or canceling a debt by a family member, or it can be complicated, like reapportioning bequests among heirs, adding heirs (after birth or marriage), or deleting heirs (after death or divorce).

A codicil must be executed with all the formality used for the original will. Like the will, the codicil must be written. The same number of witnesses is required.

There are several pros and cons for making a codicil rather than redoing the will entirely.

Reasons for Making a Codicil

One of the main reasons for making a codicil rather than redoing the whole will is to protect the terms of the will if the testator's mental capacity is questionable at the time of the codicil. Even if the codicil is rejected for lack of testamentary capacity, the will itself can still be probated.

WEALTH BUILDING PROFILE   *Using a Codicil for Limited Purposes.* George, an elderly parent, is in failing health. He made out his will several years ago, naming his friend and contemporary, Frank, as executor. He wants to name a successor to the executor named in the will. This successor is to serve in the event that Frank cannot or does not do so. However, George has become increasingly forgetful. His children think he's senile. A codicil may be advisable here. The change is not major. The original executor named under the will, Frank, is not being changed. If the codicil is successfully challenged on the grounds that the testator was incompetent at the time it was executed, the will can still be probated.

Another reason for using a codicil to make a change is simplicity. Only one or a limited number of items is being changed, so the document is short and uncomplicated. This choice can translate into savings on attorneys' fees.

Redoing the Will Completely

As long as there is no question about your parent's mental capacity, the availability of word processors leaves little reason *not* to completely redo an old will if a change is desired. Most attorneys today enter and store the terms of a will on computer disks, and a change generally becomes a minor chore (and results in minimal legal fees).

A new will can avoid the problem of conflicting clauses and the need to probate more than one document.

Letters of Instruction

It is not necessary to include every detailed wish in a will. It is customary to use a simple letter of instruction for certain matters—how the funeral and burial arrangements should be handled, for example. A letter of instruction can also be used to specify which property is to go to whom. For example, a will may leave all of a mother's jewelry to her three daughters. A letter of instruction can state which piece of jewelry should be given to which daughter. Or, a will may leave all of a father's property to his son and daughter in equal shares. The letter of instruction can provide the executor with guidance on how to divide up the property. The father may prefer that certain items go to the son and others to the daughter.

These details can be specified in a will, if the distribution is to be made binding on an executor. A letter of instruction is merely guidance for an executor; it is *not* legally binding on family members or on the executor.

→ **ACTION ITEM** ←

A letter of instruction can be stored along with the will. It may be helpful to alert relatives that, in addition to a will, a letter of instruction has been left.

Safekeeping Wills

It is usual for a will to be photocopied, in order to produce several copies. For probate purposes, the original will is required. If the original is not available, then the probate process can become very lengthy and very costly. For this reason, it is important that the original will be kept safe.

There are a few good places to store the original will. The attorney who prepared the will can hold on to it. The attorney will store the will in a fireproof safe in the law offices, or in a bank vault. Your parent can retain the will and keep it in a fireproof safe at home. You, another relative, or a friend may keep the will for your parent, if you can do so safely and are trusted by your parent to produce it when the time comes. The important point is that you or some other relative must know where the will is kept and be able to readily gain access to it.

It is *not* a good idea to keep it in a bank safe deposit box. In many states, safe deposit boxes are sealed when the owner dies. They cannot be opened without approval of the state tax commissioner or a court order. Getting such approval or a court order is time-consuming and costs money.

What is the probate estate?

All property that does *not* pass to someone else automatically.

Can a relative be named as executor of a will?

Yes, and very often that is exactly what happens. There is a risk that this can create hard feelings among surviving relatives, so the decision should not be made lightly.

When is it advisable to write a codicil to a will, rather than rewriting the will entirely?

When there is a possibility that the mental capacity of the parent can be questioned. The codicil alone might be challenged later, rather than the entire will.

What advantage does a living trust have over a will, in disposing an estate?

Depending on how they are set up, trusts can transfer property more easily, and with fewer expenses, than a will. However, it is usually advisable to have a will in addition to the trust.

How much can a parent give away to relatives and friends without incurring any federal taxes or having to file a federal gift tax return?

Up to $10,000 per person, per year, can be transferred with no taxes at all. There is no total limit.

TRUSTS

Trusts can be set up during one's lifetime or through a will. Trusts set up during life are called inter vivos trusts. Trusts set up in a will are called testamentary trusts. There are numerous purposes, benefits, and drawbacks to trusts of all types. Many of these aspects were discussed in Chapter 9. For purposes of estate planning, we focus here on trusts that are used as *will substitutes*. These trusts are set up during life and are often referred to as living trusts.

Living Trusts

Living trusts are increasingly in vogue, primarily as a means of avoiding probate. How do they operate? A person (called the grantor or settlor) sets up a trust (advisedly, with the help of an attorney). Property is transferred to the trust and held by the person named to manage the property (the trustee). The benefits of the property are enjoyed by those persons who are named as beneficiaries of the trust.

The trust is used to make property distributions. Typically, in living trusts, the person setting up the trust remains a beneficiary of the trust for life. Upon that person's death, the property passes to the other beneficiaries named in the trust document.

Pros and Cons of Using Living Trusts
Primarily for Avoiding Probate

Trust property passes automatically to the persons named in the trust document. Trust property passes outside the probate estate, so it is not tied up in the probate process. This means that there is certainty in who gets trust property. Regardless of whether a person has a will and that will is considered valid, beneficiaries of a trust will receive trust property.

Time and expense are saved. The property can be transferred quickly because no court approval is required. There are no court costs, filing fees, or attorneys' fees for probate. The trustee merely takes the necessary steps to transfer the assets according to the terms of the trust. The savings can be small or great, depending on the probate process of the state in which the grantor lives. In high-cost states, such as California, Massachusetts, and New York, the savings can be as much as 5 percent or more of the value of the property in the trust.

The use of a living trust offers another advantage over probate: privacy. Probate is a matter of public record. Once a will is filed for probate, the executor estimates the amount of probate assets. For public figures in a community, it is not uncommon for this information to be reported in the local newspaper. In contrast, a trust is a private matter. It is not filed in court, and the public has no access to the contents of the trust. Some individuals may prefer that their property holdings be kept out of the public eye.

A trust is useful to avoid possible family conflicts. Like a will, a trust can be tailored to make unequal property distributions to children or other relatives. However, it is more difficult from a legal standpoint to contest a trust than a will. Therefore, property dispositions in a trust are safer from challenge than those made in a will.

There is much to recommend a living trust, but it must be emphasized that it is not a complete estate-planning solution. First, it is virtually impossible to dispose of all of one's assets under the trust. Therefore, it does not end the need to also have a will for this purpose. Second, a will is still useful for other purposes, such as naming a guardian for a minor and having a tax clause to specify how property is to share the responsibility for estate taxes.

→ **ACTION ITEM** ←

The typical living trust does *not* save estate taxes. If the grantor has an interest in the trust for life, or the grantor retains the right to alter, amend, or revoke the trust, the property is included in the grantor's estate for death tax purposes. Therefore, if tax savings are desired, other arrangements must be made.

Naming a Trustee

The choice of trustee is very important. The trustee generally has great power over and responsibility for the property. The trustee must manage the assets in the trust, which includes making investment decisions and collecting income. The trustee must also distribute income and property according to the terms of the trust. In some instances, the trustee is called on to exercise discretion over distributions. Finally, the trustee has the obligation of filing a federal (and, in some cases, a state) tax return for the trust.

While the grantor is alive, he or she can serve as cotrustee. Whether this is advisable depends on the purpose of the trust. If the purpose is primarily to avoid probate, then having the grantor serve as cotrustee is quite common. If there is some other primary purpose (e.g., alleviation of asset management during life), then another choice may be better.

Another trustee can be a relative or friend. This person can be asked to serve with or without fees. Some states provide statutory amounts for trustee fees, based on the assets in the trust or some other measure. For very large trusts, it may be advisable to use a corporate trustee (a bank or trust company). This arrangement can be costly, but may be useful if the size of the trust warrants it.

It may be advisable to name a successor trustee or to describe the mechanism under which a successor trustee can be appointed by a court.

LIFE INSURANCE

Role of Life Insurance in Estate Planning

Life insurance has two key functions in estate planning. The first is to provide income for family members. An elderly parent may have a spouse or a dependent child who will need income after the parent's death. Life insurance can provide that income.

The second function of life insurance is to ensure adequate liquidity for estate needs. These liquidity needs include sufficient cash for the payment of federal and state death taxes (generally due 9 months after the date of death), funeral expenses (generally due immediately), debts, and probate and administration costs. Life insurance is protection for an estate's nonliquid assets. Without insurance, it may become necessary to sell off these assets. Such forced sales may yield only "fire sale" recoveries.

Types of Life Insurance

There are several types of life insurance, but they all have one thing in common: they pay a cash amount upon the death of the insured.

Whole Life

Whole life is often referred to as "permanent" life insurance because the owner is paying a fixed amount that does not change for the life of the policy. It may be possible to pay up a policy by making payments for a set number of years (e.g., 8 or 10 years). Whole life offers not only a death benefit but an investment opportunity. Depending on how well the insurance company can invest the premiums, it may be possible to receive an additional payout, besides the promised death benefit (the face amount of the policy), upon the death of the insured. A whole life policy builds up a cash value over the years. It may be possible to borrow against this cash value. Any loans outstanding at death are netted against the proceeds paid to the beneficiaries.

Universal Life

Universal life is a variation on the whole life theme. It is another form of permanent insurance. Unlike whole life, however, the premiums after the first year can vary at the policyowner's option. If premiums are not sufficient to continue the face value of the policy, then a reduced death benefit will result.

Term Insurance

Term insurance generally is the least expensive form of providing death benefits. However, as the insured ages, the cost escalates substantially and may become prohibitive. Term insurance cannot be bought past a certain age, and it has no cash surrender value.

Joint or Survivor Life Insurance

The newest form of life insurance being marketed is joint or survivor life insurance, or "second-to-die insurance." Under this policy, the lives of two people are insured. The policy pays nothing upon the death of the first insured to die; the policy pays off in full upon the death of the second insured. Due to actuarial assumptions, this form of insurance is less expensive than insuring two lives. It is especially attractive for certain people—for example, couples who have substantial nonliquid assets that they wish to be kept intact for the next generations (e.g., family businesses, art collections, real estate). Using the marital deduction (discussed below) avoids estate tax on the estate of the first spouse to die. Second-to-die insurance guarantees that there will be sufficient cash to pay the taxes for the estate of the second spouse to die.

Tax Consequences of Life Insurance

Life insurance enjoys special tax treatment under the federal tax laws. Upon the death of the insured, it may be possible to receive proceeds completely free from income tax and estate tax.

Income Tax

Proceeds paid to a beneficiary upon the death of the insured are not subject to income taxes. There is no limit on the size of this tax exclusion.

Some parents may have bought policies years ago. It may be desirable to upgrade these policies or to change to companies that are more fiscally reliable. Policies can be exchanged for other life insurance policies without any immediate income tax. Under a so-called "Section 1035 exchange," policies of equal value can be swapped without current taxation. The IRS has even acknowledged that, where the old policy has a loan outstanding, it is not necessary to pay off that loan before swapping. As long as the new policy has a similar loan feature, the exchange is treated as tax-free.

Estate Tax

Proceeds of a life insurance policy are included in an estate if the decedent owned the policy or had the proceeds payable to the estate. In all other cases, the proceeds are not included in the insured's estate and are not subject to estate taxes. Ownership, for federal estate tax purposes, has a special meaning. It encompasses a number of powers over the policy, such as the right to change beneficiaries, borrow against the cash value in the policy, or cancel the policy.

Transfers of Life Insurance for Estate Tax Savings

If your elderly parent owns a policy on his or her life, it may be possible to transfer that policy in order to save estate taxes. The policy can be transferred directly to another person as a gift. Alternatively, the policy can be transferred to a trust set up specifically for this purpose or to an existing trust. Once the policy is transferred, the proceeds are not included in the parent's estate *if* the parent outlives the transfer by at least 3 years.

WEALTH BUILDING PROFILE   *Transferring Life Insurance for Estate Tax Savings.* No one can be sure that he or she will outlive a transfer by more than 3 years, but there is nothing to lose by attempting it. For example, Paul, an elderly parent, gives a paid-up life insurance policy to his child, Jennifer. Paul dies 2 years after the transfer. The proceeds are included in Paul's estate for federal estate tax purposes—the same result as if no transfer had been made. If Paul had lived 3 years beyond the date of transfer, then the policy would have been successfully removed from his estate.

There may be gift tax consequences to a transfer. Before attempting one, it is advisable to discuss your plan with an estate planner or other tax adviser.

Death Proceeds During Life

A few major insurance companies are now offering a new option on life insurance contracts: the opportunity to tap death benefits if death is imminent or there is a medical catastrophe. This option is referred to as an accelerated death benefit (ADB). As much as 80 percent of the face amount of the policy may be payable, if a doctor certifies that the insured is terminally ill and has less than 1 year to live. One company pays out on a monthly basis to policyholders in nursing homes. Each month, up to 2 percent of the face value of the policy can be tapped, up to the set maximum. Some companies, acting as factors, may agree to buy policies for as much as 75 percent of face value, if the insured is terminally ill.

There is one compelling reason to take advantage of this option: immediate cash. However, there are many more reasons for not doing so.

Perhaps the most important good reason for declining this option is the reason the insurance was taken out in the first place: protection of heirs. If the proceeds are used by the insured during life, they are not available at death to benefit heirs or to pay estate taxes and administrative costs.

Another reason for turning down the option is the danger of jeopardizing Medicaid eligibility. If a parent is in such great need of funds that it becomes necessary to tap life insurance proceeds, then it can be assumed that the parent may be in financial straits and may be eligible for Medicaid to cover medical expenses. If the insurance funds become accessible, they may be counted as an asset for Medicaid purposes. Because this policy option is very new, there is no published statement or example case on precisely how Medicaid will treat it. One major insurance company offering an ADB has assured policyholders that the Health Care Financing Administration and the Social Security Administration will not treat this option as an available asset and a New York law adopts this approach. However, the position of some other states is not clear, and it would be foolish for someone to have this option if the benefit would only inure to the state.

———————→ **ACTION ITEM** ←———————
Before opting for an ADB, be sure to check the status of it under state law. The concept of an ADB option is recognized in 46 states and prohibited in others. Some states have yet to specify the status of the ADB option.

Exercising the option can bring adverse tax consequences. Proceeds payable on the death of the insured are not subject to income tax. However, this exclusion does not apply to proceeds payable for other reasons. The IRS has yet to rule on the tax consequences to ADBs. It is arguable that the proceeds are tax-free accident and health benefits, but there is no precedent for this position. Where policies are sold to factors, the sale is fully taxable to the policyowner.

Other sources of funds that do not have adverse consequences may be available. Loans or gifts from family members may be used to meet immediate cash needs, in lieu of tapping life insurance proceeds.

JOINT OWNERSHIP

Joint ownership means having title to property in more than one name. There are three types of joint ownership: tenancy in common, joint tenants with rights of survivorship, and tenants by the entirety.

In a tenancy in common, each tenant owns an interest in the whole property in a manner similar to that of partners who own an interest in a partnership. That interest can be passed on to heirs and does not pass automatically to other cotenants.

In the case of joint tenants with rights of survivorship, each tenant also owns an interest in the whole property. However, upon the death of a joint tenant, that interest passes automatically to the remaining joint tenant.

Tenants by the entirety is the same as joint tenants with rights of survivorship except that the only joint tenants are a husband and wife. When estate planners refer to joint ownership, they typically mean joint tenants with rights of survivorship (or tenants by the entirety).

The advantages and disadvantages of joint ownership from an income-planning perspective were discussed in Chapter 7. Here, joint ownership is discussed solely with respect to estate planning. For many individuals, the sum total of their estate planning is putting everything in joint name. There is nothing less advisable. Joint ownership will avoid probate and will ensure that property passes automatically to the intended beneficiary, but joint ownership can undermine estate plans. Joint ownership has both pluses and minuses.

Advantages of Joint Ownership

Joint ownership is easy to arrange. All that is necessary is to put property in the name of two or more individuals. For example, a parent can set up a brokerage account with a child as a joint tenant. There is no added cost for doing so. (Where separately owned property is transferred to joint name, there may be some tax and other costs. For example, the transfer of title on a deed to property may involve both attorneys' fees and state transfer taxes or recording fees. In addition, there may be gift tax consequences to consider.)

Joint ownership ensures that the property will pass to the person intended. No special document is required to accomplish this end.

WEALTH BUILDING PROFILE   *Using Joint Ownership to Pass Property to a Particular Individual.* Katherine, a parent, has two children. One child lives nearby and sees to Katherine's needs on a regular basis. The other child, equally loved, lives across the country and does not contribute in any tangible way to Katherine's well-being. Katherine may want to favor the nearby child with property upon her demise. She can put the title of her house in joint name with this child so that, upon her death, the house automatically becomes the property of the nearby child.

Joint ownership avoids probate costs. As with life insurance and property transferred by trust, jointly owned property passes by operation of law and there is no need for court intervention of any kind.

Disadvantages of Joint Ownership

Some individuals are under the impression that, because joint property passes automatically outside the probate estate, there are estate tax savings. This is not so. For federal estate tax purposes, a person's interest in jointly owned property is included in the estate. Where property is owned jointly with a spouse, half of the property is included in the estate of the first spouse to die. For property owned jointly with any other person, the *entire* value of the property is included in the estate of the first joint owner to die, *unless* the surviving tenant can prove that he or she paid for all or a share of the property. In most cases, this fact is very hard to prove.

Joint tenancy can undermine an estate plan. If individuals set up trusts under their wills or make certain bequests, there may be no assets with which to fund those trusts or make those bequests. The jointly owned property is not controlled by the will; it passes automatically outside the will.

WEALTH *Avoiding Joint Ownership to Permit the Funding*
BUILDING *of a Credit Trust.* Charles and Amy have assets of
PROFILE over $1.2 million and they want to reduce their com-
bined federal estate taxes. In his will, Charles sets up
a credit trust, designed to make maximum use of the $600,000 exemp-
tion equivalent to which each person's estate is entitled. Under the
terms of Charles's will, Amy is entitled to the income from the trust.
However, the trust does not qualify for the marital deduction; rather,
it is shielded from tax by the $600,000 exemption equivalent. Upon
Amy's death, the property passes to their children under the terms of
Charles's will; there is no additional estate tax due from Amy's estate
on this trust property. (Amy's will contains similar provisions, in case
she predeceases Charles.)

If Charles and Amy own everything in joint name, there are no
separate assets with which to fund the trust. Amy will inherit everything. Upon her death, however, that portion of property that would
have skipped her estate will now be subject to tax in her estate. The
tax cost of this error is more than $230,000 in federal estate tax!

GIFTS FOR
ESTATE-PLANNING PURPOSES

The surest way for a parent to see that property ends up in the hands
of the person he or she intends is to give away that property while still
alive. The gift is also the easiest way to reduce estate taxes at little or
no current tax cost. However, there are important psychological, tax,
and other considerations in making lifetime transfers.

Discussing Gifts with Parents

Transferring property to children and grandchildren is, for many
elderly parents, a very difficult thing to do. More than anything, it
means giving up control. Having wealth can equate with having
power in the family. Giving the wealth away saps that power. Even
people of considerable means who do not need all their wealth to
sustain them may be reluctant to part with property.

Transferring property has a measure of finality that many elderly
people are not able or willing to deal with. Giving property away is a
statement that a person has recognized his or her own mortality and

has taken steps to deal with it. This admission can be brought to bear most painfully in the case of Medicaid planning for an elderly parent. If a parent has assets over and above the resource limit for Medicaid, the parent must, in order to qualify, give away or spend the assets (see Chapter 4). Once the assets are transferred, the parent is "poor" and can never again regain those assets.

Despite these negative aspects of giving away property, it may be advantageous for a parent to do so. As already mentioned, giving away property in one's lifetime will ensure that certain persons receive the property intended for them. For example, a mother with three daughters may have jewelry that she rarely wears. The mother may want to give away special pieces to each child, to avoid having them fight over the items after her death. The mother may also enjoy seeing her children wearing her jewelry or knowing the pleasure it brings them. Gift giving may be an important part of Medicaid qualification (see Chapter 4), and it is an easy way to save on estate taxes.

Establishing the Purpose for Gift Giving

The purpose of a gift dictates its nature and extent. If a parent has only limited assets and Medicaid qualification may become necessary in the not-too-distant future, then virtually complete asset transfers may be advisable. If a parent is quite wealthy and healthy and his or her transfers are tax-motivated, then a specific gift-giving program may be useful. The wealthier parent would want to keep sufficient property to be self-supporting and independent.

Seeking the Help of Experts

It may be beneficial for a parent to discuss estate plans with an impartial outsider (such as an attorney or financial planner) and explore gift-giving objectives. This recommendation can quell a parent's suspicions that a child is acting selfishly or greedily, rather than practically.

Tax Considerations

Transferring property during life can have important tax consequences. In 1976, the estate and gift taxes were "unified" into one transfer tax system. Theoretically, whether property is transferred during one's life or after one's death, the same tax should result. Thus, each person can transfer $600,000 without any federal tax— estate or gift. As a practical matter, there are important differences between transfers during life and transfers after death.

It may be possible to give away property without *any* tax cost and even *save* on future estate taxes. Each year, an individual can give away up to $10,000 per person ($20,000, if married and the spouse joins in the gift) to as many relatives and friends as desired. There is no limit on the number of recipients for gifts.

WEALTH BUILDING PROFILE   *Using Annual Gifts to Transfer Sizable Amounts of Property Completely Tax-Free.* Frances, a widowed grandmother, has six grandchildren. She can give away $10,000 to each grandchild tax-free each year, for a total of $60,000 annually. If the process is repeated for 5 years, $300,000 will have been transferred entirely tax-free!

Income Tax

If the asset transferred is income-producing property, then the elderly parent has succeeded in shifting the income tax on that income. This is helpful if the recipient is in a lower tax bracket than the donor. For example, if a wealthy grandparent has a teenage grandchild (over 13) who has no income, the transfer of income-producing property to the teenager can mean that the income will be taxed in a lower tax bracket.

WEALTH BUILDING PROFILE   *Keeping Appreciated Property Until Death Provides Income Tax Advantage to Heirs.* Arthur, an elderly parent, owns a piece of real estate for which he paid $30,000 in 1955; it is worth $250,000 in 1992. If Arthur gives the property to his child, and the child sells the property for $250,000, the child will have a gain of $220,000 ($250,000 sale proceeds less $30,000 tax basis) for income tax purposes. The federal income tax cost to Arthur's child is over $60,000!

If Arthur holds on to the property and the child inherits it, the child's basis in the property becomes $250,000. Should the child sell the property for $250,000, there is no gain for tax purposes ($250,000 sale proceeds less $250,000) and, therefore, no income tax is charged to the child.

Although giving property away may save income and transfer taxes for an elderly parent, it may result in higher income taxes for the recipients. Special tax basis rules apply for property received by way of gift versus property received by way of inheritance.

For gift property, the recipient (donee) generally steps into the shoes of the transferor (donor). Thus, when the donee eventually sells the property, he or she will ultimately pay the income tax on the appreciation that the donor enjoyed during his or her tenure of ownership.

For property acquired by bequest, the recipient gets a "stepped-up basis": the property is valued as of the date of death (or, in some cases, an alternate valuation date that is generally 6 months after the date of death). All of the appreciation during the owner's lifetime is effectively wiped out; the heir starts clean. Thus, an heir can sell inherited property shortly after receiving it, with little or no income tax consequences. The amount of this income tax difference can be very significant.

Estate Planning by Fiduciaries

An individual may begin a gift-giving program but become incompetent before completing it. Even after a parent is no longer legally competent to act, it may be possible for an agent to act on behalf of the parent under certain circumstances.

Where a durable power of attorney specifies this gift-making authority, there is no problem. The agent merely has to act in accordance with the terms of the durable power of attorney. Those terms may be limited: the durable power of attorney may state that gifts must be limited to the annual gift tax exclusion. It may also prohibit the agent from making gifts to himself or herself or to the agent's family. On the other hand, the gift-making authority in the durable power of attorney can be very broad, giving the agent complete discretion to make gifts of any size to any person. For example, the agent may be permitted to make gifts to himself or herself or to a spouse, children, or other relatives.

Even where the durable power of attorney does not specifically mention a gift-making power, it may be possible for an agent to make gifts. In one case in the U.S. Tax Court, gifts made by an agent under a durable power of attorney were recognized for tax purposes. The document did not refer to gift making, but the principal had a history of gift making. The agent based his actions on two points: the agent was merely continuing the principal's prior activities, and the agent interpreted the power to "convey any property" as broadly as possible. He concluded that he had the power to make gifts. In this case, state law (New Jersey) did not prohibit gifts that lacked express authority. The authority to make gifts rests on the doctrine of "substituted judgment." This doctrine will be recognized where the incompetent person has sufficient assets for support and maintenance. Present needs and future projections of those needs are taken into account. This doctrine is also based on the likelihood that the incompetent would have made the gifts if he or she had been well enough to do so. A prior history of gift giving is very helpful in this situation.

Even without express authority (a specific power in a durable power of attorney) or implied authority (a broad interpretation of a general power to convey property under a durable power of attorney), it may be possible for a fiduciary to make gifts on behalf of a person who can no longer do so. A court may be willing to sanction gift giving where the purpose of those transfers is in the interest of the incompetent person. For example, a New York court allowed the guardians of an incompetent to make gifts to siblings up to the annual gift tax exclusion. The court in this case did not rely on the doctrine of substituted judgment. Instead, it asked a subjective question: what would a reasonable and prudent person do in the same circumstances? Where the gifts serve tax-saving goals for the estate without resulting in current tax or a diminution of the incompetent's standard of living or future well-being, then the gifts may be sanctioned. Where court approval is required, it may be costly to pursue the issue. Planning for gift-making power is a better course.

In providing for gift-giving authority, you should take into account family problems that can arise if a parent has more than one child but only one is named as agent under a power of attorney.

──────────────→ **ACTION ITEM** ←──────────────

To avoid family discord, it may be advisable to name all children as agents under a power of attorney for purposes of exercising the gift-giving power, even though other powers can be exercised by only one child. Alternatively, the power itself can require that, if gifts are made to the agent or agent's children, then equal gifts must be made to the principal's other children who are not named as agent.

There is a potential pitfall to granting broad (unlimited) gift-giving authority. The IRS may look on the ability of the agent to acquire all of the principal's property as a "power of appointment." If the child should die before the parent, the child's estate could be taxed on all of the parent's property. Where there is a view toward asset transfers for Medicaid eligibility, there is a need for broad gift-giving authority. The odds do not favor the child's predeceasing the parent.

Deathbed Gifts

It may be possible for a dying parent to achieve tax savings (to the extent assets are removed from a parent's estate under the umbrella of the annual exclusion) while ensuring that property passes to intended heirs. Gifts made while a person is near death are sometimes referred to as deathbed gifts.

It is important to know that, if a dying parent makes a gift by check, the gift is valid only if the check is cashed before the parent dies. There have been many cases in which estates have argued that deathbed gifts by check, which were not in fact cashed before death, should still be recognized for estate tax purposes. The U.S. Tax Court and a number of other courts have not agreed with this position. However, one court in New Jersey allowed gifts to stand, even though the checks were not cashed until after death. That court recognized that the ability to stop payment on checks ends with death.

DEATH TAXES

Under federal tax law, an estate tax return Form 706 must be filed if the value of the property in which a decedent had an interest at the time of death exceeds $600,000. The federal estate tax rates run effectively from 37 percent to 55 percent for estates subject to tax. (The top rate is scheduled to drop to 50 percent after 1992.) Each estate is entitled to a unified credit of $192,800, which operates to exempt $600,000.

When this exemption equivalent was enacted in 1981 and phased in over several years, it was estimated that fully 97 percent of Americans would be completely free from estate tax. The lawmakers failed to take into account the impact of inflation. The $600,000 figure is not as large as it seemed in 1981. Now, many more individuals than had been expected will have their estates subject to federal estate tax.

In its instructions for tax filing, the IRS publishes the tables that are the basis for calculating estate and gift taxes. These tables are reproduced here for easy reference. (See Figures 10-1 through 10-4.)

Column A	Column B	Column C	Column D
Taxable amount over	Taxable amount not over	Tax on amount in column A	Rate of tax on excess over amount in column A
			(Percent)
0	$10,000	0	18
$10,000	20,000	$1,800	20
20,000	40,000	3,800	22
40,000	60,000	8,200	24
60,000	80,000	13,000	26
80,000	100,000	18,200	28
100,000	150,000	23,800	30
150,000	250,000	38,800	32
250,000	500,000	70,800	34
500,000	750,000	155,800	37
750,000	1,000,000	248,300	39
1,000,000	1,250,000	345,800	41
1,250,000	1,500,000	448,300	43
1,500,000	2,000,000	555,800	45
2,000,000	2,500,000	780,800	49
2,500,000	3,000,000	1,025,800	53
3,000,000	--------	1,290,800	55

Figure 10-1
Unified Rate Schedule

Even if an estate's assets are valued at less than $600,000, state death taxes may have to be paid. Each state has its own rules. Some taxes have high tax liabilities; other have low or no death taxes. Some states impose estate taxes that are similar to the federal scheme; that is, the tax is imposed on the estate itself. Other states impose a credit tax or "pick-up tax," which is a variation on the federal estate tax. The amount that is allowed as a credit against the federal income tax is shown in Table B in the IRS instructions section. Some states impose inheritance taxes on the shares paid to beneficiaries. The amount of taxes varies with the class to which the beneficiaries belong. For example, children pay less tax than more distant relatives do, on the same amount of inheritance.

For decedents dying— The credit is—

1987 and later 192,800

Figure 10-2
Maximum Unified Credit Against Estate Tax

1   Federal taxable estate (from Tax Computation,
    Form 706, line 3) $_____

2   Adjustment   ___60,000_____

3   Federal adjusted taxable estate. Subtract line 2
    from line 1. Use this amount to compute
    maximum credit for state death taxes in Table C.   _____

———————————————————— **Figure 10-3** ————————————————————
Federal Adjusted Taxable Estate

Adjusted taxable estate equal to or more than—	Adjusted taxable estate less than—	Credit on amount in column (1)	Rate of credit on excess over amount in column (1)
(1)	(2)	(3)	(4)
			(Percent)
0	$40,000	0	None
$40,000	90,000	0	0.8
90,000	140,000	$400	1.6
140,000	240,000	1,200	2.4
240,000	440,000	3,600	3.2
440,000	640,000	10,000	4.0
640,000	840,000	18,000	4.8
840,000	1,040,000	27,600	5.6
1,040,000	1,540,000	38,800	6.4
1,540,000	2,040,000	70,800	7.2

Adjusted taxable estate equal to or more than—	Adjusted taxable estate less than—	Credit on amount in column (1)	Rate of credit on excess over amount in column (1)
(1)	(2)	(3)	(4)
			(Percent)
2,040,000	2,540,000	106,800	8.0
2,540,000	3,040,000	146,800	8.8
3,040,000	3,540,000	190,800	9.6
3,540,000	4,040,000	238,800	10.4
4,040,000	5,040,000	290,800	11.2
5,040,000	6,040,000	402,800	12.0
6,040,000	7,040,000	522,800	12.8
7,040,000	8,040,000	650,800	13.6
8,040,000	9,040,000	786,800	14.4
9,040,000	10,040,000	930,800	15.2
10,040,000	--------	1,082,800	16.0

———————————————————— **Figure 10-4** ————————————————————
Computation of Maximum Credit for State
Death Taxes (Based on Federal Adjusted Taxable Estate)

Tax-Saving Strategies

There are several ways to reduce the federal estate tax obligation. First and foremost, everyone is allowed to pass along up to $600,000 completely tax-free. This $600,000 is referred to as an exemption equivalent because it is the amount that is free of tax after applying a unified credit. This unified credit is $192,800.

→ **ACTION ITEM** ←

It is important to keep in mind that there is only *one* opportunity to transfer $600,000 completely tax-free. If that opportunity is used during life (taxable gifts of $600,000 or more have been made), then it cannot be used again to protect assets transferred upon death.

In addition to the $600,000 exemption amount, there are certain other transfers that can help to reduce taxes.

Marital Deduction

Transfers to a surviving spouse can qualify for a marital deduction. The transfers must be in a form designed to ensure that the property will be subject to estate tax when the surviving spouse dies. There is no dollar limit on the size of this deduction. Still, outright transfers to a surviving spouse can needlessly burden the estate of this surviving spouse.

Special rules apply where a spouse is not a U.S. citizen. Unless the transfer is made via a *qualified domestic trust, no* marital deduction is allowed.

It can be helpful to discuss marital deduction planning with an attorney, to ensure that the transfers will qualify for the deduction and that the estate of the surviving spouse is adequately planned for.

Charitable Deduction

A deduction is also allowed for charitable contributions. Unlike income taxes, there is no limitation on the size of the transfer qualifying for the deduction. If a parent wants, he or she can give away *all* property to charity and there will be no federal estate tax. For families of modest means, this may seem an outrageous and unfair thing to do—disinheriting children and grandchildren. However, in wealthier families, where children already have sizable fortunes of their own, there may be little point in passing additional wealth to the children; having charities as heirs may be a wise alternative.

Gift Giving

As discussed earlier, the only other effective way to transfer wealth with estate tax savings is through gifts. It is important to realize that, even where gifts result in transfer tax costs, they may still be advisable.

WEALTH BUILDING PROFILE *Weighing Current Gift Tax Costs Against Future Estate Tax Costs.* Paul, a wealthy parent, owns a famous painting. If he transfers the work now, it is calculated that it will cost him $25,000 in gift taxes. However, if he retains it until his death, the painting can be expected to appreciate in value and it may cost his estate well more than $25,000. In this instance, Paul may choose to pay the current gift tax as a way of saving his estate the added transfer tax cost.

———— POINTS TO REMEMBER ————

▶ A person without a will dies intestate. State law determines who will inherit the property of the estate.

▶ The gross estate is a tax term meaning all the property that a person had an interest in. The probate estate includes property passing under a will or, in the case of someone intestate, by direction of state law.

▶ A will requires an executor (or personal representative); this person is responsible for handling the terms of the will.

▶ Wills usually require witnesses to the signing; states vary as to how many witnesses are required.

▶ A codicil is a change to a will.

▶ Using life insurance policies to transfer assets directly to heirs can potentially avoid gift or death taxes.

11

Personal Recordkeeping

No doubt about it: recordkeeping is a tedious task. Yet, after a parent becomes incompetent or dies, the records left behind are the only means for you or other relatives to properly handle your parent's affairs.

Good recordkeeping not only saves those concerned a great deal of time and trouble, but it can also translate into dollar savings. It avoids the need for costly intervention by accountants and attorneys who must research information and documents or reconstruct financial data. Having organized and up-to-date records can speed up the application process for Medicaid or collection on insurance policies.

Recordkeeping is not a mindless task; it serves a vital function. It allows an elderly parent or a parent's relative to produce and prove certain information that may be required for various purposes. It is important to know:

▶ What records should be saved;
▶ How long these records should be saved;
▶ Where these records should be stored.

This chapter provides a personal recordkeeper form for collecting all the information necessary to permit family or friends to handle the property of an elderly parent in the event of incompetence or death. Completion of the form may be a chore for many individuals, but the importance of doing it as early as possible and updating it frequently cannot be underscored enough.

WHAT RECORDS SHOULD
BE SAVED

Each day, you are inundated with paper. Some arrivals are worth saving, others are not. How do you know the difference? Different forms are required or helpful for different purposes. Let's consider some of those purposes.

Medicaid Eligibility

The state agency that determines Medicaid eligibility looks at a number of personal and financial records. Financial records dating back 30 months are scrutinized. Other personal data are also required. The following is a list of the records requested for a Medicaid application in New York:

▶ Social security card;

▶ Medicare card;

▶ Private health insurance information (I.D. cards; current paid bill);

▶ Social security check (copy of face and endorsement) or benefits letter from local social security office;

▶ Pension information (payor and amounts);

▶ Benefits from unions (payor and amounts);

▶ Proof of age (birth certificate or other proof);

▶ Citizenship papers, if naturalized citizen;

▶ Alien registration number, if a noncitizen;

▶ Information on marital status (marriage certificate; death certificate of spouse);

▶ Veteran identification information (including discharge papers);

▶ Proof of residence (rent or utility company receipt; co-op or condominium maintenance receipt);

▶ Proof of burial plot;

▶ Bank account (checking and savings) statements for the past 30 months (both current and closed accounts);

▶ Other resources (cash value of life insurance; real estate; business interests; stocks and bonds);

▶ Bills or canceled checks for large expenses.

In furnishing this information, photocopies are acceptable. There is no need to provide originals of any documents or statements.

Probate

To complete probate forms and estate tax returns, various information or documentation is required. Some items duplicate those listed above; others are additional. For example, to complete the estate tax return, it is necessary to ascertain the value of all property owned on the date of death (or other applicable valuation date). To do so, you must know exactly what property your parent owned. For this determination, reference can be made to brokerage account statements, bank books, and a physical inventory of personal furnishings, jewelry, and collectibles.

Additional documents (beyond Medicaid's requirements) necessary for probate and estate return preparation include:

▶ Last will and testament;
▶ Codicils to the will;
▶ Trusts in which your parent had any interest.

For you to proceed with the probate process after your parent dies, you will need a death certificate, a receipt for funeral expenses, and bills for the cost of the final illness.

You may also need to know the name, address, and citizenship status of all your parent's relatives who outlived your parent including a spouse, children (both from marriages and from other relationships), parents, sisters and brothers, and, in some cases, even more distant relatives.

Tax Purposes

Tax Returns

There is no law mandating retention of old tax returns. However, they can serve as helpful reminders when preparing new returns or in circumstances where old returns should be amended. Old returns are essential in case of an IRS audit. The burden of proving most items falls to the taxpayer, when the IRS challenges tax positions claimed on a return.

If an old return cannot be located, a copy of it can be obtained by filing Form 4506 with the IRS Service Center in which the lost return was filed. There is a charge of $4.25 per return (e.g., $8.50 if the request relates to 2 tax years). Generally, the IRS will not provide returns older than 6 years.

Records and Receipts

Records are required as backup for certain deductions, in case a return is audited. For example, it is important to keep bills and canceled checks for medical expenses, to show the amount of the expense and the date of payment. A log of the cost of transportation to and from doctors (mileage, parking, and tolls; or taxi or bus fare) is also required if the cost of medical travel is deducted. Statements, notes, and canceled checks are acceptable as proof of interest payments on a mortgage or investment loan. Special recordkeeping is required for charitable contributions.

Records (receipts, canceled checks, Form 1099s, and so on) supporting income and deductions generally should be retained for 3 years from the date the return was filed (or, if later, 2 years from the date the tax was paid). These records will serve as proof in case of an audit of a tax return. In certain circumstances, the IRS can audit a return older than 3 years. It can go back 6 years if more than 25 percent of the income shown on the return was omitted from taxation. There is no time limit on audits of false or fraudulent returns.

Some records and receipts should be maintained for longer periods. Records are required for proving when and how an asset was acquired as well as when and how it was sold. Often, these records include brokerage statements showing when stocks, bonds, and other securities were bought or sold. These records must be kept for as long as these assets are held plus an additional period for audit purposes, as discussed above.

If your parent owns a home, it is advisable to keep records that show any capital improvements to the home (e.g., receipts for the cost of constructing a new room, installing a new roof, or landscaping). If your parent owned a previous home on which tax on the gain was deferred, then records for the previous home must also be retained. As in the case of securities records, house-related records should be retained for as long as the home is owned, plus the additional audit period.

For further information on tax recordkeeping, see IRS Publication 552, "Recordkeeping for Individuals," which can be obtained free of charge by calling 1-800/829-3676 or writing to the IRS Forms Distribution Center nearest you.

STORING RECORDS
AND PAPERS

Some records are irreplaceable, others are not. Where you store your records and papers depends in part on whether they can be replaced or duplicated if lost, damaged, or stolen. Here is a partial listing of where it is advisable to keep important records and papers:

▶ Wills, trust and other legal documents cannot be replaced or duplicated. Therefore, it is advisable to store them in a fireproof safe. Some individuals keep such documents in safety deposit boxes. This may not be the best location. In some states, safety deposit boxes are sealed when the box owner dies, and it may take a court order to open the box. This can result in expense and delay in the probate process. Some individuals prefer to leave legal documents with the attorneys who prepared them. This is certainly one viable alternative for safekeeping these documents.

▶ Medical directives (living wills, health care proxies), like wills and trusts, cannot be replaced. Once a person is incompetent to execute a new one, the loss of an original may be quite a problem. Some states permit photocopies to be used. It is advisable for your parent to keep the original in a safe place. This place should be accessible to you, in the event it becomes necessary to produce the medical directive. Photocopies should be given to your parent's doctors as well as to close relatives.

▶ Deeds are important legal documents. However, because deeds are officially recorded in the locality of the property, the loss of a deed is not fatal to a property transfer. It is helpful to keep a deed safe and yet accessible.

▶ Personal papers (birth certificates, adoption papers, marriage license, divorce decree, citizenship papers, death certificates) can be replaced. State record departments maintain records on births, deaths, and marriages. Divorce decrees are on file with the court in which the order was entered. Although these records can be replaced, it may be burdensome to do so. These documents should be kept in a safe place.

▶ Receipts for tax purposes should be kept available. The burden of proving entitlement to any tax deductions or credits rests entirely with the taxpayer. Therefore, if a taxpayer is unable to substantiate certain expenses, the IRS can disallow them. There have been cases in which receipts were destroyed in a fire and a court allowed deductions nonetheless. However, it is smart to keep receipts safe for as long as necessary.

▸ Income tax returns, as mentioned earlier in this chapter, can be obtained in duplicate from the IRS for a fee. To avoid the need to send for old tax returns, keep your returns (for the past 6 years, at a minimum) in a safe place.

?

Are photocopies acceptable for most estate documents?

Yes, with the exceptions of wills, codicils, and other signed and witnessed documents.

What important records can be obtained from state files, and which cannot?

Among the records that can readily be obtained from the state are birth and death certificates, marriage licenses, citizenship papers, and deeds. Wills, trusts, and other legal documents cannot be duplicated or recovered from state files, and thus must be kept in a safe place.

POINTS TO REMEMBER

▸ Keeping records of important life data is vital for obtaining Medicaid and other benefits.

▸ Documents supporting federal tax returns must be kept for up to 3 years, at a minimum.

▸ Records on home improvements should be kept for as long as the home is owned, and for at least 3 years thereafter; these records help reduce capital gains taxes when a house is sold or transferred.

▸ Irreplaceable documents, such as wills or trusts, should be kept in a safe place, but not necessarily a safety deposit box. In some states, these boxes are sealed until a probate court becomes involved.

▸ Use the personal recordkeeper worksheets to help organize recordkeeping for your parent.

PERSONAL RECORDKEEPER

PERSONAL DATA

Parent: _____ Spouse: _____

Date of birth: _____ _____

Social security number: _____ _____

Address: _____

_____

_____

Phone: ____/____-____

County of residence: _____

Employer: _____ _____

_____ _____

_____ _____

Date of retirement: ___/___/___ ___/___/___

Veteran: Yes _____ No _____ Yes _____ No _____

FAMILY

Date of marriage: ___/___/___

Children:
(full legal names)   Address: Grandchildren:

_____   _____   _____

_____   _____   _____

_____   _____   _____

_____   _____   _____

_____   _____   _____

_____   _____   _____

_____   _____   _____

Any children by a previous marriage? _____

Any children who have died leaving children? _____

MEDICAL/DISABILITY

	Parent	Spouse
Doctor:	_____	_____
Phone:	_____	_____
Doctor:	_____	_____
Phone:	_____	_____
Doctor:	_____	_____
Phone:	_____	_____
Dentist:	_____	_____
Phone:	_____	_____
Current medications:	_____	_____
	_____	_____

Health Insurance

	Parent		Spouse	
	Co. Name	Policy No.	Co. Name	Policy No.
Medicare	_____	_____	_____	_____
Insurance from employer	_____	_____	_____	_____
Medigap insurance	_____	_____	_____	_____
Long-term care policy	_____	_____	_____	_____
Other	_____	_____	_____	_____

Health Care Decision Makers

	Parent	Spouse
Health care proxy	_____	_____
Phone:	_____	_____
Religious adviser	_____	_____
Phone:	_____	_____
Living will	_____	_____

FINANCIAL

Income-Producing Assets

Description/Location of Property*	Value	Account No.	Owner
_____	_____	_____	____
_____	_____	_____	____
_____	_____	_____	____
_____	_____	_____	____

* Bank accounts, CDs, brokerage accounts, stocks, bonds

Monthly Income

	Parent	Spouse
Social security	_____	_____
Pension	_____	_____
IRAs, annuities	_____	_____
Rents	_____	_____
Interest and dividends	_____	_____
Other	_____	_____
TOTALS:	_____	_____

Do any sources of income have a benefit for a surviving spouse?

____ Yes   ____ No

Real Estate

Description of Property	Value	Mortgage	Cost	Owner
_____	_____	_____	____	____
_____	_____	_____	____	____
_____	_____	_____	____	____

Any interest in a business (other than publicly traded stock listed above)? _____

Life Insurance

Insured	Company	Face Value	Policy No.	Premium	Beneficiary
———	———	———	———	———	———
———	———	———	———	———	———
———	———	———	———	———	———
———	———	———	———	———	———
———	———	———	———	———	———

Does your parent own any policy on his or her own life?

——— Yes ——— No

_____

_____

Retirement Benefits

Description	Value	Designated Beneficiary
———	———	———
———	———	———
———	———	———
———	———	———
———	———	———
———	———	———

Liabilities

Description*	Balance Due	Monthly Payment	Maturity Date
———	———	———	———
———	———	———	———
———	———	———	———
———	———	———	———

* Mortgages, notes to banks, loans on insurance, other

Personal Property

Description*	Value	In Whose Name?
_____	_____	_____
_____	_____	_____
_____	_____	_____
_____	_____	_____
_____	_____	_____
_____	_____	_____
_____	_____	_____

* Cars, boats, antiques, jewelry, collectibles, other

Financial Advisers

	Parent	Spouse
Broker:	_____	_____
Phone:	_____	_____
Broker:	_____	_____
Phone:	_____	_____
Insurance agent:	_____	_____
Phone:	_____	_____
Accountant:	_____	_____
Phone:	_____	_____

Location of Important Papers and Other Items

Tax returns: _____

Bank books: _____

Financial statements: _____

Safety deposit box:

  Keys located _____

  Box number _____

  Located at _____

LEGAL

	Parent	Spouse
Last will and testament:		
Date made	_____	_____
Location	_____	_____
Durable power of attorney:		
Date made	_____	_____
Agent	_____	_____
Agent's phone	_____	_____
Location	_____	_____
Living will:		
Date made	_____	_____
Location	_____	_____
Health care proxy:		
Date made	_____	_____
Proxy	_____	_____
Proxy's phone	_____	_____
Location	_____	_____
Living trust:		
Date made	_____	_____
Trustee	_____	_____
Trustee's phone	_____	_____
Location	_____	_____

Any pending lawsuits? _____

_____

Acting as executor, trustee, or guardian for any estate, trust, or
person? _____

Ever lived in a community property state (Arizona, California, Idaho,
Louisiana, Nevada, New Mexico, Texas, Washington, or Wisconsin)?

_____

Directory of State and Private Resources for the Elderly

GENERAL INFORMATION ON AGING

American Association of Retired
   Persons (AARP)
1909 K Street, N.W.
Washington, DC 20049
202/872-4700

Administration on Aging
200 Independence Avenue, S.W.
Washington, DC 20201
202/245-0742

National Council on the Aging
600 Maryland Avenue, S.W.
Washington, DC 20024
202/479-1200

STATE AGENCIES ON AGING

ALABAMA
   Commission on Aging
   136 Catoma Street
   Montgomery, AL 36130
   1-800/243-5463 (within state)
   205/242-5743

ALASKA
   Older Alaskans Commission
   P.O. Box C, MS 0209
   Juneau, AK 99811
   907/465-3250

ARIZONA
   Department of Economic Security
   Aging and Adult Administration
   1400 W. Washington Street
   Phoenix, AZ 85007
   602/542-4446

ARKANSAS
   Division of Aging and Adult Serv.
   Donaghey Plaza South, Suite 1417
   7th and Main Streets
   P.O. Box 1417, Slot 1412
   Little Rock, AR 72203-1437
   501/682-2441

CALIFORNIA
   Department of Aging
   1600 K Street
   Sacramento, CA 95814
   916/322-3887

COLORADO
   Aging and Adult Services
   Department of Social Securities
   1575 Sherman Street, 10th Floor
   Denver, CO 80203-1714
   303/866-3851

STATE AGENCIES ON AGING *(Continued)*

CONNECTICUT
Department on Aging
175 Main Street
Hartford, CT 06106
1-800/443-9946 (within state)
203/566-7772

DELAWARE
Division of Aging
Department of Health and Social
  Services
1901 North DuPont Highway
New Castle, DE 19720
302/566-7772

DISTRICT OF COLUMBIA
Office on Aging
Executive Office of the Mayor
1424 K Street, N.W.
Washington, DC 20005
202/724-5626
202/724-5622

FLORIDA
Office of Aging and Adult
  Services
1317 Winewood Boulevard
Tallahassee, FL 32301
904/488-8922

GEORGIA
Office of Aging
Department of Human Resources
878 Peachtree Street, NC
Room 632
Atlanta, GA 30309
404/894-5333

HAWAII
Executive Office on Aging
335 Merchant Street
Room 241
Honolulu, HI 96813
808/548-2593

IDAHO
Office on Aging
Statehouse, Room 114
Boise, ID 83720
208/334-3833

ILLINOIS
Department on Aging
421 E. Capitol Avenue
Springfield, IL 62701
217/785-2870

INDIANA
Department of Human Services
251 North Illinois
P.O. Box 7083
Indianapolis, IN 46207-7083
317/232-7020

IOWA
Department of Elder Affairs
Suite 236, Jewett Building
914 Grand Avenue
Des Moines, IA 50319
515/281-5187

KANSAS
Department on Aging
122-S, Docking State Office
  Building
915 Southwest Harrison
Topeka, KS 66612-1500
913/296-4986

KENTUCKY
Division for Aging Services
Department of Social Services
275 East Main Street
Frankfort, KY 40621
502/564-6930

LOUISIANA
Governor's Office of Elderly
  Affairs
P.O. Box 80374
Baton Rouge, LA 70898-0374
504/925-1700

MAINE
Maine Committee on Aging
State House, Station 127
Augusta, ME 04333
207/289-3658

MARYLAND
State Agency on Aging
301 West Preston Street
Baltimore, MD 21201
301/225-1102

STATE AGENCIES ON AGING *(Continued)*

MASSACHUSETTS
Executive Office of Elder Affairs
38 Chauncy Street
Boston, MA 02111
1-800/882-2003 (within state)
617/727-7750

MICHIGAN
Office of Services to the Aging
P.O. Box 30026
Lansing, MI 48909
517/373-8230

MINNESOTA
Minnesota Board on Aging
Human Services Building,
  4th Floor
444 Lafayette Road
St. Paul, MN 55155-3843
612/296-2770

MISSISSIPPI
Council on Aging
301 W. Pearl Street
Jackson, MS 39203-3092
1-800/222-7622
601/949-2070

MISSOURI
Division of Insurance
Truman Building 630
P.O. Box 690
Jefferson, MO 65102-0690
1-800/235-5503 (within state)

MONTANA
Department of Family Services
P.O. Box 8005
Helena, MT 59604
406/444-5900

NEBRASKA
Department on Aging
Legal Services Developer
State Office Building
301 Centennial Mall South
Lincoln, NE 68509
402/471-2306

NEVADA
Department of Human Resources
Division of Aging Services
505 East King Street, Room 101
Carson City, NV 89710
702/885-4210

NEW HAMPSHIRE
Department of Health and
  Human Services
Division of Elderly and Adult
  Services
6 Hazen Drive
Concord, NH 03301
603/271-4394

NEW JERSEY
Department of Community
  Affairs
Division on Aging
South Broad and Front Streets
CN 807
Trenton, NJ 08625-0807
609/292-0920

NEW MEXICO
Agency on Aging
La Villa Rivera Building, 4th
  Floor
224 East Palace Avenue
Santa Fe, NM 87501
1-800/432-2080 (within state)
505/827-7640

NEW YORK
State Office for the Aging
Agency Building
2 Empire State Plaza
Albany, NY 11223-0001
1-800/342-9871 (within state)
518/474-5731

NORTH CAROLINA
Department of Human Resources
Division of Aging
693 Palmer Drive
Caller Box 29531
Raleigh, NC 27626-0531
919/733-3983

STATE AGENCIES ON AGING *(Continued)*

NORTH DAKOTA
  Department of Human Services
  Aging Services Division
  State Capitol Building
  Bismarck, ND 58505
  701/224-2577

OHIO
  Department of Aging
  50 West Broad Street, 8th Floor
  Columbus, OH 43266-0501
  614/466-1221

OKLAHOMA
  Department of Human Services
  Aging Services Division
  P.O. Box 25352
  Oklahoma City, OK 73125
  405/521-2327

OREGON
  Department of Human Resources
  Senior Services Division
  313 Public Service Building
  Salem, OR 97310
  1-800/232-3020 (within state)
  503/378-4636

PENNSYLVANIA
  Department of Aging
  231 State Street
  Barto Building
  Harrisburg, PA 17101
  717/783-1550

RHODE ISLAND
  Department of Elderly Affairs
  160 Pine Street
  Providence, RI 02903
  401/277-2858

SOUTH CAROLINA
  Commission on Aging
  400 Arbor Lake Drive,
    Suite B-500
  Columbia, SC 20223
  803/735-0210

SOUTH DAKOTA
  Agency on Aging
  Adult Services and Aging
  Richard F. Knelp Building
  700 Governors Drive
  Pierre, SD 57501-2291
  605/773-3656

TENNESSEE
  Commission on Aging
  706 Church Street, Suite 201
  Nashville, TN 37219-5573
  615/741-2056

TEXAS
  Department on Aging
  P.O. Box 12786
  Capitol Station
  Austin, TX 78711
  512/444-2727

UTAH
  Division of Aging and Adult
    Services
  120 North 200 West
  P.O. Box 45500
  Salt Lake City, UT 84145-0500
  810/538-3910

VERMONT
  Office on Aging
  Waterbury Complex
  103 South Main Street
  Waterbury, VT 05676
  802/241-2400

VIRGINIA
  Department for the Aging
  700 Centre, 10th Floor
  700 East Franklin Street
  Richmond, VA 23219-2327
  1-800/552-4464 (within state)
  804/225-2271

WASHINGTON
  Aging and Adult Services
    Administration
  Department of Social and Health
    Services
  Mail Stop OB-44-A
  Olympia, WA 98504
  206/586-3768

STATE AGENCIES ON AGING *(Continued)*

WEST VIRGINIA
  Commission on Aging
  State Capitol Complex
  Holly Grove
  Charleston, WV 25305
  1-800/642-3671 (within state)
  304/348-3317

WISCONSIN
  Bureau on Aging
  Department of Health and Social
    Services
  P.O. Box 7851
  Madison, WI 53707
  1-800/242-1060 (within state)
  608/266-2536

WYOMING
  Commission on Aging
  Hathaway Building, First floor
  Cheyenne, WY 82002
  1-800/442-2766 (within state)
  307/777-7986

ELDER LAW ATTORNEYS

National Academy of Elder Law
  Attorneys
655 North Alvernon Way
Tucson, AZ 85711
602/881-4005

American Bar Association
750 North Lake Shore Drive
Chicago, IL 60611
312/988-5000

State and local bar associations

PRIVATE GERIATRIC CARE MANAGERS

National Association of Private
  Geriatric Care Managers
655 North Alvernon Way
Tucson, AZ 85711
602/881-8008

Sources of Help

Chapter 1
Helping Your Parent

Support groups and assistance for caregivers

Aging Network Services
4400 East–West Highway
Bethesda, MD 20814
301/657-4329

Children of Aging Parents (CAPs)
2761 Trenton Road
Levittown, PA 19056
215/945-6900

National Support Center for Families of the Aging
P.O. Box 245
Swarthmore, PA 19081

Geriatric care managers

National Association of Private Geriatric Care Managers
655 North Alvernon Way
Tucson, AZ 85711
601/881-8008

Chapter 2
Budgeting for Short-Term Medical Care

Medicare

Social Security Administration
P.O. Box 17739
Baltimore, MD 21235
1-800/772-1213

Local Social Security
Administration office

Help in fighting Medicare

Health Advocacy Services, AARP
1909 K Street, N.W.
Washington, DC 20049
202/879-4700

State and local bar associations

Medigap policies

Insurance Consumer Help Line
1-800/942-4242

Health Insurance Association of America
1025 Connecticut Avenue, N.W.
Washington, DC 20036
202/223-7788

State insurance department

Chapter 3
Deciding on a Nursing Home

Nursing homes

American Association of Homes
  for the Aging
1129 20th Street, N.W., Suite 400
Washington, DC 20036
202/296-5960

Nursing Home Information Service
National Council for Senior Citizens
National Senior Citizens Education
  and Research Center, Inc.
925 15th Street, N.W.
Washington, DC 20005
202/347-8800

In-home care

Foundation for Hospice and
  Homecare
519 C Street, N.E.
Washington, DC 20002
202/547-6568

National Association for Home Care
519 C Street, N.W.
Washington, DC 20002
202/547-7424

Chapter 4
Managing the Cost of Long-Term Care

Long-term care insurance

State insurance department

Insurance Consumer Help Line
1-800/942-4242

Health Insurance Association of
  America
1025 Connecticut Avenue, N.W.
Washington, DC 20036
202/223-7788

Medicaid

Department of Social Services
  (check your phone directory for
  the office near your parent)

Veterans' benefits

Veterans Administration
810 Vermont Avenue, N.W.
Washington, DC 20420
1-800/827-8954

Chapter 5
Finding the Ideal Housing Alternative

Housing alternatives generally

American Association of Homes for
  the Aging (AAHA)
901 E Street N.W., Suite 100
Washington, DC 20004
202/296-5960

Reverse mortgages

AARP Home Equity Information
  Center
1909 K Street, N.W.
Washington, DC 20049
202/872-4700

Commission on Legal Problems of
  the Elderly
American Bar Association
1800 M Street, N.W.
Washington, DC 20036
202/331-2297

Services for the elderly

National Council on the Aging
600 Maryland Avenue, S.W.
Washington, DC 20024
202/479-1200

State agencies on the aging, listed
  above

Chapter 5
Finding the Ideal Housing Alternative *(Continued)*

Adult day care

National Institute on Adult Day Care
600 Maryland Avenue, S.W.
Washington, DC 20024
202/479-1200

In-home care

National Association of Home Care
519 C Street, N.W.
Washington, DC 20002
202/547-7424

Safety devices for the elderly

Emergency Response People, Inc.
1300 Admiral Wilson Boulevard
Camden, NJ 08101
1-800/322-8377

Lifeline Systems Inc.
1 Arsenal Market Place
Watertown, MA 02172
1-800/451-0525

Medic Alert Foundation
    International
P.O. Box 1009
Turlock, CA 95381
209/668-3333

Chapter 6
Protecting Health Care Decisions

Living wills

Society for the Right to Die
250 West 57th Street
New York, NY 10107
212/246-6973

Hospices

Foundation for Hospice and
    Homecare
519 C Street, N.E.
Washington, DC 20002
202/547-6568

National Hospice Organization
1901 North Fort Myer
Rosslyn, VA 22201
804/243-5900

Euthanasia

Concern for Dying
250 West 52nd Street
New York, NY 10107
212/246-6962

Hemlock Society
204 West 20th Street
New York, NY 10011
212/807-5548

Organ donations

National Institute of Health
9000 Rockville Pike
Bethesda, MD 20014
301/496-4000

Chapter 7
Maximizing Income

Financial planners

International Association of
    Financial Planners
2 Concourse Parkway, Suite 800
Atlanta, GA 30328
404/395-1605

Accountants

American Institute of Certified
    Public Accountants (AICPA)
Personal Financial Planning
    Department
1211 Avenue of the Americas
New York, NY 10034
212/575-6200

Chapter 8
Ensuring Money Management for Declining Capacity

*Legal assistance with mechanisms
  for financial management*

National Academy of Elder Law
  Attorneys
655 North Alvernon Way
Tucson, AZ 85711
602/881-4005

American Bar Association
750 North Lake Shore Drive
Chicago, IL 60611
312/988-5000

State and local bar associations

Chapter 9
Using Trusts and Other Special Arrangements

*Legal assistance with sophisticated
  money management
  arrangements*

National Academy of Elder Law
  Attorneys
655 North Alvernon Way
Tucson, AZ 85711
602/881-4005

American Bar Association
750 North Lake Shore Drive
Chicago, IL 60611
312/988-5000

State and local bar associations

Chapter 10
Estate Planning

*Legal assistance with estate
  planning*

National Academy of Elder
  Law Attorneys
655 North Alvernon Way
Tucson, AZ 85711
602/881-4005

American Bar Association
750 North Lake Shore Drive
Chicago, IL 60611
312/988-5000

State and local bar associations

Index

private annuities, 200
revocable trusts, 190
trusts, 186
withdrawal clauses, 186
Gifts:
basis of, 226
deathbed gifts, 228
durable power of attorney and,
168, 226
estate planning, 223, 232
expert help, 224
generally, 223
income tax and, 225
Medicaid planning, 224
purposes, 224
see also Gift tax
Ginnie Maes, 151
Granny flats, see Housing
alternatives
Grantor retained income trusts
(GRITs), 195
Grantor trusts, 193
Group-term life insurance, 145
Guardianships:
fiduciary designation, 171
generally, 158, 176

Health advocacy specialist, 31
Health care decisions:
advance directives, 115
euthanasia, 116, 128
do-not-resuscitate orders, 124
durable power of attorney for
health care, 120, 132, 166
health care declarations, 117
health care proxies, 120
hospices, 116, 127, 132
living wills, 115, 116, 120, 131, 132
organ donations, 116, 129, 132
Patient Self-Determination Act, 126
power of attorney for health care,
120
safekeeping advance directives,
119, 237
surrogate decision makers, 120,
125
Health care proxies, 120
Health insurance, see Employee
benefits, Medicaid, Medicare

Health maintenance organizations
(HMOs):
alternatives to Medigap insurance,
35, 36
generally, 38
Home health agencies (HHAs), 56,
97, 102
Homes:
exempt Medicaid resource, 75
Medicaid strategies for, 82, 83
transfer for Medicaid eligibility,
74, 91
see also housing alternatives
Homestead exemption for Medicaid,
75
Hospices:
health care alternative, 116, 127,
132
Medicare coverage for, 25
National Hospice Organization,
128
Housing alternatives:
accessory apartments, 112
adult communities, 107, 113
assisted living projects, 110,
113
continuing care facilities, 40, 57,
60, 108
downsizing, 87, 102, 105, 106
elderly cottage housing
opportunities (ECHOs), 111
generally, 87
granny flats, 111
hospices, 116
lifetime care facilities, 40, 57, 60,
108
moving in with family, 111
relocating, 102
remaining at home, 88
renting out a room, 92, 102
retirement communities, 107
reverse mortgages, 89, 101, 113
safety concerns, 99, 102, 113
shared living arrangements, 92,
112
selling to child, 92, 113
tax consequences of sale, 93, 101,
105, 106, 109, 113
see also In-home care